Staying Home Instead

Christine Davidson

Staying Home Instead

How to Balance
Your Family Life
(and Your Checkbook)

Jossey-Bass Publishers
San Francisco

Substantial discounts on bulk quantities of Jossey-Bass books are available to
corporations, professional associations, and other organizations. For details and
discount information, contact the special sales department at Jossey-Bass Inc.,
Publishers (415) 433-1740; Fax (800) 605-2665.

For sales outside the United States, please contact your local
Simon & Schuster International Office.

Jossey-Bass Web address: http://www.josseybass.com

 Manufactured in the United States of America using Lyons Falls Turin Book.
This paper is acid-free and 100 percent totally chlorine-free.

Library of Congress Cataloging-in-Publication Data
Davidson, Christine.
  Staying home instead: how to balance your
family life (and your checkbook)/Christine Davidson.—
1st ed.
    p.   cm.
  Includes bibliographical references and index.
  ISBN 0-7879-3940-4 (alk. paper)
    1. Working mothers—United States. 2. Home-based businesses—
United States. I. Title.
HQ759.48.D38 1998
640'.852—dc21   97-45097
                                                      CIP

FIRST EDITION
PB Printing 10 9 8 7 6 5 4 3 2 1

Contents

Preface   xi

1. Introduction: Is This Liberation?   1

2. The Working-Mom Rat Race   25

3. Anxiety Attacks at the Baby-Sitter's Door   41

4. Can You Really *Afford* to Quit?   67

5. Saving Money Instead of Making It   85

6. How to Avoid Being Chief Bottle Washer   101

7. Building Bridges   119

8. Making Money at Home: Nap Time,   143
    Nighttime, Anytime You Can

9. Do Try This at Home: 171
    Computer-Based Businesses

10. Moving Beyond the Traditional: 193
    Nurturing Ourselves and Others

Appendixes

    A. Resources   215

    B. Alternatives to 9-to-5 Jobs   223

Notes   233

Index   245

About the Author   249

For Alice K. Boatwright
and, most of all, Chip, Jen, and Mike

Preface

This is a book written in support of stay-at-home parents, as well as for those who aren't but would like to be. The trend in our society for more than two decades has been to give greater and greater support—both economic and moral—to those parents who work outside the home while others care for their children. Although there are men and women who might be unhappy staying at home and others who simply have no choice economically, there is a growing group of men and women who have some economic choice and feel great conflict in leaving their children. There is little encouragement for this group—for those who wish to pursue the exciting, frustrating, enlightening occupation of full-time parenting. It is my hope that this book can help parents—or those looking forward to parenting for the first time—to question the modern dictum of "Having it all."

Some of the social changes that have occurred in the last two decades have been beneficial. We no longer assume that everyone will do what his or her gender would once have dictated. Since the rebirth of the women's movement in the early 1960s, we no longer expect that the majority of women in our society will marry young, have children shortly thereafter, stay home indefinitely, and be supported by a husband who will work outside the home. There are infinite possibilities in work and in lifestyles today. But the changes and possibilities have created confusion, too, through distorted feminist philosophies and a modern myth that says happiness for women lies in promotions and big paychecks. Unfortunately, children may sometimes be the victims of this new myth, as well as the men and women who are their parents.

Both economic and social factors pressured mothers to go to work in the 1970s and 1980s. Between 1972 and 1979, eleven million women went to work.[1] They were influenced as much by real or perceived economic need as by the exhortations of the women's movement. During the last two decades, American men and women have altered their assumptions and expectations of family life enormously. Young married couples have come to expect a lifestyle equal to what their parents may have worked twenty years to acquire. "Have it all!" became almost a rallying cry. The "success ethic," a rather warped interpretation of the old American work ethic, greatly influenced the young middle class.

The feminist movement made the new lifestyles and attitudes more socially acceptable by questioning traditional female roles and creating a tolerance for various lifestyles and parenting styles. It was now OK to leave the kids and work outside the home. But soon it became not OK to stay home, even when a mother could afford to. Staying at home meant a mother was less than successful as a person; a father at home was even more suspect.

The connection between the success ethic and the push for mothers to work outside the home is discussed perceptively by the author Arlene Rossen Cardozo, who saw where we were headed many years ago in her first book, *Women at Home:*

> Women's liberation has become the latest spoke in the wheel of success-ethic mythology. The women's lib proposal that a job outside the home would provide a woman with freedom from boredom and loneliness at home was a treatment based on the equation of the success ethic with freedom.

Men chained to specialization and sub-specialization, climbing the apocryphal ladder of success, seemed to lonely women looking out their picture windows, not enslaved, but free. Liberationists sought not to change the existing success system but merely to join it themselves. Their only quarrel with the success ethic was that it excluded women; thus, they sought to ameliorate the inequity by seeking for women the same kind of "freedom" they believed men enjoyed. . . .

In theory, it appeared that a job outside the home would solve the problems faced by the women raising a family. In fact, for many women it compounds existing problems or creates new ones.[2]

There are millions of women today who have recognized—or are in the anguishing process of recognizing—that work outside the home away from their children is not necessarily the road to freedom. They are seeing that success can be measured in the emotional luxuries a woman has as well as the material ones. This book is for those women.

But it is also for the woman I was for several years: the mother who must work for basics rather than luxuries. I made many mistakes as a working mother in looking for child care and organizing a household, but most of all in not seeking alternative ways to work. Other women can learn from this experience. So for those women—single or married—who feel they have no choice about working, this book is an acknowledgment of the problems and an attempt to present practical options.

I should make it clear that in spending so much time discussing women as parents, I do not mean to imply that men do not have an equal responsibility for their children. Indeed, I feel that some men's greater participation today in the birthing and rearing of their children is one of the most hopeful trends for families in the United States.

The first edition of this book, entitled *Staying Home Instead: How to Quit the Working-Mom Rat Race*, was originally written primarily for young mothers who wished to stay at home with their children. Although the emphasis in this edition is still on women, parents who've chosen to stay at home now include many fathers. Half a century ago, when many families were engaged in agriculture, the father, as well as the mother, was an everyday presence. Today, because of the accessibility of sophisticated telecommunications devices such as modems and fax machines, this is again possible for many families.

Much has changed, of course. The fact that *stay-at-home mother* or *stay-at-home father* has become a separate designation worthy of comment—or the subject of an entire book—indicates that many people now perceive this as an unusual or archaic way of raising kids. We have come to a point where parents who want to stay at home have so little encouragement, and are so concerned that they "won't be able to make it financially," that there is a need for a how-to book on the subject. I hope this book contributes to fulfilling that need.

Most of the book focuses on women with babies or small children. This is not to say that staying home with elementary school–age children or teenagers is not also worthwhile. Indeed, the incidence of pregnancy, drug use, suicide, and sexually transmitted diseases is assuming such alarming proportions among teenagers today that there are good reasons to stay home or work part-time outside the home during these years too. I spoke to women who had begun at-home businesses in order to be home during the "early crucial years" and had continued this work or returned to it in order to be at home during the second "crucial years." This book promotes the idea that a parent's concern for his or her children at any age is legitimate and laudable, rather than intellectually suspect or "self-sacrificing." The main reason for so few references to older children is principally the scope of the book, as well as my conviction that things are physically and emotionally toughest on working parents when children are babies and toddlers.

Staying Home Instead is a discussion of some of the currents in our contemporary culture that propagandize against parents' staying at home. But as stated earlier, it is also a how-to book. In Chapters Four through Nine, I present practical suggestions from my own experience and that of men and women I interviewed, as well as from research. This portion of the book has been updated and expanded. In writing this section, I assumed that many readers might want to skip over one or two of these hands-on chapters that do not pertain to their own situation, and that's fine. Chapter Ten includes ways that our nation can improve child care and discusses how we can begin moving away from the conflicts between stay-at-home and working parents that have developed over the last twenty years.

The appendixes in the back of the book are intended to give readers additional concrete help. Appendix A provides information about support groups, newsletters, organizations, and books that either assist parents looking for alternatives to 9-to-5 work, suggest methods for economizing, or encourage at-home parenting. Appendix B is made up of interviews with men and women who have devised their own home business or part-time schedule of outside work to enable them to act as primary caregivers for their children.

I am now the parent of two college-age kids who will raise their children in the next century. My children were three and six when I started the first edition, six and nine when I completed it. They are now at a time in their lives meant for independence and exploration. As my parents told me when my kids were toddlers, "They grow up fast." I am thankful I was able to work part-time. It is nice to look back and know that I was there to enjoy my children nearly every day. And it is now more important than ever for me to help others do the same, if they feel it is the right choice for them.

Acknowledgments

In acknowledging the help I received in researching and writing this revised edition, I would most like to thank research librarian

Sara Hartwell for her invaluable assistance. My appreciation also goes to Jason Busch for his computer expertise, Jenny Noon for her editorial acumen, and, as always, to Dixie McLean for her newspaper clippings and spirited encouragement.

I also owe a debt of gratitude to those who helped with the first two editions on which this book is still based: Cheri Loveless, Janet Dittmer, Christine Compston, the faculty and staff at the University of New Hampshire, the ever-patient staff of Portsmouth Public Library, as well as the many parents, grandparents, and childless couples considering parenthood who contributed their experiences, disappointments, hopes, and plans.

Most of all, I would like to thank members of both sides of my family for their encouragement during the writing of this edition. I am grateful to my parents for indirectly influencing the writing of this book through my upbringing: to my father for teaching me how to swing a hammer and mow the lawn, and to my mother for preferring to read rather than dust. Finally, I would like to thank my husband and children for their encouragement and emotional support.

January 1998   CHRISTINE DAVIDSON
Portsmouth, New Hampshire

Staying Home Instead

1

Introduction

Is This Liberation?

Twelve years ago, in the midst of my Supermom days, two incidents occurred that eventually caused me to quit full-time work. The first happened as I was crossing the street after an appointment for a freelance writing job I was working on. At the time, I was putting in about forty-five hours a week teaching two "part-time" college classes and writing and editing a report as part of a very involved, frustrating freelance assignment. I was worn out this particular day, but I was also feeling like the Dress for Success Career Woman. My husband and I were finally doing better financially after years of after-grad-school debt. I had bought myself a striking black and brown plaid coat and a leather satchel for carrying student papers that was, well, sort of a Success Symbol Briefcase. I was even remembering to wear lip gloss.

I was feeling impressed with how much I could take on, too. The work days that occasionally lasted ten hours during that spring were logistical masterpieces: scheduling children, husband, freelance appointments, and visits to the dentist or doctor or dry cleaner. The kids were unhappy when their wonderful day-care center closed for lack of funds, but I had managed to get them into another place that wasn't too bad. So maybe I *could* have it all and do it all.

That spring day, I dashed across the street just as the light changed and energetically leaped over the curb. I looked back to wave a jaunty thank you to the young driver who'd waited for me to cross, and noticed that he had the most admiring look on his face. His look, roughly translated, said, "What vitality, what energy!"

I walked to the parking lot with a glow, but by the time I'd picked up the kids, the dry cleaning, and a gallon of milk, and finally got home to unwind, I wondered how I could have looked or felt energetic. I'd been up late writing and up early to get everybody ready to go; I'd taught all morning and taken only ten minutes to eat lunch at my desk; and I'd had a long afternoon editing session with a client. As I sat on the living room couch listening to the late-afternoon telecast of *Mr. Rogers* with the kids while the pork chops thawed too slowly on the kitchen counter, I felt that I hadn't been vital or energetic bounding across the street—I'd been hyper. The competency and vitality I projected at work wasn't really an act I was putting on. There simply were days when I was so revved up that adrenaline must have replaced half the blood in my body.

As the last soothing strains of Mr. Rogers's farewell song ended—my signal to start making dinner—I decided I didn't like feeling hyper and that if I couldn't stop being that way while working full-time, maybe I shouldn't work full-time.

A second incident that spring with my daughter, Jennifer, made an even stronger impression on me. On this particular "free" afternoon that I had scheduled for supermarket shopping and errands, we were driving by the children's center Jen walked to when kindergarten let out every day at noon. As we drove up the hill, she said matter-of-factly, "This is where I always cry a little on my way to the center."

"Oh?" I tried to sound as casual as I could so that she would keep talking.

"Yes," she said. "I usually cry right at the top of the hill."

"Why is that?"

"Oh, just because I can't go home and you're not with me. I just want to go home after school."

What Jen said hit me hard partly because she told me in such an accepting, matter-of-fact voice. She was not being manipulative. She wanted to tell me her feelings, and I'm sure she would have liked to have had things be different, but she accepted that probably nothing would change.

Making Some Changes

I decided that maybe things should be different. I had gotten on a treadmill of working, too scared to quit. For so long, I had felt that I *had* to work, that I had absolutely no choice. But I realized that I hadn't looked for choices; I hadn't investigated alternatives. I had wound myself into an either-or bind of work full-time or not at all, live well or go into debt. But when I stepped back to gain some perspective, I could see that financial problems were easing for us. We had finally paid off the loan on our second car and the home improvement loan we'd taken out to put in a decent bathroom. My husband, Chip, had gotten a small raise, and although it amounted to only a few dollars a week, it coincided with the two loan payoffs.

I did a rough financial assessment of where we stood and how things were likely to go in the future. I say "rough" because I really didn't want to go into detail for fear that the exact figures would tell me I couldn't quit. It's probably just as well. I didn't know enough then to be able to make an accurate evaluation, taking into account all the money we would save in taxes and work-related costs. I did think a lot about what I could do part-time if things got bad financially after a few months. I felt confident that I could teach at night again, and kept in contact with the director of the night program at the college where I taught. But basically, my decision to quit was made on a gut level.

After I quit in the summer, we made a number of changes to save money. My husband and I sold our larger car, which was expensive to maintain, and kept our smaller one, using it on alternate days. I read books and magazine articles on economizing and talked to people over sixty who had, as young parents, apparently accepted "not having two nickels to rub together" as an expected part of having little children. After five years of seeing my son and daughter balk at the baby-sitter's door, I was ready to listen.

We did dozens of small things to save money. We learned to turn out lights, iron only five or six times a year, buy clothes at discount stores and seasonal sales, dry some of our clothes on a rack in the winter and on the outdoor line in the summer, grow produce and buy other food at a food co-op, cut our children's hair, sell our used clothing at a thrift shop, and so on and so on and so on. These are all picayune methods of saving money—but they add up and make a difference at the end of each month.

If all this sounds like work, it is. But it is work that takes up one hour a day or less, not eight. Given the choice, I prefer putting wet clothes on the drying rack to grading papers every night. I should also add that I don't feel the pressure that I did as a working mother (except for the pressure of a high electric bill) to do these things. Sometimes I'm very consistent and could win a gold star for conserving energy and remembering to take my coupons to the supermarket every week. And sometimes I'm not. I just try to be as conserving and resourceful as possible without feeling constrained by any one method of saving money.

In the process of writing and researching this book, I have interviewed parents at home who have many different methods for saving and making money. One thing that stood out in those interviews was not just the specifics of parents' buying day-old bread at a discount bakery or baking their own fresh, but the *attitude* parents had: to hang loose, to be open to a lot of ideas, and to think up as many solutions as possible to each financial hassle. Sometimes the answer to a dilemma is not to make it, borrow it, or buy it at a discount store, but simply to do without or wait a while.

Our family found that there is such a thing as an emotional luxury as well as a material luxury. For us, having me home was a luxury we wanted more than any other, and we all had to do without other things to have it.

However, we found that there are also real material needs, and careful economizing was not always enough to keep us and our household going. Seven months after I quit work, we realized that I was going to have to bring in some money. After tossing around the possibility of waitressing, modeling, or doing copywriting, I finally decided that the most comfortable thing for me to do was to teach writing again. I called the adult education director I knew and arranged a schedule. Thereafter, I taught evening classes that ran for ten weeks, and I was usually assigned to alternate terms. During the "off" terms, I wrote articles and did freelance editing. The freelance paychecks, together with my husband's pay and our economizing measures, were enough to get us by. I knew that when our children were only a few years away from starting college, there would be a real necessity for me to work full-time again, and this is the way it has indeed turned out. But when they were young, their greatest necessity—and mine—was emotional. So I was at home most of the time.

As far as the Department of Labor statistics were concerned, I was one of those "women with children under the age of eighteen in the labor force." I was part of the statistics which inform us that supposedly record numbers of women work outside the home and that American family life has changed drastically. I worked for a part-time paycheck because I had to, but I considered myself an at-home mom because that was where my focus was.

Being a part-time working mother made life better for our family. But I would be wrong to wave a flag and proclaim that working part-time is "the answer" for every working mother who is feeling overwhelmed. That would only be presenting the reverse of the idea some feminists promote: that having a full-time outside job is "the answer" for every bored housewife. As Lee Morical points out in her book *Where's My Happy Ending?*: "The hard reality is that there are no free lunches either on the job or in the home."[1] I never liked grading papers or editing a tedious report when I was working full-time, and I'm not crazy about canning tomatoes in the heat of August, which was one of my jobs after I quit. So there is no ideal for everyone; there is no one all-encompassing answer to the rather knotty problem of surviving financially while caring for the children we love. Parents have to look at the options and balance those things that are most important to their family. It is also wise to remember that nothing is forever. Both adults and children change over the years, and, therefore, a parent's priorities and preferences change. The woman who loves staying at home at thirty may be itching to leave at thirty-five or forty. Or she may be compelled to go out to work because of the medical bills of an elderly parent or the college tuition costs for her children.

What Are the Options?

The problem I observe today is that women are no longer seeing that there may indeed *be* options. They know that their families cannot live (or live as they'd like) without their contributing, so they work full-time, sometimes barely taking a break to have babies. The result is often a complicated, exhausting situation for women as home managers, wives, and, most of all, mothers.

The response most of us give to the question, How did I get myself into this *mess?* is usually "economics." But in looking back at my own experience and in interviewing other women, I think the reason is more complex than that. Unless a woman is a single parent, she is often working for more than just the money to put food on the table and to pay for the electricity to eat it by.

There are basically three groups of mothers working: single parents (who are almost always broke); married lower-middle-income women; and married middle-income and upper-middle-income women. In general, women with small children in the first two groups work because they have to; mothers in the third group work because they enjoy having a comfortable lifestyle, or wish to use specific training or education they've had, or simply because they want to. (Obviously, this is a simplification and there is some overlapping.)

Many of us in the third group are used to living at a relatively high standard of living, whether we realize it or not. Many of the women in my generation of college graduates were raised in some degree of affluence. Our fathers were usually the principal wage earners, and whether they were teamsters or physicians, they earned enough for most of us to have quite a bit materially. In keeping with a trend that began after World War II, many of our middle-class mothers went to work when we were in high school or college, thereby ensuring more material goods and the college education itself. In our twenties, as a result of our higher education, our wanting to establish a career, and our wishing to enjoy the full companionship of a new marriage, many of us postponed having children (with the help of modern contraceptives).

The significance all this has for me now is that those of us who suffer conflicts about being working mothers often say, "But I *have* to work." Often this statement should be amended to "I have to work to maintain our standard of living." It is difficult for women of my generation to do without, to lower our sights, and to recognize that there is a difference between what is *nice* to have and what is *necessary* to have. One of the ironic things about my quitting work was that I quit just at the time when we could have begun living rather well: eating out more often, having a "real" summer vacation at a resort, getting someone in to clean several hours a week, and giving the children a lot more materially and culturally. The prospect of living more luxuriously was very tempting. But we decided instead to opt for an emotional luxury. It was, however— and still is—difficult to be surrounded by a society full of exciting things and opportunities and yet have to do without most of them.

But working to live well is not the only reason so many middle-class women with small children are employed outside the home today. Contemporary culture communicates a message that few of us miss: it's not all right for an intelligent woman to stay home.

The women's movement of the 1960s was about women having the freedom to make choices and to feel confident and well adjusted, whatever those choices were. But somewhere along the line, this idea got distorted so that thirty years later there is apparently only one choice for any self-respecting, well-educated, interesting woman: to work outside the home. Current distortions of feminism dictate that this is the only place where "real work" is done. Apparently, this "real work" should continue indefinitely, even after babies are born, or maybe especially after babies are born because quickly returning to work after giving birth proves how really liberated, tough, and enlightened a woman is.

With the perspective of thirty years, some spent at home with children and some spent working outside the home, writer Edith Tarbescu gives her view of the subtle and not-so-subtle influences at play in our society:

> I believed . . . that the "real" world—the exciting grown-up world (where people made *crucial* decisions every minute), existed outside the white shutters of my brownstone in New York. . . . When I did go back to work—as a sales rep for a Fortune 500 company, with a company car and a sample case filled with reports—I realized that the corporate life wasn't what I wanted. Only what I *expected* to want. But I was a single parent by then and ironically, I didn't have a choice. Though I didn't particularly like my job, or find it stimulating, I did enjoy talking about it. After all, I had created an image for myself, and for a while, I continued to wear my uniform and speak the language. I was afraid that without my emblems I'd disappear. . . .
>
> Now that I've seen both worlds, the three decades have formed a unifying collage for me: the '60s, when women were afraid their lives would be lonely, isolated, and boring; the '70s, when women were told "It's OK to

go back to work; what's important is 'quality time.'" And the '80s, when women . . . finally decided to see for themselves. And decide for themselves. . . .

I believe there will one day be a smorgasbord of options—for men and women. The good news is that we're moving in that direction.[2]

It was initially Betty Friedan who told us in the 1960s that being at home was boring, and those of us who'd never had children or run a busy household believed her. She is still telling people how it is and was. I once heard her speak to a large group of impressionable young college students and at first was impressed with her. Before speaking she sat on the podium looking out at the young audience, really looking, with interest and pleasure. I had never seen a renowned speaker so genuinely interested in an audience before. With her prominent nose and olive coloring, she looked for all the world like an Indian chief, and I thought to myself, she *is* the chief. Then she began to speak, and she lost me. She described what being an American woman was like before she and the modern women's movement came on the scene: "Women couldn't call themselves people. . . . There was one definition for a woman—somebody's wife or mother. . . . A woman was never a person."[3]

The friend I went to this lecture with was in her early thirties, and we both looked at each other and tried to relate Friedan's 1950s–early 1960s nonperson to our own mothers. We couldn't. Even though both of our mothers had been at home until we were in junior high, we saw no resemblance to Friedan's image of the passive, at-home 1950s mother.

It was even harder to accept Friedan's image of "nonperson" women when I thought of my grandmothers and great-aunts, especially my maternal grandmother, who, as a divorced mother of three in the 1930s and 1940s, had managed a sheep ranch in Colorado with only the help of her oldest child and an occasional hired hand. Two of the women in my father's family had come to this country with little money and few prospects, having left school early and worked as servants. From what I understood of our family lore, these women were resourceful, hard-working, courageous people who would have turned over in their graves if anyone had called them "nonpersons." One reason both men and women came to this country and later went out West was to get away from restrictive stereotypes.

Betty Friedan's own mother apparently was quite passive and conventional. Certainly there were and are such women. However, I doubt that women like the ones on both sides of my family were rare or only existed in the American West. There is frequently an implication in the writing and lectures of Friedan and other feminists that one type of passive behavior was exhibited by *all* women in *all* regions and in *all* economic strata of the country before the modern women's movement. That just isn't true.

My Own Experience

And yet, as an ambitious and naïve college student reading *The Feminine Mystique* for the first time more than thirty years ago, I accepted a lot of what Friedan and other angry women said. I could see that their writing could be repetitious and exaggerated, but I needed the encouragement at the time. I was a writer just starting out who didn't have much support. It was expected by family and old friends that I would have my artistic fling after college and then get married. I would settle down when the Prince arrived. Why not? My mother had opted happily for a family and a star role in the town's Little Theater productions now and then, instead of becoming an actress or designer. And after her children left home, she had had time to pursue other intellectual and creative interests.

But I was more intense and ambitious than my mother had been as a young woman. I wanted to put off marriage and family for several years and concentrate on learning to write without any distractions. And Friedan and other feminists gave me the support I needed.

After college, I set up house as a Young Boston Career Woman, working as a librarian during the day, writing evenings and weekends, and trying, trying, trying to get published. My life in Boston helped to solidify my perceptions—and prejudices—as a feminist. The main reason for that was simply the behavior of men in the city I had chosen to live in. I got tired of a good many things: being called a "girl," even when I was twenty-five and had a gray streak in my hair; seeing women friends who'd been Phi Beta Kappa in college making thousands of dollars less than men I knew who had barely made it through college (though they were working in the same publishing houses); sitting in a restaurant feeling helpless while my date insisted on ordering dinner for me; talking to elderly male editors who assumed that most of their women editorial assistants were working to "keep busy" or for "pin money." I loved Boston, and I don't think other areas of the country were much different, but it was easy to get radicalized there in the late 1960s.

When I got married to the kind of "sensitive, enlightened male" I'd always wanted, I had many illusions about how things would be after we had children. In spite of my allegiance to feminism, I knew I would want to stay home with any children we had while they were babies and toddlers. But I also felt that when it seemed right emotionally for me to work outside the home, I would, thereby sharing the financial burden of supporting a family with my husband. I even wrote a gung-ho article about this (never accepted for publication) in which I asserted that sharing the financial burden would result in fewer stress-related illnesses for men and probably a longer male life span. It did not occur to me that stress-related illnesses might simply *increase* for working women.

Having It All?

It also did not occur to me that when a woman "has it all," she has to *handle it all*. Ironically, the woman who wrote the book *Having It All*, Helen Gurley Brown, never had it all because she had no children herself and married a man who had only one child, a teenager who visited them only occasionally. Nevertheless, this silly book had an enormous influence, if only in its title. To those who still insist that we can have it all, I now say Yes, indeed, all of it: midnight laundry loads, weekend catch-up headaches, an early heart attack. There is nothing fulfilling about fatigue. Although Friedan and other influential feminists led us to believe that being at home with children was a consignment to boredom, they didn't remember that there are many cures for boredom, but few for the harried life of a working mother.

There is no question that many positive legislative, social, educational, and legal changes for women in the United States are a direct result of the women's liberation movement. Women now have a better chance of getting a bank loan on their own or an acceptance to law school when they qualify, instead of meeting with condescension and rejection. Women who are ambitious and committed to a particular endeavor no longer need feel that they are "unfeminine." At the same time, many men have recognized their need to nurture and to express constructively feelings like fear or anger. Society as a whole is benefiting, because in such fields as medicine, business, and law, the best qualified of both sexes now compete, rather than only men. Americans no longer assume that all little girls will grow up to be housewives any more than they believe all little boys will become farmers.

However, many of the improvements have helped those few in the upper reaches of our society rather than those in the middle, who are the majority. And, most important, there has been a tendency to throw the baby out with the bath water. Since the 1960s we have discarded legal and social traditions that protected children as well as women. The most obvious example of this today is no-fault divorce, through which a housewife and mother who may have saved thousands of dollars every year of a marriage in economizing measures or sent her husband to college is awarded so little money that she is usually unable to remain at home caring for her children for even a full year.

Some changes that have been heralded as breakthroughs for women in the workplace have had questionable value. Powerful women in politics have argued vehemently against company policies of protection against hazards, seeing these as barriers to women's advancement in certain occupations. It may well be true that the policies of some companies have been more motivated by a fear of lawsuits than by genuine concern for women's safety. However, the jubilation of feminists and workers when such barriers have been struck down in the courts should perhaps be tempered with some sobering facts.

There is medical evidence that many jobs where workers are exposed to dangerous substances are potentially hazardous not only to women and their unborn children but also to men and the offspring they might sire. An article in *Health* magazine outlines some of the dangers. "Growing evidence suggests that sperm is . . . more fragile . . . than previously thought. . . . In fact, one study found that a baby was more likely to be harmed if the father rather than the mother worked in an unsafe environment in the months before conception."[4] Perhaps the greatest breakthrough for equality on the job would be for women *and men* to be advised of and protected from hazardous materials in their childbearing years. Throwing out protections is a questionable solution to inequality in the workplace.

All in all, if I were a male employer today, I would be pretty confused by now. Some of the most vociferous members of the women's movement in the 1970s led businessmen to believe that there was nothing to doing housework and rearing children. Now they accuse businessmen of being "insensitive" to working women's responsibilities at home. Many feminists, claiming to speak for us all, led men—and young, newly pregnant women—to believe that it was a snap to have a child and go back to work six weeks later. Now, many are demanding a year of job-protected leave after childbirth as the greatest contribution to having it all.

In the sixties and seventies, there were feminist writers who criticized men for overemphasizing the discomfort or lessened efficiency a woman might experience during her menses. Now, there are dozens of articles about PMS in which some feminists complain that there was too little research done by male doctors in the past and too little concern on the part of businessmen regarding this problem. Once again, men are insensitive scum.

I am all for parental leaves of absence for men and women and for more sensitivity in the workplace. But I think one cannot have it both ways. Wanting to have it all must seem a little absurd to a man anyway; they have had it all. In the past, they often did without the emotional perk of spending a lot of time with their children. But the point radical feminists have been pushing all these years is that men are the bad guys, men are the enemy. And men have the secret to having it all. Yes, some men are selfish or prejudiced or ignorant of certain realities. Some are narrow-minded and so insecure they feel threatened by competent women. But even these men are not necessarily engaged in a deliberate, insidious, conspiratorial effort to keep us down. They may feel a distaste for the abrasiveness and paranoia of some feminists, yes, but are they part of an organized backlash or conspiracy? No.

I think women today really need to look at what they want as individuals and avoid the temptation to follow the herd or blame only outside forces for what they don't achieve by age thirty. Each woman also needs to determine what her conception of true freedom is. About the time I was questioning my participation in full-time work and considering staying home, I read the words of *Toronto Star* columnist Lynda Hurst: "After the last dazzle of the [feminist] fireworks, there was deeper darkness. You are perhaps more enslaved now than you have ever been."[5] I felt as if her words had been spoken in the deep, commanding voice of an all-knowing matriarch. I began to see that women with young children and an average job— not a high-salaried executive position—were probably leading daily lives that were less liberated than that of their stay-at-home mothers. Today, many women working outside the home have less time to pursue their own interests and are no longer their own bosses as women were when they worked as housewives.

But current attitudes interfere with the working wife and mother's seeing the absurdity of the situation she may be in. One of these attitudes involves the prevailing idea about what a woman should do with her education. *Should* is the operative word here. As the author of *Where's My Happy Ending?* points out, "The nagging persistence of the educational 'should' can become a kind of water torture if we let it; a degree will provide us freedom of choice only if we allow it."[6]

Among the middle class in the United States, there seem to be education-for-women fads. They range from the genteel nineteenth-century learning-to-be-ladies syndrome through the 1950s' no-better-way-to-use-your-education-than-raising-children dictum to the 1990s' use-your-education-to-get-to-the-top approach. There is no question that it is important for every modern woman to get the education or training necessary to be self-supporting. As one mother I interviewed put it, "A woman has to be prepared for death, disaster, or divorce."

But it is unfortunate when young women feel that education should be connected primarily to advancing professionally, and forget that for a few years or more it can be used to help a young child discover his or her world. There is a high status placed on working outside the home; we almost sanctify it. We've gone to the opposite extreme of the situation of the 1950s when motherhood was sanctified; when any woman who was married was expected to become a mother and then expected to stay home indefinitely, even when her children went off to school and she was climbing the walls. I don't think we've learned to strike a balance and to give equal value to the mother at home and the mother at work.

In the colleges where we teach the theory of infant-mother bonding in Psychology 101, we might consider discussing frankly the anguish many new mothers feel when they must leave their infants to go out to work. We might also consider instructing young women on the advantages of learning how to economize or to adapt an occupation to part-time, nighttime, or at-home work patterns when their children are young. We could discuss "early careers" and "later careers." We could acknowledge that not all working women with small children have the physical and emotional energy, the money, and the luck to blend the responsibilities of home, husband, children, and work without stress.

In the last few years, young women have slowly begun to see some of this. In a *Parents* magazine Working Life Survey, 43 percent of readers said they approved of women's staying home while men go to work, which was almost twice the number replying this way in 1989. Furthermore, "among those under twenty-five, a majority—55 percent—preferred the lifestyle of the 1950s."[7] Still, we don't do all that we could in educating young women in the realities of trying to cope with caring for an infant and working full-time.

Conflicting Messages

Middle-class American culture gives young mothers many conflicting messages today: women should breast-feed their babies and later mash and blend "natural" foods for them instead of using that awful stuff in jars. They should hold their babies often (a tough thing to do ten miles away at the office), "involve" the father, and talk and read to their babies frequently so they will learn to be "verbally communicative" at an early age. But at the same time all this extensive nurturing is going on, a woman is supposed to be "building a life of her own" and "exploring her potential."

The media, particularly advertisers, tend to exacerbate the basic problem of these conflicting messages by depicting the working woman as a glamorous symbol. She is always a "professional" on her way up, never a hairdresser or a word processor or a sales clerk. She carries (always!) a leather briefcase. The briefcase, the charge card, and the fast, fluid movements of the TV working woman imply that American women should hanker after the image of the male executive who's on the fast track.

Obviously, we are all free to reject this image. But like it or not, advertising is very influential, particularly when its message is buttressed by the colleges, news media, and some radical feminists. According to newscaster Lee Bergman, in creating this image of the working woman, most media people "responded to a real trend in the country, took it to an extreme, and ultimately distorted the real situation." What has happened is important because the media has tremendous power to "influence women and the society as a whole to accept the distortion."[8]

I think that this distortion has led to many problems. One of them is women's unrealistic expectations for themselves, which all sorts of dress-for-success and how-to books have encouraged. Frustration sets in when the expectations are not realized. It's not really surprising that they often aren't realized, either. After all, there are only so many high-paying spots for doctors, lawyers, and business chiefs—for women *and* men. The competition for those jobs is staggering. An M.B.A. and a subdued wool suit do not guarantee anything. A lot of us don't make it.

But in trying to make it, many intelligent, caring women are ignoring jobs that are also important and rewarding: the so-called female jobs like nursing, teaching, and secretarial work. As a result, we may, as a nation, wind up with less-qualified people in these traditionally female positions or suffer great shortages in some fields. Suzanne Gordon, author of *Prisoners of Men's Dreams: Striking Out for a New Feminine Future*, writes of some sources of the problem in the caring professions:

> When women moved into the marketplace, . . . we hoped to teach men to value caring, to share in women's caring work in the home and workplace, and to support

truly care-centered programs in the political arena. . . . But, in our society, the very project of human caring has been compromised.

. . . [M]ore and more American women have been encouraged to embrace the very marketplace values that have always denigrated care. New female images of success, like their masculine counterparts, preclude work in the caring professions. . . .

Some American feminists have also failed to emphasize the value of caring work in their theories and public discussions because they, understandably, fear that any widespread attempt to revalue women's caring work will be manipulated by conservative forces. . . . No wonder then, that many women who were proud to be in "women's work" felt that mainstream feminism was—and sometimes still is—hostile to their interests. . . .

[W]omen's caregiving work has become a negative standard against which we measure our progress. Our progress . . . is [now] charted in the distance women have traveled away from caregiving work, and toward traditional male activities and preoccupations.[9]

As columnist Ellen Goodman has pointed out, what we need to do is raise the status and pay for caregivers instead of encouraging them out of these occupations. As it is, "the rise in status for women is associated, for better or for worse, with entry into the male world. . . . We have . . . done a better job at letting some women into 'men's' jobs *than at raising the status of 'women's' jobs.*"[10] Eventually, as shortages occur in these jobs, it is possible that the salaries offered will become higher. In the meantime, however, as some of the most capable young women in the country reject such positions, there will be shortages.

In the business world, this situation is no better for someone trying to hire a secretary who can spell and punctuate. The business community will never be helped by a glut of M.B.A.'s and a dearth of good support staff.

I also question whether society will be helped by women being told that it is unstimulating or unchic to be at home with their young children. While the working woman is unrealistically glamorized and the single mother (or father) ignored, the married mother at home is too often depicted as a drudge; what's more, her strength in numbers is greatly minimized by the media, and her choice is both catastrophized and patronized.

For example, an article in *Working Mother* in 1997 referred to the new "simplicity movement" (which this book helped to start) as "conspiring to send working moms back home again." The author disparages the notion "that if women would just simplify their lives—that is, cut back on daily expenses—they could afford to quit their jobs and become stay-at-home moms." Referred to as the "simplists' message" (she might as well just say "village idiot"), the writer goes on to say that following this message "could have serious and irreparable consequences on your long-term earning power and future financial security. . . . You'll lose influence in your marriage," and so on.[11]

At the time this article appeared, the editor-in-chief of *Working Mother*, Judsen Culbreth, and a professor at Southhampton College, Christopher Hayes, were interviewed by Katie Couric on NBC's *Today* show in a discussion about the new trend. Ms. Culbreth was pretty scathing in her ridicule: "the theory is that if you cut back, if you can tomatoes, if you buy your kids' clothing at yard sales, if you make rugs out of pantyhose, that you can afford to . . . stay home." Ms. Culbreth went on to say that this was a "simple-minded theory" and "really defeats the image that working mothers have."[12] Hayes stated that quitting even for a couple of years was "extremely dangerous for women's economic security."[13]

There were some inaccuracies and misconceptions in both the *Working Mother* article and in the interview. For example, Ms. Culbreth said in the interview that "most studies show that women who work part-time have the worst of both worlds." In fact, most studies show the opposite, and many people know that, but Culbreth was not called on this. The magazine article quoted a working mother who said "I don't know many people who have been able to save enough to put their kids through college buying flour in bulk."[14] Such a statement ignores the likelihood that both parents would be working full-time by then. It also expresses an upper-middle-class bias, because studies show that most parents send their children to state-supported colleges and that their kids are eligible for a number of outright grants, work-study campus jobs, federally subsidized loans, and federal and private scholarships. This I know well—we're going through it all at this writing. Obviously, the exaggeration means stay-at-home parents are some sort of threat.

Certainly it's true that one drops a few rungs on the corporate ladder by staying home for a few years and that it can be difficult to make up for lost time in terms of salary (see Chapter Seven). But, of course, some of us just want to earn a living when we go back to full- or part-time work and are not *interested* in climbing that ladder. Supposedly, we have a choice, yet the media and many influential feminists often make it sound as though some of us make a very wrong choice.

There are other instances of this type of reporting on many TV programs. A short segment on *CBS Evening News* reported one night on a congressional hearing on day-care proposals. One of the speakers was Linda Burton, a mother at home, who suggested that one excellent way to relieve the pressure on day-care facilities would be to change the dependent exemption for taxpayers so that it represented 18 percent of family median income as it did in the 1940s and 1950s. This would be a good solution to the U.S. child-care crisis, for not only would it enable many married parents and some single parents who want to stay home to do so, but it would also mean less demand on overburdened day-care facilities. In addition, it would ideally enable mothers who prefer to work to pay better wages to day-care workers, who are now grossly underpaid.

What is interesting is that when CBS reported the proposal made by Burton, which one congressman described as "the most appealing . . . I have heard since . . . I have been in Congress,"[15] Dan Rather's closing comment was that it was "a return to the ways of yesteryear."[16] Too often, influential media people like Rather don't seem to understand that staying at home to care for young children is most definitely involving oneself in the present—and the future, too—more than is any other job.

Rather's remark implies that staying home with children is not only old-fashioned but also unusual. Yet statistics and studies of how women spend their time do not bear this out. A magazine or newspaper article will frequently cite the number of mothers who work, but the degree of participation varies depending on whether one is looking at single mothers or married mothers. More important, the expression *in the labor force* can mean many things. For example, during 1992, eighteen million married mothers worked "at some time" during the year, but only nine million worked full-time the entire year. Put another way, 73 percent of married mothers had "work experience," but only 37 percent were engaged in "year-round, full-time work."[17]

Also significant is that women are now engaged in a *variety* of occupations: shift work, flex-time jobs, farm labor, and part-time temporary and part-time permanent work. There also are patterns in the time devoted to paying work, which are usually related to the ages and needs of one's children. Thus the percentage of married women who work full-time who have children under the age of six is lower (31 percent) than for women with older children (43 percent).[18] The percentage of never-married mothers who work full-time who have children under six is even lower, usually because of the mothers' age and inexperience.[19]

According to another researcher, the idea that this country is full of "Supermoms who wear 'power suits,' drop the baby at a day-care center, and work downtown 40 hours a week [is a myth that] distorts the reality of mothers in the United States today."[20]

Deborah Fallows, author of *A Mother's Work*, has a large section of one chapter devoted to government statistics on women and work and how easily the statistics can be distorted. She points out that "the Labor Department's 'part-time' category includes everyone from the autoworker who was laid off for half the year and took a job on the side, to the young mother who took on a salesclerk's job for a month before Christmas to earn extra money for the family, to the woman who works five hours a day, five days a week, fifty-two weeks a year." Fallows also reminds readers that the Department of Labor statistics can be misleading because they include those who are *seeking* employment but are unemployed for the quarter the department is reporting on.[21]

According to a 1996 article in *American Demographics*, "women aren't joining the work force as fast as they once did." In the future, their labor force participation rate is projected to show an increase of less than three points.[22] As more and more women and men choose to work at home in front of a computer terminal, the statistics for Americans engaged in work outside the home during traditional 9-to-5 hours can only continue to decrease. Yet a superficial reading of official statistics will continue to mislead people and, more important, influence public opinion and public policy in Washington.

A good question to ask is how these misleading statistics can become so pervasive in the media. A journalist friend explained to me that a news reporter with a tough deadline will often look for apt statistics from the government and read them quickly, so there isn't much time to consider finer details. More often, the reporter won't even have time for this cursory reading and will instead go to the clip files of the publication or station. The files hold clippings from newspapers and magazines on a wide array of subjects. In every file cabinet, there is a file on women's issues because the topic is hot today. If a clipped article implies that women "in the workforce" means women working full-time, then this misconception will be repeated. When that newsperson's article with its misleading statistics is clipped by some other publication or station, the misconception continues *ad infinitum*.

Although there are thoughtful columnists and TV commentators who do their research thoroughly and are able to cut through the morass in order to present a clearer picture, there are always more journalists who lift statistics to fit into a quick story that meets their deadline. In addition, there are feminist interest groups who know the details but ignore the facts because they are concerned that what little money is allocated for day care by the government may be cut even more if a different picture is given. So, true work patterns for American women continue to be distorted. What is important to remember for any mom at home with young children is that, depending on the year, if well under 50 percent of mothers are working full-time year round, then the majority are at home with their children *most of the day*.

Behind the statistics are women designated as full-time workers and paid full-time wages: teachers, nurses, waitresses on night shifts, and flight attendants and other women who work the "mom shift"—a long three-day-weekend shift.[23] The fastest-growing group of new entrepreneurs in this country are women—people who work hard but can choose their own hours and often do some or all of their work at home.[24] Add to this the number of at-home child-care providers who work six to nine hours a day baby-sitting other people's children while caring for their own and the total becomes still larger. All these facts change the picture of American mothers leaving their small children in droves, thereby creating a great social revolution. Millions of American women are at home with their babies and young children most of the day. *They are the majority*.

A major change in American life has taken place, but the most dramatic shifts have been in women (single and married) working a *longer period* before having children and parents engaging in *part-time work* outside the home and in *at-home businesses*. Today, the millions of American women who are lucky enough to be able to stay home to care for their young children and who find fulfillment in doing this are sometimes denigrated as women who "do nothing." They are ignored even more than single parents and given little emotional support. They are too often treated as if they were a tiny minority, not even worth considering by the media. It is time for the other side to speak up. It is time for some support and a lot of applause for parents who choose to stay at home.

The Working-Mom Rat Race

While the mother at home deserves attention equal to her numbers, the *real* working mom laboring both outside and inside the home does too. Notice I say *real*. We are surrounded by images of an unreal Superwoman: the high-salaried attorney, the groundbreaking executive, the traveling corporate woman. The glamorous lifestyle of single women (well, some single women) has become muddled with that of working mothers. The general image represents such a tiny minority of women working outside the home that it has become a cruel absurdity. Yet even when we recognize how far from reality the image is, it influences us all.

The profile of the *real* working mother is someone who may often be tired, guilty, underpaid, or stressed, even when she likes her job but especially if she doesn't. She works in an office, hospital, school, or factory. She is not very glamorous, and that's the main reason she doesn't wind up in too many perfume ads. Even in documentaries and news features, upwardly mobile attorneys, executives, and psychotherapists are overrepresented compared to blue-collar and office workers, even though it is these workers who make up most of the working-mother labor force.

In reality, about one-sixth of all American families depend on women for their chief economic support.[1] According to the U.S. Department of Housing and Urban Development, the average median income in the United States for which there are statistics (at this printing) is $41,600. For metropolitan areas it is $44,600, and for nonmetropolitan areas it is $31,400.[2] If the income of a young mother's spouse falls below these figures, she is probably going to feel compelled to work unless she can find significant ways to economize or has some kind of housing break.

Some of those in the "real" category wind up working full-time because they put themselves in a mortgage or lifestyle bind before having children and find themselves too financially insecure to quit. Many naïvely believe that it will be nothing to give birth to a cute little bundle and go back to work a few weeks later. Only recently have there been magazine and newspaper articles that question the wisdom of returning to work right away or that indicate some of the pitfalls of combining parenting with a full-time job outside the home. And there is little in our culture today that encourages economizing and doing without for a few years for the sake of staying home with young children.

New mothers in their late twenties and early thirties whom I interviewed said that they had given hardly any thought to quitting their job when they were pregnant. They had read little that even began to describe the attachment they would feel to their own small baby: "Those tiny pinhead fingernails, and the velvety hair and skin . . . the way they look up at you and reach out to you with their little hands." "No one prepared me for the work and exhaustion that was involved in having a baby, but they said even less about the magic of it all."

In my own case, working outside the home kind of crept up on me. I had always assumed that I would work hard writing and teaching before having children, take off perhaps eight years to enjoy their preschool years, and then get back to work, still writing and teaching, I hoped, when I was a little old lady. That seemed sensible and, from what I'd observed, pretty realistic during the years when I was first married. But there were some financial surprises in store for us, especially when my husband went back to school for a graduate degree a year after our daughter was born. We borrowed a little money from a relative and applied for veterans' educational benefits to cover tuition, my husband got a work-study job at the graduate school, and I got a job teaching writing at night just to manage living expenses. By the time my daughter was a year and a half old, I found that I could work on lesson plans and my writing during her blissfully long naps and for an hour during *Sesame Street*. Because I taught and prepared classes for only fifteen hours a week, things went easily. I was very happy in all that I was doing, especially in my life as a mother.

I had had a hard time adjusting to motherhood the first few weeks, mostly because Jenny was premature. She was very frail the first two weeks after birth and could not be taken outside because of some minor damage to her lungs when she was born. I have always been susceptible to claustrophobia, but during the first couple weeks out of the hospital I wondered if a person could actually *die* of cabin fever! But once I got through the early period and Jenny began to gain weight and strength, the good times as a mother began to roll. I found I loved taking care of a small child. Things that at first bothered me, such as having milk burp-ups on the shoulder of my blouses, didn't seem particularly important after a while. I got into perspective what really mattered to me. Spending the day loving a small person seemed a pretty wonderful way to live. I found motherhood an involving, exhausting, stimulating job.

Her first year, Jenny went out with me every day after our morning writing and nap time. On the coldest days of winter, I would wrap her in a yellow quilt and hold her close as we walked in the brittle white New England sunshine. During the spring and summer, I would put her in her orange umbrella stroller and take her for a leisurely outing downtown to window-shop and get to know the assorted dogs and cats, bubblegum machines, chain-link fences, traffic cops, and other neighborhood wonders.

Jen was a jolly, inquisitive, stubborn little kid, and we thought she was the most fascinating being that ever was. We spent a rather idyllic summer as a young family. We would eat early in the evening and then go for walks around the neighborhood. My husband would carry Jenny on his shoulders, and she would pluck blossoms from flowering trees and shower them down on us. My days with her were spent almost rhythmically as she settled into her own definite schedule of eating, playing, and sleeping, and I wove my jobs of cleaning, washing, and writing into that schedule.

During the two years that my husband was in graduate school, I continued to teach at night and occasionally had articles published in local newspapers and magazines. When he received his degree and we relocated for his new job to the seacoast area north of Boston, I was happily pregnant and excited about our move. I think I assumed that my time of working even part-time would be over for a few years. After our son, Michael, was born, I was content to enjoy him and our daughter, fix up the old house we'd bought, and write during morning and afternoon nap times. However, by the time our son was six months old, graduate school debts as well as the expenses of a house and a new baby made it clear that I would have to go back to work at least twenty hours a week.

The summer my daughter was three and a half and my son seven months old, I got a job in a department store evenings and, the following September, a position teaching composition at the local state university. As time went on, I worked longer and longer hours. One of the reasons this happened was the house we had bought: an eighteenth-century colonial that had originally been an eight-room home but had been converted into a duplex during an economic depression in the 1800s. The house was about fifty yards from a cove where ducks and snowy egrets came to feed and was just down the hill from a tiny neighborhood beach.

Unfortunately, the water view and the price were the only things the house had going for it. We bought what I'm sure was the last $25,000 house in New England. Some of its more interesting drawbacks included a bedroom ceiling whose lead paint was peeling so badly that I had to vacuum it more than the floors; a bathroom toilet that was fast sinking into the cellar; and a stove with an insecurely attached oven door that would come off in your hands when you pulled it down. Our realtor had called the house a "handyman's special" with "lots of potential."

We soon learned to expect crazy experiences in every room as we slowly fixed up our "special." When we finally replaced the downstairs toilet, we used a big mixing spoon to scoop up the mushy, rotted subflooring. When we took down the sagging plaster ceiling in the family room, the yellowed carcass of a small animal fell from the rafters. At neighborhood parties with friends undergoing similar experiences with old houses, our traumas now make hilariously gruesome stories.

But I have to admit that at the time it was not always so hilarious. We had to spend money and time almost every weekend fixing and patching up the place. I had to work to help support the effort. Also, we learned during the first two years of renting out half the house that we were not cut out to be a landlord and landlady. In the hundred years that the house had been set up as a duplex, no owner had ever done any soundproofing. This was a big problem for us, as we always seemed to rent to people who either kept late hours or had a baby who did.

So when our third tenant moved out, we decided to take over the entire eight rooms. We finally had some room to breathe, and it was wonderful. But I had to keep working, and working hard, now that we had no rent money to help us make payments on the mortgage and on a home improvement loan.

In some ways, this was not difficult. I liked my job. After a couple of years, I was teaching composition part-time on the university's main campus, teaching the same course at night in the adult division, doing occasional freelance editing and writing jobs, and managing to squeeze in a little time for my own writing. My job—or jobs—were fun and stimulating. And I had the freedom to work as much as I wanted each term just by teaching an extra writing course or by scouting for a freelance job. But having this freedom made it easy for me to overextend myself, particularly because there always seemed to be some financial emergency. My last two years when I was working full-time I organized my work so that I had two half-days a week when I could be at home with my children. My work-week consisted of a four-hour day, followed by a thirteen-hour day, followed by another four-hour day and thirteen-hour day, and ending with an eight-hour day. I am sure this schedule every week contributed to my feeling exhausted and harried. But it was very deliberate. I wanted my children to have two half-days a week when they could invite friends over or spend time reading and playing with me.

I look back on this now as "playing 1950s mom" because so often my children were downstairs watching some dumb cartoon while I was upstairs grading papers. I would yell downstairs to pipe down or to be a big girl and get your own juice. So to a certain extent, my "quality time" with my children was a fraud. But it was an attempt at providing them a few hours a week with what I had had as a child every day: Mom at home.

On the long days, I felt guilty about being away from my children both day and night and about our inability to find a good day-care situation that *lasted*. And no matter how much I might intellectualize about how stimulating my career was, I missed my children. I had a sense of "How did this happen? I never intended things to turn out quite like this." I was as maladjusted a working mother as Betty Friedan was an at-home mother. What saved me from bitterness was what saves a lot of working mothers, especially single ones: I had to work, so I had to make the best of it.

The Demands of Housework

Like most working mothers, I had no household help. In the area where I live, getting someone to clean house and do laundry one day a week was extremely expensive. I was a university instructor on a low pay scale. My husband was an administrator for a nonprofit agency. We had often joked about the low pay and demanding schedule we had: doctor's hours, teacher's pay. But it was no joke that there was a lot of work to be done at home and very little time for either of us to do it.

When we were first married, we had split household work 50–50; well, maybe 60–40. Anyway, we had a small, efficient apartment to clean occasionally; three laundry loads a week; two cereal bowls, two plates, and a few glasses to wash every night; and no yard work or general house maintenance to do.

But after several years of marriage, we had a crazy, broken-down, eight-room house; triple the laundry load; lots of dishes to wash; and sundry objects to pick up from any surface that could serve as a landing site for a toy or bottle of juice. And, of course, there was also the work of caring for a baby and a preschooler, which I still thought of as a demanding job in itself.

My husband spent a lot of time with the children, did the dishes most nights, cooked dinner Friday night, did his own laundry, and occasionally vacuumed on the weekends. This was all he felt he had the energy for, but it was only about a quarter of what needed to be done. I knew he needed rest at night and on the weekends as badly as he needed food and sleep to stay healthy. He left his job enervated, whereas I left mine refreshed at least half the time. I had much more control and freedom in my job because once I closed the door to my classroom, I could do as I wished as long as the students learned what they had to by the end of each term. But in spite of understanding—and rationalizing—all this, the fact was, the unequal division of labor at home caused me a good deal of stress.

Since quitting, I've thought about the unequal division we had and that I've noticed among other married friends. I have tried to analyze why I so often did things we had originally agreed my husband would do, such as vacuuming the upstairs after I had done the downstairs. He would be too tired to do it Saturday morning and too tired or busy on Saturday afternoon, and I'd finally figure, oh, what the hell, I'll do it. Now I ask myself, why did I do that? Why did he let me? I was probably just as exhausted as he was.

But I felt an *obligation* to do housework in a way that my husband did not. And I'd been conditioned to do it since I was ten. It was somehow *my job*. I think, too, that cooking and cleaning had a kind of rhythm for me that I could step to unconsciously. For my husband, it was a new dance. Why I didn't teach him how to dance, I don't know. I guess it was easier just to do it myself.

But in spite of being familiar with what had to be done, I really was not a particularly efficient housekeeper, and housework was the last thing I felt like doing. There were times when I'd finally finish cleaning on a Saturday afternoon and feel like saying, "Freeze, everybody—don't eat off another plate or pull another toy or book off the shelves."

As the kids got older, things improved a little. A five-year-old can clean a room, clear and set the kitchen table, and even do some vacuuming. But beyond that, I felt that there was not much I could or should expect from my young children. So the responsibility was still mine, and so was 80 percent of the work.

The thought occurred to me at the time that maybe I could just handle the frustration of dealing with a myriad of petty household chores better than my husband could. He really was not refusing to help me. Aside from his inexperience, he appeared to have a truly low level of tolerance in attending to the daily pileup of small tasks at home. I later learned that there is some medical evidence that such a response is typical in men. Women apparently have greater tolerance for dealing with multiple tasks than men do. Endocrinologically, men have "a good quick response to acute stress but their hormonal make-up is not good for chronic stress. . . . Adrenalin in women is released slower and over a longer period of time. . . . Because of the difference in brain development, women can apparently deal with more things at the same time than men."[3]

However, the last thing the doctor who did this research would want is for someone to use it as an excuse for the average husband's not sharing equal responsibility for the housework. If a man has a quick, short-term hormonal response, then surely he can do household chores and errands in a quick burst of male energy. Nothing really explained why I was doing so much more than my husband; it was just a pattern that we got into.

Feeling Inadequate

At the time, I was convinced that other working mothers did not have problems keeping house to the extent that I did. The storybook success articles had influenced me so much that I really thought that other working mothers could have it all and do it all.

I looked for help in different "coping books," but I found little awareness of the problems of the average, nonexecutive working woman. The books were usually written by highly paid career women. One book had a section on housecleaning and lifestyle that I still find a hoot. The authors discussed the pros and cons of live-in help, daily cleaning services, weekly cleaning help, and European *au pair* girls. The book gave advice about buying more easy-living appliances, sending out the laundry as well as the dry cleaning, and being good to yourself by eating dinner out often. All sound advice for the family with a six-figure income.

The sense of inadequacy I developed extended beyond just household management to the general image I had of "the working woman." Without realizing it, I, like many women I later interviewed, became afflicted with what psychologist Lee Morical calls the syndrome of "Everybody's Got It Together Except Me."[4] TV commercials, popular books, and magazine articles and ads portrayed the working woman as one who juggled job, husband, home, and kids, smiling all the while because "I love my work so much, it's worth it."

This woman, who loved her work and her family (and most of all, herself?), seemed to be everywhere, jaunty and free, with a briefcase swinging at her side. She was an executive, a mover; she had everything under control. After all, she had a "career," not just a job like most of us. This career provided her with "real fulfillment" and gave her family a chance to buy "those little extras."

Throughout my years of working, I felt surrounded by this woman, this image of success. She was often working in the field of business or in some previously male-dominated field. She was moving ahead—fast—and she had money. Friends, especially male friends, who have listened to me disparage the current "selling" of the Successful Woman have asked whether this image isn't better than the old soapy one of the housewife worrying about the shine on her floor. I think the answer is that both images are unrealistic (and, by the way, we certainly haven't gotten rid of the first one). But any woman with common sense can laugh at and even feel superior to the Anxious Housewife image. The second image is discomfiting because many of us have the uneasy feeling that maybe this Competent, High-Salaried Beauty is the woman we *ought* to be.

Even though she is the minority among working women, she has become important, especially among young women in their twenties. She represents a goal, the ultimate. According to psychiatrist Avodah K. Offit, many young women "long for magical, marvelous gratifications in work."[5]

The image of the woman who fulfills her dreams and succeeds in a previously male-dominated field has even invaded the women's movement. The woman who is a groundbreaker, preferably on high-salaried ground, gets all the applause. Writers Richard Moore and Elizabeth Marsis have written about this in a scathing and sad commentary:

> Corporate feminism is alive and well, nurtured by enterprises that want to whitewash their sexism or simply make a buck. The bleached, coopted version of the feminist mission is increasingly passing for the real thing in the business world—and even in some segments of the women's movement. . . .

Macy's and *Working Woman* magazine co-sponsored a "special event" to unlock the secrets of success for women. . . . And though the affair promised to take "a complete look at the business of being a woman," there was scarcely a word about discrimination or harassment, sisterhood or equality. . . .

By cultivating powerful but deceptive ideals of equal opportunity, business leaders hope to conceal their pre-dominantly male hierarchies and let the steam out of calls for collective women's actions. . . .

The current campaign introduces a new variation on an old theme. If women buy designer clothes and play along, they can "go places" in a man's world. In indus-try after industry, women see . . . [that] the prosaic facts of their working lives conflict with the media myths about them.

Segments of the women's movement, intentionally or unwittingly, are feeding the corporate fiction that femi-nism is really another word for "making it." From *Work-ing Woman* and Ms. to [celebrity] self-help books, individual achievement and stardom are beginning to consume much of the feminist agenda. . . .

The struggles of average women, in whose name suc-cessful women are supposedly breaking barriers, have become incidental to barrier-breaking itself. Image (or tokenism, as it used to be called) has emerged as the driving force of this brand of feminism.[6]

I think that the goals of the women's movement have become quite confused. Because a lot of women don't think of themselves as part of the "feminist" or "women's lib" movement, this develop-ment would not matter except that the confusion isn't confined to the women's movement. There seems to be a growing rejection of femaleness in the push to succeed. In the media, in colleges, in the business world, "equal" seems to mean "like a man."

In an article written in the early 1980s, entitled "The Gender of Success," writer and teacher Patricia L. Dombrink explores this subject with wonderful insight:

> Each year a major magazine for women devotes an entire issue to the topic of success and profiles 10 women who epitomize this concept. After diligently saving these special issues for several years and admiring the role models, I began to notice an ominous pattern. The successful women were those who had careers in heretofore male fields. . . .
>
> The message was clear: only those women most unlike their traditional sisters are worthy of being considered successful. Where does that leave the very successful women in the so-called service professions? Are they not successful, even when they lead happy, fulfilling lives that make a significant difference in the lives of countless other people? Have we been defining success in the wrong terms? Does the idea of success—in itself—include the requirement that a woman has broken through that previously solid barrier of prejudice that prevented her from reaching financial heights and power in such fields as engineering, architecture, law or business? Should women in traditional career fields be ignored, lest their younger sisters do something so gauche as choose a "female" career? . . .
>
> [The] notion of aping men is . . . [also] found in the dress-for-success look widely depicted in women's magazines. The successful women are shown wearing two-piece . . . suits, tailored shirts, and carrying the obligatory attaché case. They are schooled in what to say and eat

as well, in order that "feminine" characteristics do not intrude in the "male" domain of business and high finance. Prof. Henry Higgins of *My Fair Lady* would undoubtedly rejoice to find today's women "more like a man."[7]

Taking Responsibility

Although it's easy to point a finger at advertising, the news media, and various individuals, books, businesses, and organizations, women themselves must finally take responsibility for what is happening. We've unintentionally created and tolerated problems for ourselves. For all the rhetoric about sisterhood and solidarity from feminists, I fear we are growing apart, not together. For all the talk about power, in our daily lives we sometimes behave as if we were powerless.

Many of us play what I now call the macho-feminist "I Can Take It" game. Though we may speak frankly with friends about the conflicts between home and job sometimes, we also make an effort to show people, especially bosses, that we can hang tough, we can take it. I fell into this game mostly because I was afraid some Powerful Someone (probably male and above me in the university hierarchy) would shake a finger at me and say, "See, you can't do it, Sister. Go home and put another layer of wax on the kitchen floor." The words of opponents of feminism that I heard when I was a young woman stayed with me a long time: women are irritable and erratic once a month when they've got "the curse"; women job-hop; women always quit as soon as they get married. Women, in short, are not dependable or serious about their work.

In the 1960s, women countered such ill-informed criticism with statistics on women's long work records, charts of women's sick leave that did not coincide with their menstrual cycles, and other proof of women's physical soundness, loyalty, and diligence. We insisted that we could be dependable and dedicated to a profession or a specific job. Thirty years later, we're trying to do that; it's just that it's nearly killing us. Married women with families who work "just" part-time are in fact working full-time; those who work full-time are working at least time and a half; and single mothers working full-time are working double-time. As one writer put it, "There are, and always have been, women who can successfully cope with all the conflicts of career and family. . . . They are exceptionally hard working; they are exceptionally competent. . . . But there are, and always will be, children and women who are not so strong and resilient."[8] No doubt, Betty Friedan was the first type, but a lot of us are the second type.

Men, too, are not always resilient and full of energy. There is a lot of stress in two-paycheck marriages. Psychologist and family counselor Marjorie Hansen Shaevitz states that working women "more frequently than they like to admit, give their partners . . . only the time that is left over—*after* the work is done, the kids' needs are met (or they are in bed), the dishes and laundry are finished, and the phone calls returned. What that usually means, of course, is that partners get the time around eleven or twelve o'clock, when the body is exhausted, the libido is quavering, and the mind is cluttered."[9]

Sometimes couples don't even see each other during the week—literally. According to the U.S. Census Bureau, 5.6 million married couples work split shifts. One study found that "one-tenth of these couples have no overlap at all in their work hours. . . . And 6.3 percent of the couples have only one or two hours of overlap."[10] According to Katherine Yost, a family therapist, "this way of life is a real stresser. . . . Messages, thoughts, and feelings can get lost in the shuffle."[11]

Because wives still do most of the housework, there is bitterness about working time and a half. Husbands sometimes "help" with the housework or "baby-sit" the children in the evenings, but many still do not *share responsibility*, and there is a big difference. Fixing the sink or mowing the lawn once a week doesn't make up for the disparity, particularly because some "liberated" women have also taken over these chores. In too many families, it's chic for a woman to learn how to perform men's work but it's unchic for men to learn to do women's work.

The bitterness and general exhaustion lead to some marriages' being ruined. A woman who was a corporate executive in New York and was interviewed for a *New York Times Magazine* article on working mothers said, "I was working 60 hours a week, nursing and getting no sleep. And my husband didn't help me. When I saw how he was willing to exploit me, to let me work until I dropped, I lost faith in him and in our marriage."[12]

Not everyone has such a difficult time. The woman who doesn't have a high-level job and never brings work home with her has it much easier. But then, by media standards, she's not considered successful, either. It is ironic that the image that has been shoved down our throats is not that of just *any* working woman but of the high-salaried working woman on the fast track. Yet it is these women who must, if they are to continue to succeed, put in tremendous physical, creative, and mental energy, *and time*. A woman I interviewed who had been the head of a department in a hospital said, "You simply cannot make it unless you put the time and energy into it. I worked at home, I worked at the hospital, I worked weekends both places sometimes. To continue that with a baby and a husband who traveled extensively was impossible for me after I went back. I was afraid I would go crazy." Not everyone with a high-level job feels that desperate. And middle-of-the-night feedings and extreme exhaustion ease off after a few months for any new mother. But unless she hires help, the mother on the fast track has almost as much trouble as the single mother. Almost invariably, the career woman who successfully juggles home, husband, children, and work is a woman who has unusually high reserves of physical energy or has the means to buy help.

Freedom or Sacrifice?

There are, of course, women who become mothers and are unhappy or bored at home, even after giving themselves time to adjust. If they can leave their house and children to go out to work and everybody's happy, great. I would hate to see us return to the rigidity and narrow expectations of the past. But in an effort to replace the detergent box or the baby bottle as the symbol of American women, we have come up with the two-ton briefcase. Is the harried life of the business executive really freer than the life of the housewife-mother?

Many leading feminists have written about women spending their lives as housewives and mothers caring for others and feeling lonely and unappreciated. They consider these women self-sacrificing, as people denying their own needs. But a woman working full-time in a job outside the home can have exactly the same experience. The problem is self-sacrifice itself, and we can experience that in the office as well as in the home. All that is necessary is a woman willing to be sacrificed. The biggest difference is that in the old scenario, only the needs of the woman were sacrificed; now the needs of some American children are being sacrificed as well.

3

Anxiety Attacks at the Baby-Sitter's Door

Sacrifice is a strong word, and in using it in the preceding chapter, I do not mean to join the ranks of conservative child development experts who warn of great dangers for children raised in day care. I do not believe that early care by someone other than the parent *necessarily* results in confusion about who is Mom or Dad, or low academic performance in school, or later inability as an adult to form close interpersonal relationships. I don't think anyone will ever be able to devise a test that will tell us whether such things are affected by parents' working outside the home. There are too many variables to consider—from the particular type of "other care" to the individual child receiving it. But I do believe that many families are suffering in the present child-care crisis in the United States.

Social Contradictions and the Working Woman

The historian William O'Neil once commented that society in the United States "demands that women work, but when they do they and their children must suffer. No other developed western nation has such vicious, irrational and self-defeating policies toward working women."[1] The problem seems to be getting worse rather than better. In a 1973 article on day care, Ms. magazine used the title "The American Child Care Disgrace" and decried President Nixon's

41

veto of the Comprehensive Child Development Bill of 1971. What was called a "disgrace" in 1973 is now a disaster.

A number of child-care bills have failed in Congress. Finally, in the spring of 1990, after much debate, the House of Representatives passed the Early Childhood Education and Development Act. President Bush initially threatened to veto this bill because of the billions of dollars involved and the provisions for regulating day care, but the bill was finally passed after the provisions for effective regulation were watered down and the price tag lowered. It is estimated that under back-to-work welfare reform initiatives supported by Congress, ten million more kids will need day care as their mothers go back to work. But the funds allocated for day care for these children are not adequate.[2]

It is understandable why Congress (and the taxpayers back home) object to expanded funding for day care. After all, we may cry for "the government" to do more for American children, but the government is us, and sooner or later we have to pay for everything spent. However, the issue of funding is also one of allocation—where are we going to spend our tax money and for whom? We spend far less per capita on services and programs for children than for each American over sixty-five.[3] We spend millions on subsidies for various industries. In Washington, the wheels of government are choked with committees and subcommittees, whirling in their own little spheres of influence and often duplicating the efforts of other government committees and agencies. Private individuals and PACs spend millions to influence representatives and senators and so do we, every time we buy an item from a company that has lobbyists in Washington or a highly paid CEO who contributes heavily to campaigns.

There *is* money out there—it's how it is allocated and to whom that is significant. All surveys and studies indicate that things are getting progressively worse for children. The 1990 National Commission found that today's children are "less healthy, less cared for, less prepared for life than their parents were at the same age."[4] According to economist and child advocate Sylvia Hewlett, "Although the United States ranks No. 2 worldwide in per capita income, this country does not even make it into the top ten on any significant indicator of child welfare."[5]

When it comes to helping parents who wish to stay home with their children—whether they live in the ghetto or suburbia—we falter just as badly. According to former senator Lloyd Bentsen, "Over the past decade, more than anywhere else in the world, women in America were forced to leave their children in someone else's care and seek work."[6] Yet ironically, U.S. economists have found that the average American family was economically less well off in the mid-1990s than it was twenty years earlier. "[M]edian family income fell by over $1,400 or 3.4 percent despite a substantial rise in both 1994 and 1995."[7] Middle-income and lower-middle-income families have been especially hurt by tax increases and comparatively lower adjusted gross incomes in the last twenty years. Bentsen felt that "we should earmark at least part of [the] peace dividend for American families who got so little from the policies of the 1980s."[8]

Over the coming years, defense savings may free moneys that could be used to help parents stay home or to subsidize child-care programs for those who must work outside the home. But what is also needed is a *will* to make changes and some consensus as to what will help children and families. I think conservatives need to realize that there are women who will go out to work whether they approve or not and that those women deserve to have safe, accessible, nurturing care for their children. Liberals need to realize that some of us will want to care for our children ourselves for as many hours a day as possible.

Parents who have made different choices—or responded to financial imperatives in different ways—do not have to be placed in two opposing camps. Going out to work and staying home with kids are really not mutually exclusive. More and more women live their working lives in sequence, moving in and out of the workforce, sometimes needing day care, other times not. And more and more men are involved in jobs that can be adapted to at-home work. Most of us who are highly committed to caring for our children ourselves have worked full-time in the past and will again in the future. It would be nice if we could stop taking sides and get together to help the children of this nation.

As of this writing, there is little clout behind funding bills either to help parents stay home in order to care for their children themselves, or to help them find accessible, affordable quality care while they work outside the home. The United States rates abysmally when compared to other industrialized nations; in some regions of the country, we don't do well when compared to third world countries. We have no nationally accepted policy of how best to care for the children of this country. In the history of the human race, in both so-called primitive and civilized societies, this situation is extremely rare. There are some societies in the world in which absolutely no care is available for children outside the basic family or small social group, and there are a few societies in which the only daily care for children is outside the family. But in settings that represent those two extremes, such as nomadic Saudi Arabian tribes or institutionalized kibbutz nurseries in Israel, there is a prescribed way of caring for children that is understood, consistent, and agreed upon by the majority.[9]

It is important for those of us who wish to stay home to let congressional representatives know how we feel about leaving our children to go out to work. Changes will have some chance to occur when individual congressional representatives and senators know how their constituents feel. Surveys and studies indicate that the majority of women would prefer to work part-time and care for their children most of the time.[10] But representatives will not know this unless we tell them. They'll listen to those who speak the loudest.

In the meantime, little has been done for mothers who feel that they must work, particularly those in the lower-middle and middle class. Women's contributing to the family economically is nothing new, especially in a country like the United States, with its strong agricultural roots. But working outside the home is. After more than twenty years of seeing women with children steadily, though often regretfully, join the ranks of workers outside the home, we still haven't figured out how to care for children in a changed world. As a result, the average working mother with young children has a hodge-podge of possibilities for child care to choose from—or put up with.

It is ironic that in the last thirty years, women with children have in some ways lost rather than gained in status. In her excellent though disturbing book, *The Day-Care Dilemma*, author Marian Blum states:

> There are long traditions of women and children being first. In fiction and in fact, particularly in times of disaster—since it was first issued as a naval order during the sinking of the *Birkenhead* in 1852—the maxim has been "women and children first." But it is an empty maxim, for women do not come first, especially when the economic realities of their lives are examined. . . . The conflicts between work and child-bearing become, most often, no-win situations. . . . [W]hen it comes to working versus staying home, they are damned if they do and damned if they don't. Women of the fifties were caught smack in the middle of a great social and political upheaval; they had grown up expecting one set of values and common goals, and were told, in the middle of it all, that those values and goals were all wrong. If life was good, then the woman was a parasite. If life was desperate, it was because of a male, chauvinistic society. Those mothers of the 1950s who went to work early were made

to feel guilty and negligent. Those who stayed home were made to feel guilty and lazy.[11]

Marian Blum goes on to say that this same problem continues to plague women in our society so that "women are more *last* than first."[12] It seems that in the effort to gain equality and the recognition that we were not so weak we needed a man to open the door for us, we've wound up having the door slam in our faces. Many of us were very ignorant about what was involved in having children in general, and in having both children and a career in particular. Some of us have been surprised by a divorce or economic problems and find we have no choice but to combine children and a job. Whatever the situation, we are all living in a country in which the ambivalence or disapproval or confusion of those in power has resulted in no policy emerging in the last thirty years for caring for the nation's children. Even with an increase in the number of women staying home in the late 1990s and perhaps beyond, we need policies.

I think it is important to recognize that there *is* a problem. Many of us pretend that there isn't, particularly to our bosses. We walk in to work, after crying in the parking lot for ten minutes, with a strong, competent-woman lift to our chins. But the fact is, leaving a child is stressful and sad and, yes, gut wrenching. Boston writer Christina Robb chronicles some of the emotions many mothers have felt:

> For me, returning to work when my baby was 6 months old was culture shock. Suddenly there were women who smiled in compassion from behind the payroll window or the coffee urn and said, "It broke my heart, too. I did it three times." . . . At work in the last minutes I felt exhausted, as if I were pulling against some basic force of nature—and, of course, I was. . . .

[Later,] after several feedings and huggings and kiss-
ings, I felt normal again, just in time to put her to
bed. . . . I know . . . that to stay in touch with my daughter, I will have to feel an awful pain each time I leave
her. If I stop feeling the pain, at this stage, I will stop
being connected enough to her. This kind of premature
separation is called for so often in American life that
almost everyone I talk to who isn't actually going
through the same thing tries to tell me it's not so bad.
But it is. It is so bad.[13]

Christina Robb's description fit my feelings exactly—and those
of other women I interviewed. One young professional woman said,
"The first day back, I had to pull over to the side of the road twice,
I was crying so much." Though many of the women in my generation were unprepared for the depth of our attachment to our children, it is nothing new. The late Golda Meir, prime minister of
Israel, articulated the feelings of many working women: "At work,
you think of the children you've left at home. At home, you think
of the work you've left unfinished. Such a struggle is unleashed
within yourself. Your heart is rent."[14]

The one difference today is that, for many families, the children
are not "at home"; they are at a day-care center or at the home of
someone else, a situation that may or may not be satisfactory. Leaving babies and toddlers is tough, but leaving them in the care of
someone we're not entirely happy with makes things ten times
tougher. According to a survey of working parents done by the
National Child Care Survey, 26 percent felt that they would choose
a different form of child care if it were possible to do so. In another
study, only 13 percent of the working parents responding said they
had been able to get the child care of their choice. The survey was
of people making above-average salaries at the time, supposedly the
group most able to get high-quality care.[15]

Child Care Outside the Home—
Helpful or Harmful to Children?

One of the things that is hardest on a working mother is that there is no way of knowing whether care outside the home by someone other than a close relative is harmful to children. I found that reading the opinions of child development experts and the studies done by researchers at day-care centers (as well as the published discussions of the research and discussions of the discussions) did nothing to clear the mud. To illustrate, let me quote from an article in the *Los Angeles Times* that highlights the conflicting findings of major studies and the influential experts the article quotes:

"When a child spends . . . his waking day in the care of indifferent custodians, no parent and no educator can say that the child's development is being promoted" [the late Selma H. Fraiberg, well-known child psychiatrist]. . . .

"Several studies indicate low morale on the part of the nonemployed mother and, though it is not deliberate, an encouragement of dependency" [Lois W. Hoffman, a University of Michigan psychology professor]. . . .

Still other experts . . . say their studies show that boys are likely to *suffer* more from a mother's absence than are their sisters, or that black children seem to thrive academically and emotionally when their mothers work but white children do not, or that the ultimate impact on the children may depend on their fathers, not their mothers. . . .

Both elementary and secondary students living in two-parent homes perform worse on [standardized achievement] tests if their mothers work. The more hours that a woman works outside the home, the lower her children's scores will be.

The difference in test scores between the offspring of working and nonworking mothers tends to be greater for elementary school students than for secondary school students.

But the *Los Angeles Times* summary also quotes studies done by the National Academy of Science which "concluded that the children of working mothers do just as well in school as the children of mothers who stay home. . . . Parental employment in and of itself—mothers' employment or fathers' employment or both parents'—is not necessarily good or bad for children."[16]

Nobody really knows how harmful—or helpful—care outside the home is for children. Some of the most prominent researchers now believe that day care may harm the infant-mother attachment for children under nine months, but many factors are involved in the development of the infant-mother relationship. Thus, no study has been able to give absolute answers to those who worry about leaving an infant in another's care.

Most researchers contend that day care is not harmful for preschoolers "assuming it's a good program."[17] I found that all studies that are positively inclined toward out-of-home care or that see few differences between children raised in outside care or parental care, qualify their findings with such phrases. But, as I and others have pointed out, how easy is it to find a high-quality program, particularly if a family has limited financial resources? For those who don't feel they have the best possible care, the hedging of researchers doesn't provide much solace.

I doubt there will ever be a definitive study that will tell us "how it is" for the children. For one thing, a wide range of care exists that any one family can wind up with. Here is just a partial list:

- Sister, grandmother, or close friend

- Elderly neighbor

- Baby-sitter registered by the state

- Baby-sitter licensed by the state

- Unlicensed, unregistered baby-sitter (the majority)

- Nursery school with extended hours

- State-subsidized community day-care program

- Federally subsidized day-care center

- Church-supported day-care program

- Nonprofit private day-care facility

- For-profit day-care center open ten hours or more

It is obvious from this list that in addition to the variety of people who can care for children, there is also a wide range of places where children are taken care of—from a brightly lit, well-equipped private or subsidized facility with an extensive playground, to a dimly lit church basement or a grandmother's cramped apartment.

There are also a great many individual family situations and attitudes that can affect the way children feel about going to day care. Some parents are happy about going out to work and getting out of the house—they say they are better parents for it. Some hate their jobs and resent being away from their children and home most of the day. Parents may have their individual self-esteem enhanced or harmed by their job situation. They may make a lot of money or very little.

In their personal lives, working mothers may be happily married or in the midst of grief and recovery from a divorce. They may like or dislike the sitter or day-care center. All these attitudes and life circumstances can affect children, who, in turn, have their own range of feelings and experiences. An individual child may be jolly and outgoing or quiet and unusually sensitive. If there are other children being cared for, the individual child has to learn how to interact with them. They, of course, may range in personality from hypersensitive to callous. These factors alone make it clear that deciding whether or not care by someone other than the parent is good for a child can only be done on an individual basis.

In addition, many of the studies done on the subject are irrelevant to the experience of the majority of working mothers because the studies have been conducted, almost invariably, in high-quality, university-based day-care centers. Yet less than a quarter of American families using day care employ day-care centers for their preschoolers, and these are certainly not all university-based, excellent facilities. Therefore, data from the studies done *"cannot be generalized to the entire world of day care."*[18]

If all of us who work full-time outside the home had our children in the ideal pilot-study kind of day-care center (perhaps after the children spent their infancy at home with a grandmother), then this chapter would probably be unnecessary. But most of us don't. The majority of parents have their young children in an environment that is unregulated by state or federal agencies. And yet, even having a child in a sitter's home or a day-care center that is registered or licensed is no guarantee that the care is excellent. Few states or cities have the personnel to inspect and monitor child-care facilities.[19]

The Ideal and the Reality

One can argue forever about what constitutes "excellent" child care, but there are some basics that I think most of us can agree on: safe and pleasant indoor and outdoor spaces, age-appropriate play and learning equipment, supervised interaction with other children, nutritious meals and snacks, quiet rest and reading times, and, most important, affectionate, sensitive adults who can make a commitment to caring for the children for at least a year. National research conducted also indicates that small group size is important, more significant than the ratio of adult to child. And, although the general level of education for the child-care provider does not matter much, it is important for providers to have training in child development.[20]

These are really no-frill standards, the basics that all children deserve. But many working parents will tell you that they have been unable to find such care *consistently*. This is particularly true if the parents are single, live in an area that has little care available, or are poor. Millions of women fit this description. At best, they have dependable but mediocre care; at worst, unkind or abusive care. The incidence of sexual or physical abuse is less than 1 percent in regulated child-care centers.[21] We do not know what the figures are for unregulated child-care facilities, but they are apparently higher. Although there has certainly been much publicity that would indicate otherwise, 95 to 98 percent of all child abuse takes place at home, not at day-care centers.[22]

Studies have found that a more common problem is inconsistency and unavailability of care, which may result in neglect. Sometimes this means that children go from pillar to post, with a frequent change of sitters and surroundings. Among low-income families, it may mean no care at times. In an article on children's safety, Jack Levine, director of the Florida Center for Children and Youth, points out in an interview that, in his state, thousands of children are on waiting lists for subsidized care, and many more are eligible.

> We're talking about roughly 40,000 to 60,000 children
> in Florida under the age of 5 for whom there is no room
> at the inn. The reality is neglect. . . . Many people [do]
> not . . . make the association between waiting lists and
> actual damage to children. A waiting list is not a safe
> place to be. It is limbo, danger, crisis. There are no car-
> pets on a waiting list, no toys, no trained adults to watch
> over and help children. A child on a waiting list is most
> likely to be neglected, molested, abused.[23]

A study conducted by two researchers at the University of North Carolina School of Public Health corroborates Levine's statements. Researchers found that families with consistent access to child care "have the lowest rates of substantiated child abuse—6 percent for those who have full-time child care, 38 percent for those who have no regular child care."[24] Many incidents of injuries or death because of neglect or physical abuse have occurred at night. Fewer than 5 percent of child-care facilities can give care after 6:00 P.M., yet many single parents work at night or on a swing shift.[25] It is at such times that children may be left alone or with someone who is unreliable or abusive.

More common among all income groups and family situations is mediocre, custodial care; the millions of children in this group are what Carolee Howes, a researcher and development psychiatrist at UCLA, calls the "middle clump."[26] The difficulty in these situations is not abuse, but indifference or unkindness. Let me give you an example. Let's say a two-year-old throws a ball several feet in a strong straight line. It is the first time he's managed that, and he's very proud. A parent or grandparent standing nearby might share in a child's excitement, acting as if this is surely the cleverest thing a little kid ever did. Obviously, such a response is very good for a child's self-esteem and self-confidence. A good caregiver might express this same kind of excitement and affectionate pride. Then again, she might not. If she is baby-sitting in her own home, she might simply not notice because she is so busy with her own children, the other children she cares for, and her household concerns. A third response some caregivers might make is to speak sharply at the child's cry of joy after throwing the ball so far: "OK, so you finally threw the ball somewhere. Just watch my kitchen windows next time. And pipe down." I have heard all three kinds of responses from child-care providers when a young child accomplished something new.

It is true that a mother or father could also give a response that is not positive for the child. The problem comes when the parent would give the child an enthusiastic response but has hired a caregiver who would give an unenthusiastic or negative one. Then we end up having our children raised by people who are not giving the kind of encouragement and praise we want.

Unfortunately, there are not enough of the loving, sensitive child-care providers that we all wish our children could have. The following essay describes the experience of one professional woman vainly searching for child care:

> I missed my children when I was gone. I worried about how they were being dressed, fed, cared for. I worried that their bright inquisitiveness was being dulled by the housekeeper who, while a kind and decent person, lacked a certain intellectual vitality. I was almost relieved when my housekeeper quit. I came back home to attend to my children and, again, searched for child care. Diligently, and over what came to be a period of two years, I searched for child care everywhere from the local town newspaper to the best nanny schools in London, Wales, and Scotland. I talked to friends. I tried to recruit at senior citizens' centers. Although I will admit to a prejudice against institutional day care, I even investigated that.
>
> And I discovered that there were millions of mothers like me trying to hire the same sort of person I was. No matter where I . . . looked, a long waiting list of mothers had been there before me. All of a sudden, the notion occurred to me that perhaps the elusive, almost mystical "she" was not out there. After all, here we were, 17 million women trying to hire someone to replace ourselves. We all wanted someone warm, wonderful, motherly, and loving. All of a sudden common sense just told me that there simply weren't enough warm, wonderful, motherly, and loving people to go around. And even if they *were* out there, it was clear that they didn't want to give priority attention to my children. They wanted to take care of their own children. . . .

I had wanted someone with a driver's license, good English, a sense of fun, and an alert lively manner. I wanted someone who would encourage my children's creativity, take them on interesting outings, answer all their little questions, and rock them to sleep. . . . Slowly, painfully, after really thinking about what I wanted for my children and rewriting advertisement after advertisement, I came to the stunning realization that the person I was looking for was right under my nose. I had been desperately trying to hire me.[27]

The kinds of experiences this woman describes are not unusual for the mother in search of the perfect caregiver. I knew from what I'd read and courses I'd had in college that what I wanted was a kind, grandmotherly woman who would care for our children in our home when they were infants and early toddlers. When they were about three years old, this could be supplemented with an excellent day-care center or preschool for half the day. But I could not find anyone who was good who would come to the house (though I did find someone who was lousy and was willing to come to the house). I could not afford to pay above minimum wage, and I also did not have the money to provide paid vacations or insurance or Social Security deductions. I did not have the space or inclination to have a student live with us and (again) no money for a high-priced nanny. So we did what millions of parents do: we took the children to a sitter's house.

We had several sitters over the years—what is known as family day care. These women were, for the most part, dependable, decent people. But somehow we always seemed to get sitters who switched on the TV the way we switched on the lights when we came home. The TV was on when we dropped the kids off, when we picked them up, and the few times we called or came by early. It was always tuned to soap operas in the afternoon, which we felt had subject matter that wasn't appropriate for young children. Two of the sitters seemed to care more about having a clean house and having their day's laundry neatly folded on top of the dryer by the end of the afternoon than playing with our children. Even in warm weather, our children and the sitter's other charges were rarely taken outside.

I know now that my husband and I did not work nearly hard enough to find someone we were all happy with. On the other hand, you can't be picky when there's not much to pick from. In conducting interviews, I have since realized that we were not alone in our bad luck and occasional anguish.

Some women I talked with confessed to a fantasy of living next door to an elderly woman who would take an interest in their children and love them like a grandmother. This kind, encouraging woman would become "one of the family." She would never move away.

But the reality is different. One woman I interviewed said that she had advertised for a sitter who would have her own transportation and would come to the house, but people answering the ad always wanted the opposite arrangement. In general, she found that "the kind of person you want is the kind of person you can't get." She had one sitter who forced her four-year-old to eat a hot dog he was too full to finish "till he threw up." Another sitter, an elderly widow who seemed to fit the grandmotherly fantasy, was in fact a resentful, complaining woman who didn't really seem to like the children and told them that their father was "a bad man" because he'd divorced their mother. "They were so little then they didn't understand how I contributed to the divorce, so her words really upset them. So that was the end of her."

In an effort to find a good baby-sitter, many of us change sitters several times. Sometimes this creates real improvement, and sometimes it simply contributes inconsistency to the children's situation. Though I spoke to mothers who had found good, permanent care for their children, they tended to be women who were in a high-income bracket. Even those who could afford the at-home care they wanted, and got it, described occasional difficulties. One woman, who had the space and income to hire live-in help, said, "We've had excellent women, but a *succession* of excellent women."

When a sitter isn't satisfactory and you fire her or she quits, the drawn-out process of looking for a replacement begins, and it's easy to get pessimistic about finding a person you really want to hire. You often give in and just look for *someone*, anyone, who will start right away. That you can literally lose child care overnight leads to further inconsistent care and sometimes poor care. According to one child-care expert, "Once you have found a caregiver, you are relieved, you think you can sit back. But child care is like a used car, once you find it, you have to keep fixing it."[28] Joan Emerson, a California counselor who helps parents find child care, found that in looking for care, "Parents tend to be desperate, and that is the basic thing that leads to low-quality care."[29]

Even when parents can find a sitter they like and their children love, there are situations that can lead to inconsistent care: the sitter can get sick for a few days, her own children can get sick, or there can be some other emergency. Some of the best sitters are professionals who may go back to school or find a much better paying job after a year or two. One single parent, who had had a succession of both good and bad sitters during a twelve-year period, said, "In all those years, I never had a sitter longer than a year. Even the ones who said they loved my kids had some reason for going on to something else."

The Day-Care Center

Because of similar experiences, my husband and I got ourselves on a waiting list for a day-care center and finally got our children in. Though my eighteen-month-old son had a terrible first two weeks adjusting, he later loved it, and the center was the best experience we had. It was not affiliated with a university, but it was excellent,

with energetic, affectionate young workers and a well-organized program. Because there were a number of day-care teachers and a
backup list of substitutes, we never had to worry about a phone call
at 8:00 A.M. telling us that we were on our own for the day. This
alone took a burden off us. Once the children got used to the place,
it was a pleasure to take them there, and the high point of my day
was picking them up and seeing them happy. But the center, one of
those "high-quality facilities" a child development expert would
give high marks to, closed a year and a half after we had placed our
children there, due to lack of funds.

We were able to get our children into another place, although
the adjustment to another school was especially difficult for my son,
who was three by that time. The new place was disorganized and
confused. Though it appeared to give high-quality care, it was in
reality borderline unsafe simply because the supervision was so poor
for my son's age group. Twice I drove into the parking area and
found a three-year-old playing alone at the edge of the driveway,
waiting for her parents to pick her up.

Although the day-care center we first had was wonderful for us,
I have since learned that, apart from closing for lack of funds, centers also have many drawbacks for some parents. One problem is
their institutional nature, which concerns a lot of parents who have
infants or children under the age of three. This also concerns a good
many child development experts and psychologists, although there
have been studies that concluded that being away from the parent,
particularly the mother, and cared for by outside caregivers did not
affect a child's sense of security as long as the care was of high quality. However, the newer studies indicate that care for children under
nine months, particularly for male infants, may harm the infant-
mother relationship and, thus, the child's general sense of trust and
security. In several studies, psychology professor Jay Belsky found
that for children beginning day care under the age of eighteen
months, the incidence of insecure feelings was almost double that
for a child raised at home.[30] Other researchers who disagree with

these findings concede that a great deal depends on the quality of care, the individual child, and, sometimes, the gender of the child.[31]

Even when a family finds an institution that is good, there can still be a problem of inconsistency. In other words, the actual facility doesn't change, but the people working there do. Day-care centers have the highest rate of staff turnover of any human services profession.[32] The reason for the heavy turnover is a combination of low pay, low status, and physical and emotional exhaustion— burnout. Caring for several young children requires tremendous physical stamina, intelligence, and patience. We all have great sympathy for the woman who has sextuplets, but we forget that the experience of being a day-care worker is similar. A woman (and usually day-care workers are women) who is tempted to quit may try hard to stay on because she knows that the children are attached to her and that her leaving will mean one more adjustment for them. But it's logical that if this person has a degree and can get a better job, sooner or later she will leave an occupation that has high demands and low status and pay. "Caregivers in most licensed day-care centers earn less than golf caddies and parking lot attendants."[33]

Considering all the reading I have done and my experiences with my own children and their friends, my own feeling about day care for preschoolers is, when in doubt leave it out. The younger the child, the less institutional the care should be. Avoid using a day-care center unless it is significantly better than any sitter you can get (in our case, the first center we used was). Be sure there is a great deal of physical cuddling and holding and eye-to-eye contact between the caregiver and your baby or toddler. Be sure, too, that there is a strong sense of order at the place and that kids know what is expected of them. There is so much emphasis today on "allowing the child to feel free" and "stimulating the child's intellect and sense of self" that we often forget how important order and a dependable universe are for a small child.

My advice for anyone who must work outside the home and hire caregivers is to find the best possible sitter or center available and fight like hell to get it. Call frequently, get your name on a waiting list, ask if there is anything you can do that would give you a better chance of getting in. (I know someone who shoveled snow every winter at an excellent school that she otherwise could not have afforded.) Don't let yourself get so tired and discouraged that you convince yourself that the quality of even part-time care "isn't *that* important." We all know that if an intruder came into our home in the middle of the night, we would do everything we could to protect our children from possible harm. Considering how important good child care is for the welfare of children, I would advise any parent to take that same passion to protect, and use it to find the best possible care.

Learning Independence or Growing Up Too Fast?

In spite of the drawbacks to outside care and the amount of work involved in getting the best, there are some parents who will speak in glowing terms of their two-year-old's time at the day-care center. They will say, "Oh, she's learning so much; she's so much further ahead intellectually than she would be if she weren't in day care," or "He's really having to learn to be independent at the center." I don't necessarily think that this is rationalization. In such cases, I think parents are genuinely pleased and feel that their day-care situation is very good for the child. Learning independence seems to be one definite benefit to the child's being cared for away from home. I said so along with everybody else.

But I am no longer sure such "advances" are necessarily beneficial to small children. Is there something inherently good in a child's learning to do things early? Some of the learning that seems to give children a boost when they enter school can be gained through an hour of *Sesame Street* every day. There is little to indicate that a child's knowing the ABC's or how to tie shoes at three will ensure that he or she will become a great physician or famous government leader or an inventor at thirty. In fact, a good many high achievers in U.S. history have been slow learners. And, in emotional development, is early independence a guarantee of adult independence and self-confidence? No one can say yes with certainty.

A letter from a young Ohio mother raises some of these same questions: "It seems our culture is rather obsessed with making children independent because, of course, an independent child makes life more convenient for us. [But] dependency is partly what childhood means. . . . If a child feels loved, secure, and good about himself, he will naturally, on his own time table, become independent."[34]

Each parent, of course, has to determine whether a push toward independence, either in the day-care situation or at home, is taking place too early. But it is important not to assume blindly that early is necessarily better or that a child who appears self-reliant really is—or ought to be. Dr. David Elkind, author of *The Hurried Child*, reminds us that there is something to be said for "growing up slowly."

Children and Illness

When I look back, the incidents most distressing to me now are those that involved our not allowing our kids to be kids: scared or angry or unsure. Or ill. Illness in children is one of the things that some of the often childless "professional feminists" never talked about in espousing the notion of having it all. Yet preschool children—*healthy* preschool children—get an incredible variety of contagious diseases like colds and the flu and chicken pox, as well as occasional ear infections and stomachaches.

When our children were sick, I felt that we ought to be ready to stay home and make them chicken soup or Jell-O, to keep them in a warm bed and stroke their heads as my mother and father had done for me. Instead, we grilled our children to see how sick they were and whether one of us really *had* to stay home. Of all the hassles I had as a working mother, this one was fraught with more conflict and guilt than any other.

A typical scene would run something like this: at three in the morning, our daughter would jostle my elbow. "Mommy, Mommy,

Michael is throwing up. He's throwing up so much, he woke me up."
My husband and I would get out of bed to clean up Michael, change
him and the bedclothes, take his temperature, give him water, rock
him to sleep again, and soothe our daughter so that she could get
back to sleep. We would then pile back into bed at four.

An hour or two later the alarm clock would ring, and we would
get up for work—maybe work. We would check Michael, trying to
decide what to do. If he was hungry and fairly happy and had not
thrown up by seven or eight o'clock, I would take him to the sitter
or center at eight fifteen, praying that he would not be sick there.
Out of all the times I did this with both children, there were only
two times when they were so sick that we were called at work to
come get them. So we were lucky. I guess.

But I always felt guilty no matter what happened. I was guilty
about taking advantage of the sitter or center and terribly guilty
about leaving my kids when they were sick. If I had not been working, we most certainly would not have taken them away from a
warm bed and our care when they were feeling sick and unhappy. I
would also not have taken them to a place where they could expose
other children to whatever they had.

But one of the reasons it happened so often was because we felt
we had to save our sick leave for times when the children were
really ill and had to be quarantined for a week with chicken pox or
had strep throat or the flu. So I did not stay home with the kids
when they had something we deemed minor, though sometimes the
minor sniffles became major a few days later.

According to health care professionals, a recurring problem in
day-care centers—and, no doubt, in family day care too—is that
parents don't always keep children home for illness, and when they
do they often bring the children back to day care before they have
fully recovered. Such children then have low resistance and easily
pick up infections from other ill children. It is no wonder that "day
care transmission of disease is probably one of the whole nation's
major health problems."[35]

But as a parent with a job, what can you do? About the only thing that works is to use sick leave for your children instead of for yourself. A nurse I interviewed said that this was so common in the hospital where she worked that she and her colleagues had an expression for it: "kid sick."

One divorced woman I talked to about illness was a junior high school administrator with a primary school–age daughter. One winter, the child had a severe ear infection, followed by a bout with the flu, followed by a croupy cough. The mother had no recourse but to stay home with her daughter at first, because her ex-husband lived several hundred miles away, and she could find no sitter who would care for her child. But it became more and more difficult for her to call in and say that she would be out again because her six-year-old was ill. After a couple of weeks she was lucky enough to find a friend who worked at home and was willing to look after her child while she went in to work for a few days. But later in the winter, when her daughter was sick again, she phoned the office with her hand over her nose and said that *she* was sick.

Many women feel that they simply cannot tell a boss or even some colleagues why they are out for fear that it would seriously jeopardize their job. For a single mother, telling the truth is not worth the risk, particularly if she is in a previously male-dominated job. It's all very well to say, "Well, women should just create a simpler lifestyle and wait till their children are older before working outside the home." But for some parents, particularly single parents, this simply isn't an option financially.

Eventually, of course, the hassles of children's getting sick lessen. Children get older and have fewer illnesses and accidents and emotional upsets and mysterious stomachaches. They can stay home by themselves when they do get sick, with someone looking in on them at lunchtime. Children are great survivors.

Parents are great survivors, too. We solve problems as they come along and try not to concentrate on the frustrations. We swap desperation stories with other working parents and learn to set up a network of friends, relatives, neighbors, or part-time sitters to help in emergencies. And some parents finally find the "perfect" child-care setup.

In the course of interviewing two former day-care workers, I came to recognize the mistakes we had made in looking for people to care for our children. I could see that we had not worked hard enough to find sitters whose values and priorities were the same as our family's. When we lost a sitter, we did not labor hard enough or long enough to find really good replacements. However, at the time I felt you have to take what you get, and it was easy to become pessimistic. As Linda Burton points out in her essay, there simply aren't enough people out there providing excellent care. More alarming is that in this country, some parents who must work to stay off welfare cannot find any permanent care at all. So a child of four or five is shuffled from temporary sitter to neighbor to friend to, occasionally, the back seat of the parent's car, or is left in an empty house. "So you have parents, usually single parents, struggling to overcome that AFDC [welfare] syndrome by working. It becomes evident that for lack of affordable, safe day care, neglect seems to be the only option. If people want to press criminal charges against the mother [of children who are hurt or killed], we would also have to put legislators on the accomplice list."[36]

There are various policy changes and concrete improvements that could be made on federal and state levels. But as it is, federal and state subsidies for child care are inadequate for low-income parents. There is no help for middle-income and lower-middle-income groups, apart from some private and community referral groups in some states. Fortunately, there are a growing number of corporate on-site child-care facilities. Still, there is not enough adequate care, and thousands continue to be on waiting lists for both subsidized and nonsubsidized care.

Single parents who work sometimes make so little money after paying day-care expenses that it is only the unpleasant alternative of welfare that keeps them going. Yet middle-income married women who want to stay home have financial difficulty doing so. The legislative push is for day care, particularly institutional centers rather than a mixed approach, with parents who prefer to stay home or work part-time dissuaded, making the space squeeze at centers worse. Divorced middle-income women who might be able to afford to work half-time or during school hours often can't because the courts do not consistently prosecute ex-husbands for reneging on child support. Among these men who fail in their responsibility are professionals and successful business executives.

Those of us concerned about all of this are left with many questions. I fluctuated between feeling that maybe children with mothers at home in the 1950s and earlier were indulged, to feeling that children are vulnerable, needy, powerless beings who cannot adequately articulate their wants and needs. I ask myself whether the rough-and-tumble of a day-care center is good for little children. Or do they need, when they are tiny, as much protection and holding and individual attention as they can get? Does growing up with a group of children help children learn to interact with their peers? Or simply cause them to be overly aggressive or susceptible to peer pressure? Do the disappointments children feel when nobody can leave work to drive them to an after-school birthday party, or to see them in a school play, make them tough and resilient? Or simply insecure and sad? In short, when we accept, even promote, a childhood for the nation's children that is less secure and nurturing and consistent than what many of us benefited from, are we being rational—or simply rationalizing? Is anyone being liberated?

4

Can You Really *Afford* to Quit?

By the time I quit, I felt that I would rather eat spaghetti every night than keep us all in the working-mom rat race. I simply didn't care about the money. When I quit in the summer, I figured—pretty vaguely—that if things got bad financially by September, I could probably get a teaching job at night for a few hours a week. Once you've gotten to the point where you are ready to quit full-time work and stay home with a child or children, it's tempting to quit on the spot. But I don't recommend it.

No matter how stressful the home-work situation is, it's best to quit after at least a little forethought and two weeks' notice. This isn't just courtesy and kindness talking, it's practicality too. You never know how many years it will be before you want or need to go back to full-time work, and sometimes an old job is the first and best place to look.

I also think it makes life easier for everybody in the family if some preparations have been made ahead of time. Sitting down with paper and pencil and making some evaluations of your finances, emotions, and community is wise. And if the financial assessment looks grim for you as a one-paycheck family, then it helps also to look at the possibilities for part-time or at-home employment.

Making a Financial Assessment

The best assessment to do first is definitely the financial one. This is just a cousin of the monthly budget most of us are already familiar with. If you have never done a budget, go to the local public library or paperback bookstore for references. There are also booklets you can buy at stationery or discount stores that are written specifically for itemized budgeting. When listing your present expenses, keep in mind that it's crucial that you remember *all* expenses.

According to financial experts, when people review their finances, they're often worried that they will only learn what they can't do. But according to these same experts, planning gives you "greater control and well-being." Parents who want to have the mother stay home have to change their financial priorities and "recognize the need for trade-offs."[1]

Once you have a basic budget for the average amount you spend on items each month, take a close look at the individual items and begin putting values on things: what you *need* and what you *like*. On two separate sheets of paper, transfer budget items to a "Need" list and a "Like" list. A working couple with one child might wind up with something like Tables 4.1 and 4.2.

When both lists are complete—and it usually takes a week or two to think of *everything*—type or print out the lists and make at least two photocopies of each list. That way, you can play around with scratching out and reentering items without totally obliterating the lists.

As you've probably guessed, the purpose of these two lists is to figure out what you can comfortably cut out of your Like list and cut down on in your Need list. The key to doing both successfully is to find a lower-priced replacement for an item, rather than dropping it entirely. Cutting out the basic things on the Need list is impossible, and removing everything from the Like list can lead to problems: resentment on the part of the person working outside the home, and a feeling of being "stuck" or "poor" for the person at home. So avoid being savage.

Table 4.1. "Need" List.

ITEM	COST
Monthly bills paid on time:	
Mortgage	_____
Utilities:	
Gas	_____
Electric	_____
Water/Sewer	_____
Fuel	_____
Installment payments:	
Car loan	_____
Refrigerator loan	_____
Credit card bill	_____
Insurance premiums	_____
Bills coming in twice a year or more:	
Medical and dental bills	_____
Maintenance costs on house and yard;	
condo or co-op apartment fees	_____
Transportation/automobile maintenance costs	_____
Taxes:	
Property	_____
Residence	_____
State	_____
Federal	_____
Dues for professional organizations	_____
Clothing:	
Work	_____
Recreation and home	_____
Children's	_____
Personal grooming:	
Haircuts	_____
Cosmetics	_____
Other	_____
Furniture for children and house	_____
Food:	
Groceries	_____
Snacks and coffee breaks	_____
Lunch out at work	_____
Savings	_____
Unexpected expenses	
Entertainment (leave blank until Like list is completed;	
alter after doing emotional evaluation)	_____

Table 4.2. "Like" List.

ITEM	COST
Entertainment:	
Weekend movie twice a month	_____
Dinner out once a week	_____
Lunch out on weekend	_____
Other treats:	
Concerts	_____
Party with friends occasionally	_____
Racquetball one night a week	_____
Travel:	
Occasional weekend trips	_____
Summer vacation	_____
Long winter weekend away	_____
Lessons and classes:	
Art	_____
Music	_____
Aerobics	_____
Books and CDs or tapes	_____
Children's books and toys	_____
Charitable contributions	_____
Gifts	_____
Extras:	
Full liquor cabinet	_____
Other: _____	_____

Reducing Expenses: The Need List

Though it may seem that the most you can hope to do in order to economize is take things off the Like list only, you can usually change more things on the Need list than you'd expect.

Buying a House

If you are thinking about a major purchase, such as a house, think again. More young mothers get caught on a treadmill of working because of high monthly mortgage payments than for any other reason. Sometimes there is no way of avoiding this. As one young woman said, "If you want to have children you don't want to raise them in an apartment, and sometimes renting a house is almost as expensive as making monthly mortgage payments."

However, if you are thinking of buying a house, but haven't yet, consider all the alternatives carefully: a smaller house than you originally planned; a house located in a modest family neighborhood; a duplex or house with an apartment you can rent for income; a basic house you can build, acting as your own contractor; an old house in need of cosmetic improvements you can do yourself; a large house that could be renovated and made into a bed-and-breakfast for paying guests or some other venture. High mortgage payments are the number one nemesis of stay-at-home mothers, so consider a home purchase carefully.

Utility Costs

These costs can be reduced in several ways. For specific help on saving energy, contact the utility companies themselves, and read state and federal pamphlets (available at the local public library), as well as magazines or books relevant to the subject.

Loan Payments

If, like our hypothetical working couple with one child, you have loan payments, check to see how far along you are in paying off the loans. You might want to pay off a loan before quitting, reduce it, or sell a second car so you don't have an item like "car loan payment" on your Need list at all.

Medical Expenses

No one can do without medical attention for a serious illness or injury, but you can read up on what symptoms indicate a severe ear infection or simply a mild cold that a parent can treat without paying to be told how. I have spoken to a couple of women who have found good, sensible books on herbal remedies and other home medical treatments. Attending to some medical needs yourself is definitely a growing trend. Some of the books available today are what my husband calls "quack books," but others are dependable and written with sound medical advisers. In fact, one of Dr. Spock's original purposes in writing his famous baby book was to assist parents who did not live within easy access of a doctor.

Preparing chicken soup and offering a cool hand for a feverish forehead are, by the way, in the best tradition of a mother at home. So, using care, try to determine what savings are possible for you in health care. Look into HMOs, community clinics, free testing at health fairs and hospital open houses, subsidized well-baby clinics, and other alternatives.

Home Maintenance Costs

Moving down the list, maintenance costs on a house can be greatly reduced by doing as much as possible yourself. Again, there are lots of books and other resources to help you here. One of the most significant savings in maintenance I made my first year at home was in repairs I did myself that were crying to be made: replastering small holes in the hallway walls, applying roofing cement to a low roof that leaked, and caulking around the windows outside. I knew nothing about these things initially and regarded the replastering job with great trepidation. But an unexpected bonus in muddling my way through these tasks was that I learned some new skills and had a boost to my morale as a woman who did not have to rely on hiring a man to do such jobs.

Automobile Maintenance Costs

One of the best ways to save on this item is to keep a car as long as possible, preferably five years after the last car payment has been made. This is not an easy thing to do if you live in a Midwestern or Northeastern city where salt is used on the roads in the winter. To get rid of the corroding residue of salt, wash the car regularly. If it is too miserably cold to wash the car at home, look for high school car washes and do-it-yourself car wash establishments, which are a little less expensive than the regular drive-through places. Try to find time to change the oil, antifreeze, and other liquids yourself. As the car ages, buy plastic filler with fiber in it at the local discount auto parts store to fill any small holes that develop on the bottom of the car. To take care of rust spots, sand with fine-grit sandpaper, clean, swab with Extend Rust Treatment, and then paint over with a small vial of matching paint available from the dealer or auto body store.

Taxes

If only they and death *could* be avoided. But, according to writer and new father Peter Spotts, whose wife stayed home with their baby, this item on the list can be tamed. By changing the allowable exemptions on federal W-2 forms and state income tax forms at the father's workplace, your one paycheck can yield additional money for monthly expenses. Many parents who quit say that at tax time their family's lower tax bracket means significant savings for them.

Clothes

These parents also cite substantial savings in clothing when they quit. Clothes for work usually cost more than those worn around the house. And at-home parents have time to shop for sales, to find good discount stores, to get kids' clothing at thrift shops, and to buy adults' clothing at upscale, Junior League–type thrift shops. So figure on a cost reduction in clothes, even if you're not planning on doing any sewing. How to save money buying clothes is discussed in detail in Chapter Five, "Saving Money Instead of Making It."

Food Costs

Increases in food costs in the last decade have meant that this budget item on the list takes a much bigger percentage of our monthly income than it used to. But it's possible to get around this problem by growing some of your own food, joining food co-ops, buying in bulk, and using supermarket savings gimmicks, as described in Chapter Five.

The Importance of Savings

Sylvia Porter and other economists insist that you set aside money for savings and unexpected expenses no matter how small your income. Even if the amount saved is only five dollars a week, you should still set this money aside. Some at-home parents earmark about 60 percent of all the Christmas and other gift checks that come into the family for savings when they don't have any surplus after budgeting basic expenses.

Adding Up Income You May Not Have Thought Of

If you are like we were, your Need list total expenditures may add up to an amount that's close to that of the one paycheck you have to live on. But don't be discouraged. One other step is important in determining exactly where you will stand financially: add up the money you will have coming in apart from the one paycheck, such as bonuses, interest on savings or NOW accounts, gift checks from relatives, likely tax refunds, income on the sale of a car or extra TV, and so on. Think of all this as money in the till, money to live on—because it will be.

Also, if you have never taken deductions on your federal income tax forms or have hired an accountant to do your taxes, consider spending several hours learning to do your own taxes in the spring. Find out what kind of free help is available at the local IRS office or public library. But be sure to go early, in January or early February, when staff people will have time to help you individually. Use the library's copy of the IRS handbook for the current tax year and become knowledgeable about what donations, taxes, and loan interest payments you are entitled to deduct. It is still possible to take deductions for donations to your church or synagogue, home mortgages, state and local taxes, and medical expenses, to name a few items. It takes me at least a full day to do the forms each year, but we get IRS refunds of $90 or more and save still more by not hiring an accountant to do our taxes.

Reducing Expenses: The Like List

When you've done all you can to determine your new income and your essential needs, look at the Like list. Knock out, cut down, or find inexpensive substitutes for as many items as you can. In doing so, remember that this is not forever. There will be a day when your children are older, and you'll have two paychecks again and can put all the items back on the list.

How to Make Money-Saving Changes

Let's say you have "aerobics class at health club" one night a week on your Like list. In finding an alternative, you might consider whether it could be replaced with a less-expensive kindergym class with your child at a local community center. Or you might decide simply to walk or ride a bike more. One woman I interviewed said that she was able to keep her weight down consistently (and also get "time away alone") by taking long walks in the evening while her husband got the children ready for bed.

A week's summer vacation at a resort could be replaced by a week in a national park cabin or a visit with old friends or relatives, which would later be reciprocated. On some U.S. and Canadian college campuses, it's possible to stay for a week or more in a college dormitory during the summer for a half or third of what it would cost to stay in a nearby motel.

"Likes" That Are "Needs"

Once you have performed surgery on your Like list, it's important to put the items you can't bear to strike out onto your Need list; then toss out the Like list (you might as well get used to doing without the extraneous). It may seem odd to add these items to the Need list, but if you have had trouble crossing off an item or finding a replacement, it is probably because it really matters to your family, so it is a need—emotionally.

I cannot stress enough how important it is to include important

Likes on the Need list. The more rest and relaxation you have, the easier it is to drop *things* from the Need list: a new piece of furniture, a new car, a large wardrobe, and so forth. The idea is to attend to the basic, physical needs you have without going into debt and get the same *or more* recreation and relaxation. The purpose of the financial assessment is not to consign families to a sterile, static lifestyle but to determine what they really need in order to remain physically and emotionally healthy as individuals and as a family.

Making an Emotional Assessment

That last point brings me to the next evaluation that you need to make: an emotional or psychological assessment. This involves an honest questioning of whether everyone in the family can eliminate things from the Like list, find alternatives, and shift priorities. In short, can everyone handle doing without for a few years? This question follows logically from the financial assessment because in making that assessment first, *what* is really important *to whom* comes out pretty dramatically—and that there is going to be a lot less money becomes obvious. Assessing your ability to live in slightly (or greatly) reduced circumstances is more important to your success than determining precisely how much you'll save on transportation costs or how many discount stores are located near your home.

Individual Needs

There are some people who, in honestly questioning themselves, may decide they cannot do without. For example, a woman who was the youngest of several children and the recipient of large numbers of hand-me-downs and, at thirty, is a compulsive clothes buyer might be such a person. However, continuing to work is not necessarily the answer. There might be several other solutions to this problem, from professional counseling sessions to learning how to sew clothes instead of buying them. But it is crucial to acknowledge a partner's difficulty in doing without, because one of the great things about a mother's quitting her job is what good things it can do for her marriage. Such things won't happen if one partner has a lot of resentment or insecurity about the family's reduced income.

One woman I spoke to was married to a man who was insecure about money in spite of his relatively high salary and the hefty sum they had been able to save before their baby was born. He was upset that his wife insisted on quitting her job permanently. Ironically, they eventually saved more money each month when she was at home because she changed her clothing- and food-buying habits. But whether she saved money in a given month or broke even, she put everything down on paper to reassure him that things were OK, that they were going to make it.

As the characters of cartoonist Berke Breathed remind us, we all have a "closet of anxieties." Sharing the financial responsibility of raising a family has been one of the bonuses of the women's movement for men, and taking this bonus away in part or completely can be very unsettling. As one husband said, "This feels a little like launching a rowboat with only one oar." It's important to keep lines of communication open and, especially the first few months after quitting, to keep a constant eye on how well funds are holding out.

In evaluating your psychological and emotional attitudes, avoid "shoulds" and "should nots"—toward yourself as well as toward your partner. For example, "I shouldn't care so much about replacing the ratty living room couch with a new one; staying home with my three-year-old should be enough." If getting a decent-looking couch is important to you, it's important. So before quitting, have it recovered, buy a new one, or get one at an upscale yard sale. Avoid expending psychic energy telling yourself how you "should" be feeling.

Which Parent Will Quit?

Deciding who will quit to stay home full- or part-time is sometimes very obvious, sometimes not. Type of work, scheduling, income differences, bosses' attitudes, proximity of home to work, and possibilities for at-home income—all are important to consider. It also happens in some cases that parents can share caregiving by having one parent at home for a couple of years and then the other parent. But the decision is often dictated by emotional as well as economic considerations. An attorney who wanted to be a full-time mom while her children were young is quoted in *A Mother's Work* as saying that, although her husband was a schoolteacher and might seem to be the logical one to stay home, she "was much more suited in certain temperamental ways" for at-home parenting.[2]

The communication process that is involved in making some of the other assessments described in these pages should help a couple express feelings and sort out who should stay home and for how long. One source of inspiration is Arlene Rossen Cardozo's book *Sequencing*, in which she describes women who experience work and parenting and work again in sequence.

Social Pressures and Isolation

In addition to dealing with personal hangups and fears about finances, it is also helpful to look at your family's social life and immediate community for any pressures that may be there. What are the social expectations? Are you living in an upper-middle-class community where children go to private kindergarten at five and have a ten-speed bike by the time they're nine? Do you belong to a social or athletic club where people think little of spending fifty to a hundred dollars on a Friday evening?

In our own case, my husband and I have never gotten into this kind of social milieu, and we live in a neighborhood that is pleasant but hardly chic. Because I quit when they were three and six, my children became accustomed from an early age to doing without, "buying used," or setting aside allowance money for various things. But in some areas, particularly in suburbs of large cities, there is a lot of pressure to consume and compete. In such areas, it's tough for the kids of a stay-at-home parent to keep their feet on the ground in their factory-second sneakers. It's well to keep all this in mind if you're in the market for a house; you want to be sure you're living in a neighborhood where your values won't be out of place.

In making a family evaluation of feelings, you should also think about the disadvantages of staying home, the isolation and loneliness a parent can feel initially—or sometimes longer. This usually is not a problem once you meet other parents who are at home, and there *are* millions of us out here. But having both a husband and wife identify disadvantages to staying home can sometimes lead to surprising results if both earn roughly the same salary. I know of two situations in which the wife's salary was enough to support the family, so the husband stayed home with the children while she got out of the house. In one case the husband did part-time consulting when the children became of school age, and in the other the father was content to involve himself in rearing the children for several years. It is important to be flexible and open to the possibility that in some cases it is better for the father to stay home.

Whoever winds up at home, it is wise to create a short transitional period before quitting work, during which the family tries out living on one paycheck. Although the transition may be a little misleading financially because you don't save on commuting and other work-related expenses, it is still helpful. It enables you to see what it's like to live modestly, with low-cost alternatives for both basic and emotional needs.

Assessing Your Community

Once family members get clear on everybody's feelings about living on a reduced income, it's important to take a look at the area where you live, analyzing how it can help you to economize and also enjoy life in spite of having a reduced income. Are there brand-name outlet stores in your town where you can buy clothes and shoes? Thrift shops where you can buy and sell clothing? A dairy farm, bread factory, or day-old bakery outlet where you can get inexpensive milk and bread? Is there an open produce market, meat market, dockside fish market in your city? Are large, individual garden plots on town land available to residents in your community? Is there a food or baby-sitting co-op in your area? Finding the answers to these questions can make for some interesting "field trips" for your children and can enable you to see how much you can save in your own neighborhood.

If you live in a wealthy urban or suburban area, where most residents have little interest in economizing, this whole process may seem a bit discouraging. But over time, you will become aware of things that will provide savings. And if you do quit working full-time, you will meet a number of people in the same boat through your children's activities.

"Cheap Thrills"

In analyzing how your community can be a source of savings, take note of what is available purely for recreation—"cheap thrills," as one couple put it. Check out the parks, public tennis courts and swimming pools, local "Y's" and community centers, state colleges, churches, synagogues, and public libraries. Even places that charge admission, such as museums and botanical gardens, may have low or free admission during certain hours or seasons. Theater tickets are free in some regional theaters if you usher or provide some other service, and movies usually cost less at matinees. There is probably a great deal more available than you realize, especially if you live in or near a city with a population of more than twenty-five thousand people.

Living in the Country

If you live far from a city or town, then it's likely that you're in a rural, physically beautiful area. There's a lot to be said for swinging on the bough of an old beech tree. In the country, a stay-at-home parent has a special opportunity to revive practices like maple sugaring, raising animals that produce dairy products, or heating with wood—practices that save money and give children good skills and experiences as well as provide family enjoyment. There are advantages and disadvantages to any location that a family might live in; the parent at home needs to concentrate on the advantages and make the most of them.

Alternative Employment

After looking at finances, individual feelings, and community advantages, you may feel that your family cannot get along happily with only one paycheck. At this point a woman committed to staying at home can delay quitting her job for several months, saving at least half of every paycheck so that she can later afford to stay home. This approach can be a little risky, however. As a four-year practitioner, I finally dubbed this the "Mañana Syndrome." It can go on indefinitely.

It is sometimes better to assess what opportunities are available for what I call "alternative employment": part-time, evening, temporary, half-day, short-term, or at-home work. There are growing opportunities for this kind of employment today. One out of every five jobs in the United States is part-time, and more of these positions are opening up every day. According to a number of studies and surveys, the number of voluntary part-time workers continues to increase. *Black Enterprise* magazine has estimated that more than twenty-seven million Americans are home workers.[3] Though part-time jobs and at-home occupations have traditionally been low paying and nonprofessional, this is beginning to change, especially in flex-time and job-sharing situations and in computer-related home businesses.

One of the first places to look for a part-time job is at your present job, assuming that one of the reasons you want to quit isn't your dislike for your present occupation. Women I have interviewed who have transferred from full-time to part-time hours have said that a job that was overwhelming five days a week became wonderful three full days a week or five half-days.

There are also weekend and evening jobs, though they may not pay well. However, if what you care about most is fitting paying work comfortably into your life as a mother, these are sometimes the best jobs to get, especially if you only want one for a few years. Sometimes, they also lead to friendships with other mothers who have similar needs and priorities.

Although it is unusual for a parent to survive financially with part-time work if he or she is divorced, unmarried, or widowed, it has been done. It helps if you have only one or two children and some savings, as well as a network of emotionally supportive relatives or friends. A single mother with a baby son described trying to find "the right balance between earning an income and being at home" and wound up doing day care in her apartment in the mornings, teaching at night a few hours, and occasionally offering parenting workshops. "All of these jobs combined don't take me away from [my son] as much as one office job would, and I'm free to rearrange my schedule." As she herself admitted, not all single parents have her "particular set of skills or . . . drive." Nonetheless, she thought that for most women there are "alternatives if they want to stay home with their children."[4]

The alternative for many parents, both single and married, is to set up a modest business at home. For someone with a lot of energy and organizational skill, doing this offers a challenge and can sometimes turn into a larger, more lucrative business when children in the family get older. In deciding what specifically to do, it's best to consider your community's needs and then write down your education, experience, and interests. As many at-home businesses have developed from parents' interests as from their original full-time occupations. (For more information on part-time work both inside and outside the home, see Chapters Seven, Eight, and Nine, and Appendixes A and B at the end of the book.)

Enjoy Being at Home

Recently, some excellent magazine articles and paperback books have been published on how to set up a business at home. Unfortunately, some of the how-to information gives the impression that if a woman doesn't work for pay outside the home, she's got to work for pay inside the home, which simply contributes to the Superwoman Syndrome. If you are thinking of quitting, and it isn't immediately necessary to bring in some money, then don't—just enjoy being at home. Often, even with a financial assessment, a couple can't tell how well they will eventually manage to do without the second paycheck. So, if you have enough savings, it may be best to wait a while before plunging into a part-time job or at-home business. Running a home and raising small children is a more than sufficient occupation for many of us.

5

Saving Money Instead of Making It

Although I did not know enough at the time I quit my job to make a formal assessment of our family finances, I knew that we would have to make a great many changes in our lives in order to stay solvent on one paycheck. I was going to have to figure out ways to save money, because I wouldn't be making any for a while. My children were three and six, old enough not to need constant attention, so I figured that one thing I would have would be time, which I could use to economize. Many of the changes we made as a family and incorporated into our daily lives were picayune and were, by themselves, inconsequential. But coupled with some major changes, they made a big difference. They added up at the end of the month, and, maybe more important, they reflected a change in attitude: we became more questioning, self-aware, and resourceful.

In making individual changes, flexibility—bordering on off-the-wall looseness—was a big help. I found some unusual ways to save money. My family's favorite was the time my daughter had outgrown her ballet slippers two weeks before her spring recital and last lesson. In the past we had decided that it was OK for the slippers to be snug by the end of the school year so that we wouldn't have to buy another pair. When my daughter outgrew the slippers early that spring, I was not about to buy a new pair and have them sit in her closet all summer after being worn twice. So I lathered saddle soap onto the slippers to soften them and then stretched and pulled gently at the leather in the toes to make more room. Then I hung the slippers from hooks on the bathroom door and weighted them down with smooth stones from the beach to stretch them some more. Two days later, the slippers fit perfectly.

My daughter thought her mother was "very strange" and did not want me to tell anyone about the way we had managed to avoid buying new slippers. But two years later, at age eleven when she was growing so fast that we had to buy a pair of slippers twice during the year (and even then the second pair was snug by April), she asked me for instructions on how to stretch her slippers. A few hours later I found the soft pink slippers swinging on the bathroom hooks, stuffed with small stones.

Sources of Information on Saving

Though we invented many of our own methods for saving, we also borrowed from some excellent sources. One of the best was a used book entitled *The Heart Has Its Own Reasons*, which describes a wide range of ways to save, from major considerations like housing to minor ones like using rags or newspapers for cleaning instead of paper towels. I found that used books stores, the public library, and the paperback section of the local bookstores were invaluable for finding the help I needed. If you want a book but it's too expensive to buy, ask your librarian to order it for you. Many people forget that most public libraries have what is called an acquisition budget. Librarians like to know what books their "customers" want, so don't ever hesitate to ask for a specific book or periodical. There are books on budgeting with money-saving tips that I have taken out of our library three or four times.

During my first six months at home, I read various pamphlets on saving energy, and articles in women's magazines on food management. I had always looked down my nose at how-to-stretch-your-food-dollar articles when I was working. I didn't have the time or patience or energy to try their recommendations. But I set aside my skepticism and began reading such material carefully. I also sent away for information and attended two free workshops on energy saving given by our state university's cooperative extension service.

Now there are also a number of thrift newsletters and a collection of the *Tightwad Gazette* newsletters first published in the early 1990s when the quest to stay home and survive financially first caught hold. Jim and Amy Dacyczyn, the couple who published this popular newsletter took care of their large family in an old farmhouse in Leeds, Maine, while dispensing money-saving tips. That their newsletter, and others that have followed, have had success in finding subscribers certainly indicates that there are a great many people who are eager to establish a more frugal, family-centered lifestyle. (For more information on budget-conscious newsletter subscriptions and books on saving, see Appendix A at the back of the book.)

On a different note, I also reread Peg Bracken's book *I Hate to Keep House*, which I had received years before as a wedding present from some discerning true friend. When I stopped working, I had mistakenly assumed that I would miraculously turn into a wonderful housekeeper just because I was at home. We were all sorely disappointed in this. In fact, with three of us at home all the time, the house had the potential of getting into a bigger mess than ever. But such books helped me to keep a sense of humor and to realize that I could do only so much. Besides, my shocking deficiencies as a housekeeper saved us money—the less I vacuumed the house, the more electricity we saved. The more I served carrot and celery sticks for the vegetable at dinner instead of chopping and cooking them, the more gas we saved.

How to Get Organized When You Don't Have the Time and books by Heloise and Mary Ellen can all be a big help. The materials I read encouraged me in my hope that time—instead of a second paycheck—could be our hedge against inflation. So I urge anyone who is quitting full-time work, or thinking of doing so, to check out all the resources available.

Specific Ways to Save Money

From such resources I gleaned dozens of ways to save money. Here are a few, with some contributions from several other families, just on clothing and personal appearance items:

- Buy children's and adults' clothing at regular store sales or at factory outlet stores and dependable thrift shops.

- Sell all clothing you're not wearing to thrift shops, or have a yard sale; what you don't sell, give to charity, estimating the fair market value and taking it as a charitable deduction on your income tax.

- Dry clothes on the clothesline outside; inside, on a drying rack.

- Iron only a few times a year; when you do iron, do a lot all at once.

- Spot-clean or brush woolens whenever possible; air-dry wool suits to keep them fresh.

- Wash knitted woolens in cold water and mild liquid soap.

- If you have the talent, make clothing, tote bags, bedspreads, curtains, and other things, preferably using sale fabrics and remnants.

- Cut hair at home or go to a barber rather than to a hairdresser; consider having Mom's hair shoulder length so that frequent cuttings are not necessary.

- Ask for expensive perfumes, makeup, and after-shave lotions for Christmas or birthday presents when relatives ask what to get.

- "Cherry-pick" for soaps and shampoos (that is, check out prices any time you're at a supermarket, dime store, or drug or beauty outlet store, and stock up at the place that sells a good brand for the least amount).

- Buy appliances on sale but buy very good appliances; the same goes for anything else that the family uses daily or that is expensive to repair.

- Store soap out of the wrapper to minimize its gooeyness when it's wet, thereby lengthening its "life." The stored soap also perfumes drawers.

- Buy dress shoes and other shoes you don't wear frequently that are made of high-quality vinyl. Save your money for leather boots and shoes you wear every day.

- Buy high-quality underwear, but try to buy only at sales.

- Buy supermarket stockings, and stick them in the freezer for a day to lengthen their life.

- Buy a minimum of all clothing, in fabrics that are long-lasting.

- Color-coordinate clothing for both children and adults so that everything goes together and nothing is "wasted."

- If you have a baby, use cloth diapers instead of disposables.

- Let your children wear minimal clothing in the summer—shorts and no shirt, for example. Get them in the habit of wearing layers of clothing in the winter inside the house.

- If you're really well organized, keep a small notepad with you at all times on which you can list prices for the same item at various stores; this way, you know who sells what for the least amount of money.

The list could go on and on. The point is, you can revive and invent all kinds of saving methods once you start thinking about what life was like before paper towels.

I will be the first to admit that some of the economies are a pain in the neck. As a result, I, as well as many other at-home mothers, do not stick rigidly to all our methods of saving at all times. Often you can stop saving in one particular area that no longer seems "worth it," and rigorously, consistently save in another area.

Saving Money on Clothes

Sometimes children dictate changes. While your children are young, it's wise to take advantage of their not knowing—or caring about—the difference between brands. Babies do not know when they are wearing secondhand clothing. Three- or four-year-olds are more aware, but if clothing comes from an admired older neighbor or cousin, their secondhand clothes can actually be a source of pride.

School-age children are sometimes bothered if all their clothes come from a thrift shop or a neighbor child. Older children care a lot. But in that case, you can buy at good outlets, ask for clothes from grandparents for birthdays, and also let children buy some items with an allowance or earned money. If free or inexpensive clothes are a source of delight rather than an embarrassment for you, it's likely that they will be for your children too. Writer and at-home advocate Mary Ann Cahill, author of *The Heart Has Its Own Reasons*, reminds us that "it can be said unequivocally that there is no evidence that a child suffers any mental or physical trauma from wearing secondhand or handmade clothes; the same cannot be said when substitutes are made for mother-at-home."[1]

Saving Money on Housing

Babies and little children are also quite unaware of how large or well decorated their houses or apartments are. So the home itself might be a place where you can make major savings. As I said in Chapter Four, high housing costs can be a real nemesis for parents-at-home.

In responding to this challenge, it's important, once again, to be very flexible. If you have not yet bought a house, can you wait? Or can you buy a smaller house? An older home? A duplex with another couple? Or could you be happy buying a large house that has separate living quarters for a tenant or an elderly, rent-paying relative? Do you have the interest and background to act as a "house parent" in a halfway house or home for retarded adults? Could you buy a nice house in an inexpensive neighborhood that's "coming up"? Would you be interested in joining an established rural or urban commune? Do you have the minimal skills and patience needed to fix up a solid but neglected older home? Or to build a small house with plans from a house plan company? What about buying a condominium or townhouse with a community yard and garden? Would it be possible to buy a place with land that you could (and would like to) make income-producing?

There are many, many possibilities for home ownership besides the conventional concept many of us have grown up with. Books such as *Cooperative Housing Compendium: Resources for Collaborative Living* and "alternative lifestyle" publications like *Mother Earth News* and the less glossy architecture magazines and plan catalogues are good resources. In considering housing, keep in mind what your priorities are for family life. For:

> there is something terribly sad about a residential street where house after house stands silent and empty during the day, heavily bolted against modern predators. The adults are out working—quite often to pay the high housing costs—and the children have been dispersed to various caretakers. Is the house serving the people, or are the people in service to the house? When parents and children are at home only in the evening and on weekends, *the tab for housing, per hour of its use, is very high*. In terms of enjoyment for the whole family, the return on the investment is truly low.[2]

In order for the parent to stay at home full- or part-time, many families simply rent an apartment for a little longer than they'd originally planned. But rents can be high, too, particularly in nice apartment complexes. Renting offers fewer alternatives than does home ownership, but there are still some options. I spoke to four women who lived in low-income housing subsidized by the federal government, by their city, and, in one case, by a combination of city, state, and federal funds. Two of these places were described as "not the greatest, but OK for a few years," the third was "nice—lots of young couples with kids and middle-aged divorced women with teenagers to baby-sit," and the fourth was "super," located in a wooded area near an academic community.

In looking for this type of housing, you have to be careful, because some subsidized apartment complexes (or "projects") are favorite targets for vandalism, among other problems. But some can be very good, too. The best often have long waiting lists, so it's wise to get on the list as soon as you hear of a place.

One benefit in many apartment complexes that have lots of other families is that there are usually opportunities for baby-sitting exchanges, food cooperatives, and splitting the costs of everything from a daily newspaper to a side of beef.

In finding any place to rent that's reasonable for a one-paycheck family's budget, it is wise to ask around and check out all possibilities. Sometimes the best deal can be caretaking at a museum or living in the mammoth house of an elderly lady who spends half the year in Florida. These particular options are not available everywhere, and I don't mean to suggest that they are. But there *are* innumerable possibilities for both renting and buying.

Reducing Medical Costs

After housing, medical and dental insurance and medical bills are big expenses that put dents in a good budget. You can either regard them as essentials and cut down somewhere else, or you can look for alternatives. If you are near a university dental school, you can have routine checkups and cleanings done there and have more complicated procedures done by a dentist who's been in practice for many years. Considering the relatively low cost of toothpaste and dental floss, it's also a good idea to strongly encourage all family members to brush and floss often and to stay away from sweets.

Because of recent changes in the health care field, people should look on health care as a "buyer's market." Doctors and hospitals are becoming more and more competitive. There are HMOs, urgent-care centers, shopping center doctors' offices, and health insurance HMOs, to name a few of the current options for health care. So you don't have to stick with the insurance policies and private physicians you may have had for years. If you are healthy and are not planning to have any more children, you can consider getting what I call "disaster insurance"—the minimum medical coverage for a disabling illness or accident.

Visits to a doctor for a cold or the flu can be cut out by becoming knowledgeable about common symptoms and methods of relief. The expense of visits for an illness you are uncertain about can be kept down by going to a clinic with sliding-scale fees. Also keep an eye out for freebies at health fairs and mobile Red Cross or visiting nurse units where you can have your blood pressure or cholesterol level checked or get a free breast exam. If you have preschoolers, check out community health programs, which sometimes immunize young children free of charge or on a sliding scale.

It's also wise to practice preventive medicine at home by learning as much as possible about nutrition. It's fun and interesting to teach your kids nutritional values as you learn them, cooking and making snacks together.

One tip about paying medical bills—or any bill, for that matter: if you have a problem paying a large bill, be forthright about your financial difficulties. Doctors, nurses, hospitals, and utility companies are providing you with services in good faith and expect to be paid in full promptly. If this isn't possible for you at some point, let them know immediately and set up a monthly payment plan that you can handle. A bookkeeper for a doctor once told me of a family of six that faithfully paid four dollars a month on a bill month after month. In such a situation, a medical office or utility will not send your name to a collection bureau as long as you pay each month. The practice to avoid is "letting a bill go," with the illusion that next month it will be easier to pay. After a few "next months," the bill collector may be beating on your door.

Speaking of bill collectors, many authors of books on economizing strongly recommend getting rid of credit cards, and I add my voice to the chorus. It's usually best to cancel all charge accounts, keeping one or two charge cards for gasoline or a bank card to be used only in emergencies. Some families have card-cutting parties to celebrate the event.

Cutting Transportation Costs

In addition to saving on housing and medical and dental bills, my husband and I took a careful look at transportation expenses in trimming our household budget. We realized that millions of cars in North America sit idly in parking lots for eight hours a day, and that two of ours had been among them. We decided to sell the larger of our two cars. Two or three days a week my husband had the car we kept. On the other days I drove him twenty minutes to and from work so that I could have the car. Driving him was a pain in the neck, and yet it took only forty minutes out of a day that was otherwise mine. Later, he was sometimes able to get a ride to work with friends.

As two busy people sharing one car, we did experience frustrations and occasional arguments. But we saved so much in automobile insurance, repairs and maintenance, tires, and gasoline that it was worth it. We and the children learned to get to places riding bicycles and walking. We didn't buy a second car for four years, until the lack of a second car began to hinder my efforts to work part-time. We then spent a lot of time discussing the pros and cons, shopping around, and reading manuals. We finally bought a 1950

Ford that, unlike the other used cars in good shape that we could afford, would appreciate rather than depreciate in value over the years. It cost very little to insure and register and was technically simple enough for my husband to do some of his own maintenance on it with parts from a mail-order house. Later, we replaced the Ford with a ten-year-old car that had no rust and low mileage, donated by a retired California relative. We've since replaced this car with one that had been leased for three years, called a "program car" by car dealers. Some dealers also have cars that have been rentals for one year; these have low mileage and usually have been diligently maintained.

There are many small ways to save in running a vehicle, most notably by changing your own oil, washing and waxing the vehicle yourself, pumping your own gas, and, if you don't have too complicated a car and can borrow the tools, doing the tuneup. I learned to be very gentle with my car, for example, by taking my foot off the gas when I saw a stop sign ahead, instead of continuing at the same speed and putting on the brakes just before the sign. This both lengthened the life of the brakes and saved gas. I also tried to discipline myself to fill the gas tank once every two weeks on payday. I wasn't rigid about this, especially if I could save money on an item by driving to a store having a sale. But I combined errand running and food shopping within that two-week period such that I still had plenty of gas for weekend drives and enough for coasting into the gas station on payday.

Saving on Fuel

We saved on fuel for our furnace by using a wood stove we'd installed years before as the primary instead of secondary source of heat. Because we live in an area that is heavily forested, we take advantage by buying discounted green wood every summer and letting it season in the backyard until fall. Initially, the stove heated only our kitchen, so we tore down the walls between it and the family room and breakfast area. We put a grate in the kitchen ceiling so that my study above was heated. Four rooms in our house are now heated with the wood stove, and another two we don't use much are heated moderately well. We wear a lot of layered clothing in fall and winter, and when the house gets unpleasantly cold between December and February, we turn on the furnace for supplemental heat.

Not everyone has—or wants to have—a wood stove for heat. But the point is that you can find savings on heat whether you live in the city or in the country. If nothing else, you can learn to dress differently.

Supplying the Family with Food

In our efforts to grow some of our own food, we had the problem many people do: very little land. Our front yard, which faces south, is five feet of asphalt, mostly owned by the city. But our backyard is large enough to cram in a sixteen-by-twenty-foot garden plot, a ragged but healthy row of raspberry bushes, and twelve strawberry plants that we got free with a vegetable seed order. Two years before I stopped working full-time we had planted dwarf peach and apricot trees in the side yard, and they began to be good producers the summer I quit. And surprisingly, all this food-producing vegetation still left room for a jungle gym and a small grassy area for the children to play in.

I am convinced that the important thing is not how much land you have but what you *do* with what you have and being determined to find a way to make it productive. I know of one woman who decided to stay home with her preschool child and also take art courses part-time in order to change careers when she eventually returned to work. She and her husband devised a number of ways to save money, but one of the most touching was the array of plastic tubs of tomato plants and other vegetables that helped fill out their sparsely furnished house as well as their daily menu. Someone who wants to quit full-time work badly enough and has just barely enough money to do it *can* find alternatives: food co-ops, container gardens on the roof, ethnic open markets, or shared bulk orders with other families. The point is to look at a whole range of possibilities and ask yourself, What am I doing with what I've got?

I did find that there were some "side effects" connected to a few of our methods for saving money. For example, I hated the heat and fatigue involved in standing over a steaming pot of hot water in order to can the vegetables that came out of our prolific garden; they usually all got ripe during the hottest weeks of August and September. But I finally decided the sweat and strain were what my kids would call the "yucky" part of my new job. I had to put up with it.

For the grain products, cheese, and other products we could not grow in our garden, we joined a food co-op where I worked one hour a week. We also, of course, shopped at the local supermarket and drug store, and even there we learned to save. Instead of stopping at the shopping center every other day on my way home from work, I began shopping for food and other supplies once a week at night when my husband could stay with the kids. I could then go down the "no-brand" aisle without my children whining that they wanted a particular brand that was advertised on TV. And uninterrupted, I could do the mental arithmetic necessary to decide which of two brands or sizes was the most economical. By shopping alone, I could avoid arguing with my children about our buying Chocolate Bon-Bon cereal or plastic prince and princess sets. I didn't need either the irritation or, when I gave in, the loss of revenue.

I once ran into a friend with her children in tow during an early evening trip to the supermarket. She looked at me enviously. "Oh," she said, "your husband is taking care of the kids so you can shop alone. How nice. Mine never takes them at night except for important stuff." I smiled and waved goodbye as her children dragged her away and I thought, But this *is* serious stuff. I am spending money from an operating budget. This is business.

Using a Food-Buying Strategy

The best approaches to saving significantly at the supermarket are outlined in books by Rodale Press (also a good source for books on herbal and preventive health care). The basic strategy is to plan meals and list foods carefully, to buy large amounts of the products you like when they're on special, and to stockpile like crazy. Such books recommend using store brands rather than advertised national brands or (sometimes lower-quality) generic labels. And they caution against psychological lures and gimmicks.

One way to buy in bulk is to join a warehouse food club, such as Sam's Club or B.J.'s, which combine sales of general items with food. To make joining a club worthwhile, you should buy a lot each time you go. Usually participants have to join as part of a group, just as in a co-op. Most clubs issue an I.D. card when you join that you have to show each time you go to the warehouse. Warehouse clubs should not be confused with food clubs or freezer meat clubs that are solicited for over the telephone. You should be careful of any solicitations to join something sight unseen.

Another word of caution regarding shopping specials at regular supermarkets: sometimes a store will have a big display that *tells you* something is a great deal, so you buy ten of the item and come home to find that the supermarket where you usually buy that item sells it for ten cents *less*. It's a good idea to use a pocket-size notebook to keep track of items you commonly buy and their lowest price. Or type up a food and supply list with prices and keep it with you at all times, folded in a plastic sandwich bag to keep it from getting dog-eared.

Stockpiling canned goods and perishables seems impossible for anyone living in a small house or apartment. But even grains can be stored—by first freezing them (to kill all the critters lying dormant therein) and then stowing portions bagged in plastic in boxes at the back of a deep cupboard or under a bed. Though the obvious criticism of this method is that few people have the money to buy large quantities in addition to their regular food items each week, those who practice this insist that it can be done by gradually using a bigger and bigger percentage of the grocery money to buy quantities of sale items. One way they suggest to start is to plan meals for a week using up what you already have on hand so that much of your grocery budget for that week is freed for large-quantity buying. Some families get started by using a birthday or Christmas check to buy store specials in bulk.

One big dividend to the practices outlined in these books is that after a while you have such a good stock of food stashed under your bed that, except for fresh dairy products, you don't *have* to go to the store. As a result, if you should happen to have a financial or medical emergency, you can use money usually budgeted for groceries to cover the emergency and still eat. Your stockpile just goes down.

Using Coupons and Bargains

In almost any discussion of food budgets, I find that sooner or later somebody asks me about couponing. Stories abound of "the 'coupon queens' who buy over $100 worth of groceries for a few dollars and a wad of coupons."[3] Over a hundred billion coupons are issued every year by a wide range of manufacturers.[4] They *can* save you money, but it's important to remember that you can also lose money if you get something with a coupon that family members don't like or if you buy an item that is more expensive than another brand even after you deduct the coupon savings. I don't know how many times I've picked up a brand of margarine that I had a coupon for, done a quick price comparison with the store brand I usually bought, and found that my usual brand was several cents cheaper. Manufacturers give consumers coupons "to promote three types of sales: getting people to try a new product, keeping old customers, and taking customers away from competitors."[5] Coupons are best used to buy products you know well, like giant boxes of your favorite laundry detergent. Other than that, use coupons with caution.

The difficulty with any good strategy is that it takes discipline and consistency to make it work. Sometimes the best money-saving methods in the world seem so tedious that it's hard to be consistent. However, the various methods really do need to be thought of as part of a business. When you give them "the thought, concern, and organization you [gave your career], you'll find the routineness wears off and ingenuity settles in."[6]

Whenever anyone says to me or to another at-home mother, "But with all your education, doesn't it bother you that you aren't using your mind?" I can rarely keep myself from laughing outright. For those of us in families with a middle or lower-middle income, never have we had to use our minds more. I became better at creative problem solving after two years at home than I was after six years of higher education. As a mother at home, I had to resist the temptation to solve a problem with money and instead had to think up as many solutions as I could. I really had to *think*.

Developing a Positive Attitude

All the methods of saving described in the various commercial, governmental, university, and community publications you can get are greatly enhanced by your having the right attitude. What I did in a small New England city, parents in Manhattan or Los Angeles perhaps could not do. But they might be able to do things that I couldn't. Determination and commitment to simplicity contribute a lot to saving money no matter where you live.

When our family discussed—sometimes fought about—things we wanted to buy on our limited budget, we had to concentrate on what our priorities were. We had all agreed that we wanted to have me at home. This was an emotional luxury that we'd agreed was more important than some of the material luxuries we could have had if I'd continued working. An important thing to remember after a few years of living on a shoestring budget is that it won't last forever. Most of us eventually go back to work to save for our children's education or simply because we want to have a regular outside job again. In the meantime there are lots of freebies out there to enjoy.

6

How to Avoid Being
Chief Bottle Washer

Being happy at home is easy for some women who've been in the working-mom rat race for years and are glad to get out or, never having been in it, are proud of their choice to stay home and enjoy it fully. I, for one, had no adjustment problems. But this isn't true for everyone. In her book *Where's My Happy Ending?* Lee Morical points out that today "we are confronted by a . . . scenario in which marriage [and motherhood] are pictured as the answer to 'saving' a woman from life on the fast track by once again returning her to the comforting warmth of the hearth. . . . It can be tremendously fulfilling. But like the job outside the home, it can never be *the* answer."[1] Life at home, especially with babies and preschoolers, has its own pressures and hassles. A number of studies indicate that many women initially suffer a loss of self-esteem when they give up a paying job to stay home to care for children. Although there have been no surveys done on stay-at-home fathers, most of the men I spoke with expressed some sense of isolation and a loss of self-esteem, or at least a loss of esteem in the eyes of their community.

But there are some things you can do for yourself that will give you a good chance of being very happy at home: (1) get your identity and priorities straight, (2) find inexpensive ways to enjoy life by yourself, with your spouse and friends, and with your children, and (3) clarify to your children, in-laws, and friends what your values and priorities are. Writer and at-home advocate Deborah Fallows points out that it is also important for most women to get "involved in something *besides* raising children."[2]

The first task is not easy to accomplish with the heavy emphasis today on the question "And what do you do?" I once went to a brunch on a spring Sunday morning after I'd been up half the night with my young son, and encountered this question when I was feeling rather irritable. When I went up to the buffet table shortly after our arrival, I noticed a young woman leaning on the bookcase next to the table, sipping a Bloody Mary. She had long, frizzy, permed hair and long brown-lacquered fingernails and was wearing a long, thin, cinnamon-colored jumpsuit. We exchanged pleasantries about the food and the flowers on the table, and then I introduced myself. After giving me her name, she asked, "What do you do?" with a heavy emphasis on the *do*. I didn't want to say I was a housewife because I felt that I was much more a mother and a wife than a *housewife*. I didn't feel like telling her I was a *former* writing teacher, and there was something about the woman that made me feel uncomfortable about saying what I *had been doing* just hours before, cleaning up a little child who'd been throwing up half the night.

So I told the young woman with the long brown nails that I ran a twenty-four-hour-a-day child care center. Her eyes bugged out behind her mascaraed lashes.

"Twenty-four hours? Are you on call twenty-four hours?"

I assured her that I was because I was the director of the center. In fact, I was on call twenty-four hours a day, seven days a week.

"Oh, it must be a demanding job," the woman breathed.

"Yes," I chuckled. "Worse than being a pediatrician."

"But a challenge, right?"

"Right!"

A psychologist I consulted in writing this book, who does part-time counseling and is a gifted craftswoman, answers the question "What do you do?" with a satisfied "I'm at home with my children." If someone else in the room asks to borrow her doctoral dissertation or asks whether she sold a lot at the handcrafts fair last weekend, she will certainly talk about those things. But her primary work is raising her children, so this is her initial answer.

One woman said that she always says, "I'm at home with kids" and then goes on to elaborate on all the free time she spends at the beach and at museums, the stained glass course she's taking, the bike rides she enjoys every afternoon with her children. "I don't stop until I see that their eyes are green with envy. After all, they wanted to know what I *do*."

So, before you come face to face with this situation, if you think it could make you feel uncomfortable, decide what your standard answer is going to be to the "do" question and say it with pride and satisfaction. *How* we state our occupation makes a difference in the way we think about ourselves and in the way others perceive us.

It *is* easy to feel that the occupation of at-home parent is rare. But this perception, promoted by the media, is not even accurate. At-home parenting is becoming more desirable and common. According to a survey published in *Parents* magazine, about 54 percent of the mothers responding who were at home with their children did not plan on reentering the workforce until their children were in elementary school, and 11 percent planned on waiting longer, perhaps until junior high or even high school.[3] Those who aren't at home are expressing their desire to be in increasing numbers. According to David Blankenhorn, president of the Institute for American Values, "There is a cultural shift at least on the level of attitude." The Institute calls the apparent change in values "The New Familism."[4] In the *Parents* magazine readers' survey, when asked how they viewed each other, 49 percent of mothers working outside the home said they envied at-home moms, whereas only 11 percent of at-home mothers envied their counterparts.[5] The findings of a recent poll commissioned by the Merck Family Fund show a national trend toward "downshifting" to a lower-paying job or shorter hours—or quitting all work outside the home in order to spend more time with family, to reduce stress, or both.[6]

Men as well as women have the desire to spend more time at home with family members. In his book *The Nurturing Father*, psychiatrist Kyle Pruett describes the men he interviewed and their role as nurturers: "The nurturing instinct is a human instinct, not specifically the property of one or the other of the sexes."[7] As more and more men work at a computer at home, the number of fathers caring for their children as a primary or sharing caregiver will increase (see Chapter Nine).

Setting Priorities

It is really up to us to make the job of caring for children a good one. It is easy to get caught up in household work and in small people's needs. When children are babies, there is no way to get around this. But once this period is over, you can move on to other things. It's important to figure out what you *want* to do; in other words, to set priorities. As one writer-housewife put it: "Review what the job entails and choose from among its components which to keep [and] which to forget."[8] Elsewhere she writes: "More than anything else, I think this is the secret of home making: creating a place that makes people feel good. . . . It means creating a home where people will want to linger over dinner; where they will want to snuggle up with a quilt and a book on a rainy day instead of escaping to the shopping mall. What it does not mean is spending all day long with a can of Lysol in our hands."[9]

Making physical changes in our lives (such as quitting a full-time job) does not necessarily mean that our lives will change, unless *we* change. If you were trying to be a Superwoman as a working mother, you can try the same trick as a mother at home. Depression is common in housewives. Some of this depression is caused by the low value the housewife's job is given by society, but it can also be caused by women's trying to be perfectionists in a job that has no end. It can also be caused by poor time management. The following suggestions can give you a good start on getting rid of both problems:

- Set a schedule.

- Get out of the house.

- Assign tasks to your children.

- Be assertive about your needs.

- Get rid of the notion that you must be perfect.
  No one is, so if that's your goal, you're bound to fail.

- Finally, keep your sense of humor. It's everyone's best
  weapon against stress.[10]

Adapting to At-Home Parenting

When Arlene Rossen Cardozo, most famous for her book on sequencing, was a young mother living in Cambridge, Massachusetts, she helped organize a newcomers' group made up of women from all regions of the United States. While doing this, she investigated why some young mothers were happy at home and some were not by comparing their attitudes.

> [Happy women] did what was necessary . . . not a speck of dust more. This allowed each woman to distinguish between housework—much of which was unimportant—and the care of her children, which was of prime importance to her. . . . One sharp contrast was that the woman who enjoyed being at home used her ingenuity and creativity to retain existing interests or to develop new ones while at home, but the woman who was unhappy at home often could not function productively away from school or office without someone else to give her assignments and deadlines. It never occurred to her to find new ways to use her abilities, if being at home precluded her doing things in old ways. Nor did she develop new interests if old ones couldn't fit into her new routine.[11]

Cardozo has lamented that the women's movement "did not support the woman at home by helping her to *alter* the causes of her boredom and loneliness."[12] Instead, women were encouraged to get an outside job. But as many of us found out, doubling the workload is no help. Much more important is establishing your own priorities and interests.

Getting Organized

I found that the most important part in finding fulfillment and happiness at home was organizing my life around my priorities. I made a list of general priorities and interests, such as writing and spending time with the kids; then sometimes I would also have a daily list of priorities, such as getting some curtains measured and cut or picking tomatoes before they rotted in the garden. The housework was never on a priority list, yet it was a responsibility I had to meet. Eventually I devised a method for doing household chores that I have since dubbed the "incidental system of housework."

As usual, I would decide each evening or early in the morning what I wanted most to do on a particular day. After that I would write down what I *had* to do—for example, doing three loads of laundry and the usual kitchen chores. The first thing I would do in the morning after getting the children fed was to organize the laundry and do one load. After playing with my son and getting him interested in a game he could play by himself or with a neighbor friend, I would do the thing I cared most about, interrupting myself for nothing, including the sound of the washing machine's concluding spin. Later, I would take a break, putting the clean clothes on the line or in the dryer and starting a second load of laundry. Around dinner time I might get the third load of laundry into the washer and dryer and later ask my husband to fold. By the end of the day, I would have taken care of the laundry, but I would have spent very little physical and psychic energy on it.

Now that my children are older and in school, I don't have any more interruptions that can't be ignored, so I get even more done. But my house certainly does not look beautifully tended by a full-time housewife with six hours each day to do housework. I have learned that there is a big difference between homemaking and housekeeping. I like the first but not the second, and I know that making a home for the people I care about is more important. So daily chores like dishwashing get done when I'm in the kitchen preparing meals. I wash breakfast dishes when I'm taking a tea break at 10:30 or warming up leftovers for lunch. Lunch and snack dishes get taken care of while I'm preparing dinner. Dinner dishes are done for me either by young hands or by my husband, or I do them when I'm talking to the kids about their homework at night. Laundry gets sorted and folded when I'm taking a break from writing or editing a manuscript; the phone gets dusted when I'm talking on it; mending gets done when I'm talking to my children about how their day went at school. In short, the chores are incidental to what's really important in my life. But *somehow* my responsibilities to the house and the family are met by the end of each week using my method of domestic indifference. Well, most weeks.

Using Your "Prime Time"

Another method I've discovered that helps me get what I want out of being at home is to think about what part of my day is "prime time" for attending to my own special interests. When the children were little, prime time was nap time and an hour or two during *Sesame Street* and *Mr. Rogers*. Now it's when they are at school, involved in afternoon sports or play practice, or spending time with their friends.

But prime time is also when I'm at my prime. I am definitely a morning person, so that's when I need to do anything that requires concentration or a lot of creative energy. I discovered this one Saturday morning when I was paying bills and felt frustrated and stymied, with a lot of nervous energy. I realized that I was writing checks and licking envelopes—something I could do half asleep—when I was full of energy to dig in the garden or paint the front door. Now I schedule my day so that I do interesting, energy-consuming tasks in the morning. I use the afternoons for quiet times with my children or for shopping, bill paying, vacuuming, or a short nap. As a result, I find that I'm a lot more in tune with myself physically and mentally and not as tired at the end of a full day.

If you dislike housework, be sure you don't schedule it during either type of prime time or you will begin feeling like a drudge. And if your children are three years old or older, be sure to start them young helping you around the house. Encourage their natural desire to "be grown-up and help." You can give them your own tools or get miniature brooms, mops, and snow shovels at yard sales or from willing grandparents who will buy them.

Getting Children to Help

Once kids are of school age, there is a great deal more that they can do to help. At this point it's important to think of yourself as "the manager, not the maid"[13] and delegate responsibilities. According to one writer, "Family members need to understand that a mother has limits of time and energy, and that the family's efforts to help with order will free her to do things that will benefit everyone."[14]

Let it be known that everybody has to take his or her part in doing the "yuck chores." Even small children can understand elementary concepts of fairness, and obviously it would be terribly unfair for only one person—you—to do all the work. Here are some tips for getting people in your family to help:

- Explain to family members that you're an equal opportunity employer.

- Discuss your household situation honestly and calmly. Determine what needs to be done daily, weekly, monthly.

- If thorough cleaning is impossible each week, set priorities and decide what *must* be done.

- Decide how work can be divided. Is there a logical person to do certain tasks, based on preference, ability, or time?

- After agreeing on this division, make lists of each person's particular duties. This clarifies what needs to be done, serves as a reminder to do it, and eliminates "I forgot" as an excuse.

- Be sure family members know how to do various tasks, and be willing to teach.

- Consider setting aside a specific time—an hour on Saturday perhaps—when everyone pitches in. A "we're all in this together" approach can encourage cooperation.

- Be flexible and willing to experiment. If one method of sharing chores doesn't work, try another.

- Don't criticize if tasks aren't done exactly to your standards. Keep comments constructive and instructive.

- Remember that humor helps. Nagging is counterproductive.[15]

If your children are too small to help or for some other reason you don't have the assistance you need, figure out a way to get help—team up with a friend to clean at each other's houses a few hours a week, exchange specific cleaning chores with a friend or neighbor, find a willing high school or college student, hire a retarded adult who's had janitorial training, hire a professional cleaner for two hours a week squeezed onto the beginning of another customer's full or half day.

Whether you get outside help or not, use all the resources available to enable you to become more efficient at home. Check out the books in the library that have suggestions for managing time. Some of these are geared for mothers at home, and some of them are for women working full-time. I use them all. They have tips on everything, from installing a phone with a long cord in your kitchen so that you can cook while you talk with friends, to rubbing the runners of drawers with candle wax so they don't stick. They all discourage mothers from becoming slaves to their children.

If you ever have the temptation to straighten the messy room of a school-age or teenage child, figuring "I just work part-time" or "I'm home all the time now," find a cold washcloth and slap it across your face. The child can do the room alone or with minimal assistance from you. If you want to do something for your children, bake cookies as a snack when they come home from school or take time for a long talk together over ice cream cones. These are the kinds of things that make memories for them. Remember, you are working as a nurturer, a maker of Home, a shaper of young lives.

Do the basics, keep the place sanitary, and save as much money as you can by doing things the old-fashioned way, but most of all, enjoy the job. When you're not enjoying it because of an overdose, find someone to look after your children for an hour or more and get out.

Time Out

Here is one piece of advice that I heard many times and did not act on often enough. Sometimes a community can help you to get out of the house. There are now senior citizen and church-sponsored Parent's Day Out services for young parents, to which you can bring your baby or preschooler for an entire morning once a week. There are also baby-sitting co-ops in many areas. The organization FEMALE (Formerly Employed Mothers At the Leading Edge) is invaluable for meeting other at-home moms and sharing family activities. If there isn't a chapter where you live, you can start one (see Appendix A). And, if you can afford it, there are many preschools in most areas, offering a wide range of prices and programs. One fringe benefit to any of these possibilities is that if you don't know many other at-home mothers, you can meet them through your children's participation in a group.

There are also at-home parents who have started Parent's Day Out services as a part-time business, similar to home day care but for only one morning a week. Sometimes the fifteen or twenty dollars they make while moms and dads go out is used to purchase their *own* time out.

Networking

Another way to overcome isolation or loneliness is through "networking"—getting together regularly with others to exchange ideas and experiences. Business people have been doing this for years, not only for business referrals but also to overcome *their* loneliness. Many parent networks grow out of a church or other existing group. But you can also start one yourself with a free ad in a nonprofit newsletter or shoppers' flyer, or with a three-by-five-inch notice on a supermarket bulletin board. In networks, parents meet at each other's houses or in low-cost community space once a week or once a month. Usually one mom or dad looks after the children while the others socialize and exchange information. Some groups may be all-female, which can be a little uncomfortable for fathers at home. If this is the case for you, try to find a mixed group, or start a group yourself during evening hours for fathers who have a desire to do more nurturing, whether full-time or part-time.

Local Parenting Newsletters

Sometimes, parent networks produce newsletters and local magazines. Regional parenting magazines are thriving, with some big city magazines, such as *L.A. Parenting* and *New York Family*, becoming small businesses for the parents involved. Such publications have articles on local children's events and general child-rearing tips. Usually, they have a surprisingly large number of classified ads advertising everything from British nannies to free pets. Most of these local newsletters and magazines are free, supported by advertising dollars alone.[16]

Baby-Sitting Exchanges

When my children were toddlers, I occasionally set up baby-sitting exchanges with neighbors and friends. Generally, we used these for just a few hours of free time, but occasionally we exchanged children for a whole weekend when the kids felt comfortable with the idea. When the kids got older, they made their own friends, and "sleeping over" for a weekend became a great treat.

Recreation

When I go out for a couple of hours by myself, I do things like walking on the beach or window shopping. Every now and then, I go to a poetry reading or an art film with a friend. These are all fun or soul-nourishing or both, and they cost nothing. They are my own brand of "cheap thrills."

My husband and I also have our cheap thrills. Almost every Saturday night we go out on a "date." If we have money, we go to a movie or to a nice place for dessert. If we don't, we go "cruising" down Main Street or out on the highway that leads into the country. We usually are alone on our "dates" and use a lot of the time to catch up on what we're doing and how we're feeling.

In finding inexpensive recreation to enjoy with children, Bonnie Watkins, a contributor to the newsletter *Welcome Home*, suggests that families take advantage of the community: "Visit a pet store, a car wash, a bakery, an airport. . . . Look for free exhibits and displays at shopping malls, reduced movie prices at bargain matinees, public library programs. Learn which recreation centers and museums offer free programs for children. Frequent the public playgrounds, parks, and swimming pools instead of expensive summer camps. Check community school classes (usually a few dollars' tuition) for courses children can take."[17]

Watkins also suggests that parents avoid the toy store and have children play with simple, nonbreakable household items like pots and pans. I found that if I had my children watch mostly public television instead of commercial TV programs, their whining for new toys was lessened because they didn't see them advertised. I have never been very good about setting up creative projects for my children every day, but I did have them draw and color a great deal. Watkins suggests that if you use lots of paper at your house, call a company that uses computers and ask if you can pick up their used paper. You can get decorative paper for wrapping birthday presents and for crafts by asking wallpaper store owners for their canceled wallpaper books and half rolls.

The local public library has magazines and books for children that have recipes for making play dough, finger paints, cornstarch "goo," and bubble soap. You can also send away for lots of freebies (see Appendix A).

Gift Buying

When our kids were young, we encouraged them to make instead of buy Christmas and other gifts. Even before I quit work the children had enjoyed making gifts, so we made this a yearly practice at Christmastime. One year we got kits with coloring markers and "plate papers" to color on, which we then sent to a craft company in Texas, where the drawings were incorporated into plastic plates. Another year we gave cups made in the same way, and the year after that, I had the kids draw designs on cloth napkins with fabric paints.

Now that our children are older and have jobs, they can buy presents at the mall. But they are careful with their money and sometimes still make some gifts out of wood scraps or leather remnants that we got from a local import-export business. When we buy Christmas presents at a store instead of making them, we have a set budget of, say, five dollars a person. The children take time to make sure these are very thoughtful presents. Though they might want to buy a sweater for a grandparent or a twenty-dollar golf book for a favorite uncle, they will wind up instead with a small photo album with pictures of themselves selected for it, or "World's Greatest" printed on a plain T-shirt. As corny as it may sound, we truly have found that these presents, whether made or bought, have helped us understand what giving is all about, maybe because the children are giving a lot of themselves in deciding on them. As far as the relatives and friends receiving them are concerned, creativity and care make up for what we lack monetarily, and the gifts have been a big hit.

For gifts within the family, it is important to us to avoid buying expensive or trendy items for Christmas. Often my husband and I buy a series of small presents for each other that cost only two or three dollars apiece. They may include something like bakery bread or imported sour candies, luxuries we wouldn't ordinarily buy that are relatively inexpensive. In buying for both ourselves and our children, we pay with cash or by check only. We never charge anything or "borrow" from the savings account. To manage this, we start buying things for the children in late summer or we let money build up in the checking account and buy everything in November and December. Obviously, we can't buy many expensive things paying only in cash, but everybody understands this. We start singing the old Shaker song "'Tis a Gift to Be Simple" around the house even before Halloween, and by Christmas, the message has sunk in for our kids.

Learning to Live with Less

There have been times when not having much money at Christmastime—and plenty of other times—has been a source of frustration to me. I was surprised to find that our house helped me to keep things in perspective. I had always cursed the inadequacies of our old house: the outdated plumbing, the shallow closets, and the bizarre lighting arrangements that had been installed in the early 1900s. I can't say I had a Zen conversion to peace and serenity the first year or so at home, but I did learn a great deal from my venerable house in spite of myself.

One thing that had especially annoyed me about the house was that the closets—what few there were—had a depth of only about twelve or fifteen inches. Instead of a pole for hangers, there was only a strip of wood in the back studded with old-fashioned hooks and rosehead nails. In the one little closet in our bedroom, my clothes were hung in layers on the hooks. I realized one day that these few hooks had seemed quite adequate when they'd been put up because the eighteenth- and nineteenth-century occupants of the house hadn't had many clothes to hang up. Thereafter, instead of cursing the inadequacies of the closet, I tried to concentrate on the fact that I had an awful lot of clothes to hang up.

In *The Success Ethic and the Shattered American Dream*, author Blaine Taylor reminds us that even a low- or moderate-income American is relatively rich compared with people of other eras and other regions of the world:

> Music, news, and every variety of cultural input is constantly available. Almost everyone has a camera. One hundred years ago, not even the richest king could look at the pictures of his children and of his grandchildren, and relive the past highlights of his life with clear images memory had not dimmed or forgotten. . . . At the turn of a switch or dial, almost any American may watch a man step on the moon or visit the Grand Canyon. He may enjoy from across a continent a sporting event or a Broadway play.
>
> In a world of famine and shortage, most Americans have fresh meat, fruits, and vegetables out of season. . . . Americans eat better than kings did in previous centuries.[18]

Obviously, in the midst of a staggering array of material goods, many of us forget these facts. One thing that helped me remember, apart from my old house, was reading other books like Taylor's (purchased at a used book store): *The Future Is Not What It Used to Be: Returning to Traditional Values in an Age of Scarcity; Voluntary Simplicity;* and *Small Is Beautiful.* I also reread Laura Ingalls Wilder's Little House books with my six-year-old the year I quit. Times change and people change, but we *can* do without and survive.

As children get older and begin to have more expensive material wants, it can be difficult to explain why they cannot have things that some children acquire with apparent ease. Sometimes it helps simply to explain in clear language why there isn't much money and why you feel it is important to have a parent at home. But this period in your children's lives may signal the time for you to get an outside full-time job or to expand an existing part-time home business—that is, if your children's wants are important to you. If they aren't, sometimes it's better to help children figure out how to get things they want themselves: through their own part-time job, an allowance savings plan, or a yard sale.

As a result of our talks about this kind of thing, my daughter purchased baby-sitter business cards when she was twelve in preparation for the day she could baby-sit. My son gathered together old skates, his bike, and some nearly new toys one Saturday morning, printed "For Sale" signs on cardboard for passersby to see, and sat in the driveway for longer than he'd have liked until he made sixty dollars. When he was twelve, he started a shoeshine business, first shining shoes on a busy street corner and later making more lucrative "house calls" at brokerage firms and credit unions to shine executives' shoes. Both kids made some money selling peaches from our tree, lilac boughs, and the old standby, lemonade, at a little table they set up on our street with their best friends.

I have always worried that not having a lot of material things or having to work so hard themselves in order to buy them would make my children grow up to be materialists. Several years ago, I was worrying about this quite a bit during the Christmas season, hoping that the early foundation we had laid and the efforts we'd made to let our children know what mattered most to us would have a lasting influence on them. But I wasn't sure. My daughter at that time (age eight) had rejected PBS educational programs and was watching two hours of commercial TV every afternoon, with its barrage of Christmas commercials for toys and dolls every ten minutes. She frequently called me in to see a commercial for something she "especially wanted," which was just about everything. She was wise to the fact that Mom and Dad were Santa Claus.

I finally sat her down one evening when the television was shut off and told her that her grandparents were already getting two of the big things she wanted. Her father and I would give her the usual stocking stuffers and small things and *one* large present. I wanted her to calm down and think.

"Of all the things you could have, what one thing do you want the most for Christmas?"

"What do I want the *most?*"

"Yes."

She seemed to relax a bit as if this simplified everything, and then she looked very serious. "Most of all, I want . . . I want *world peace!*"

Enough said. I decided that maybe she wouldn't grow up to be a raging materialist after all.

7

Building Bridges

Some parents find that no matter how happy they are at home or how diligently they work at economizing, there comes a time when they feel they must go back to work, either full- or part-time. Recently, there has been a lot of scare talk about how disastrous it is for a woman to stay out of work caring for children for more than a short time. The following is typical: "It is important to know that as a woman you will beyond doubt have to work for money to support yourself a large part of your life and to do that you will need skills, and that if you stay home for much more than a year your skills will need retooling."[1]

Except for jobs in high tech and in the medical field, this description may be an exaggeration. I'd amend "a year" to "five years" for most of us. For the woman who takes courses in her field now and then during the years she's home, serves in a professional organization, or does volunteer work related to her field or applicable elsewhere, I'd add a few more years. What's more, we learn a tremendous amount at home and often acquire new skills that are later marketable. Before I stayed home with my children I had only two marketable skills: writing and teaching. After six years at home, I now have some others: wallpapering, painting, and light carpentry—not very glamorous but good to fall back on during recessions, when white-collar jobs can be hard to find.

In discussing this issue, it's important to keep in mind that "the average worker under thirty-five years of age goes about job hunting once every one-and-a-half years! And the average worker over thirty-five, once every three years."[2] Granted, the job hunting cited in such general statistics includes unattractive, nonprofessional jobs as well as the more attractive positions you might seek, but the fact remains: workers in the United States change their employment often. The days of the worker who stays at a firm all or even half his or her working life are fast fading.

However, there is a difference between changing jobs and leaving a career for several years. A study conducted by two economics professors of more than 2,400 career women, interviewed over an eight-year period, found that women who interrupt their careers, particularly for child raising, never make as much money as those women who do not. The economics professors who authored this study called these women "gappers" because of their inability to close the wage gap between them and their colleagues even twenty years later.[3] For the individual mother the question is, of course, How big a gap? Another question a woman needs to ask herself is whether the gains of a higher salary are worth leaving her kids if day care is unsatisfactory. Still another is whether it is possible to alternate which parent stays home for three- or four-year periods.

If you choose to stay home full-time for several years, you can minimize the effects of the salary gap by viewing motherhood as a job, as well as a pleasure and responsibility. Every now and then, jot down those tasks that you have learned at home that are managerial in nature or could be marketable in the future. Pursue interests that could turn into a new career five or ten years down the road. Also, keep in mind that there are ways to write a résumé and generally present yourself that can maximize what you have to offer a potential employer. You can also stay involved in your career by taking an active part in a professional organization or writing for an occupational newsletter. Knowing about the salary gap may also influence you to continue working part-time at home or outside the home.

Part- or Full-Time?

One of the toughest decisions to make when it seems to be the right time to get a job outside the home is whether to work part-time or full-time. Full-time work is usually 9 to 5, but there are more and more employers who will let you work an early morning or evening shift so that your spouse or someone else can fill in during the hours when your children are awake and you're away. If you can still get time alone with your spouse, this can work well. In both full- and part-time work, a wide range of possible hours is now developing in the workplace. Among the most common are the following:

- *Mother's hours,* which parallel local school hours.

- *V-time,* in which workers agree in writing to shorten their hours by as much as 50 percent for six months to a year. They keep their benefits and position, but have reduced incomes commensurate with the reduction in hours. At the end of the prescribed period, employees return to full-time hours or renegotiate their hours. (This is a good system for a new mother who can't afford to quit but is unhappy at the idea of having only six or eight weeks with her new baby. Unfortunately, it's unusual outside California and New York.)

- *Regular part-time,* which usually means between ten and thirty-two hours of work a week. The more hours you work, the more likely it is that you will get benefits.

- *Flexible time,* or *flex-time,* both of which refer to full-time work but on a schedule that's best for the individual: 7:00 A.M. to 3:00 P.M. every day (the "Dawn Patrol"), or 9 to 5 three days a week and a long weekend, or . . . the possibilities are endless. Some employers willing to set up flex-time do insist on certain "core days" or "core hours," meaning that you

have to be there every Monday morning, let's say,
because important staff meetings are held then.[4]

These are all possibilities for the parent who is returning to work
after being out of the workforce for a while, as well as for the parent who has a full-time job and wants to alter the hours. Some job
counselors specializing in these new ways to work suggest that if
you wish to return to the workforce or enter it for the first time, you
should look for jobs that interest you, even if they have conventional full-time hours. Once you've been offered the job, present a
strong case for tailoring the hours to your needs and negotiate with
your potential new boss.

The interest, indeed demand, for more flexible work schedules
is growing in this country among both men and women, and in both
professional and blue-collar jobs. Nearly a third of all American
companies now offer some form of flexible scheduling for their
employees. A survey of 521 of America's biggest corporations
revealed that more than 90 percent offer alternative work schedules to their employees. According to a Du Pont spokesperson, "The
single strongest message from our employee surveys is that they want
more flexibility of time." Employees today are more frequently asking for more balance. In a poll taken by Robert Half International,
eight of ten people polled said that in exchange for more family
time they were willing to make less money and have slower
advancement. Aetna Life & Casualty Company now has 125 job-
sharing teams, whereas just five years ago they had only a few.[5] (For
more about job sharing and flex-time, see the section in this chapter on job sharing.)

Negotiating with a Present Employer

If you are now in the working-mom rat race, but are certain that
you cannot afford to quit completely, talk to your present boss.
There are many employers who simply *do not know* how difficult it is

for a woman with small children to juggle everything. If your boss is a woman, you may be in luck—but not necessarily, especially if she has no children. If you have a boss who is male, he may be in the dark about the difficulties, especially if his wife doesn't work. In a study of fifteen large corporations over a five-year period, it was found that two-thirds of middle-managerial and executive-level men had spouses who were not employed outside the home.[6]

If things *look* all right to your boss, then he or she is not going to know otherwise. Although there are now many articles in women's magazines that chronicle the stresses and strains involved in juggling work and family, most employers don't *read* women's magazines, so they frequently have no conception of the problems. Also, if they're the kind of men who think that housewives and mothers don't *do* anything all day, then the media image of the working woman who easily blends all her responsibilities helps to compound their basic prejudices.

Therefore, if you want to continue at a particular job, but with reduced hours, you must clearly, frankly explain how difficult things now are for you. I was surprised to find that when I started writing about the difficulties of juggling home, job, and family, colleagues from the university where I had taught would make such comments as "You are the last working mother I would have thought was having problems." Obviously, I faked it well. Keep in mind that you may be too, without realizing it. As with so many things, communication is essential. You will get nowhere if you keep your mouth shut.

Working Mother magazine gives some tips on "How to Sell a Flexible Schedule" to a present employer, which are adapted here:

- Do the work yourself. Don't ask your boss to dream up a new schedule for you.

- Keep your company's goals in mind and let superiors know "what's in it for them."

- Make yourself a test case. Suggest that the firm try out your new schedule for a few months.

- Be flexible yourself. Demonstrate willingness to field
  important questions at home and occasionally come
  in for a meeting during "off" hours.[7]

Job Hunting—Presenting the Skills
You've Gained as a Homemaker and Parent

If you are one of those people who has been out of the workforce
for several years or who has never worked outside the home, don't
feel that you haven't got a chance to land anything but a low-
paying, low-status job. One writer found that "employers value the
sense of responsibility and the experience in getting along with people that a mature woman has."[8] I interviewed the highly successful
manager of a branch office of a large company based in Ohio who,
during her years at home, had done extensive volunteer work,
taught adult education classes, and briefly worked as a legal secretary. Rather than leave a gap of several years on her résumé, this
dynamic and forceful woman listed her volunteer positions on her
résumé and described the many organizational skills she had
acquired. One study estimated that eighty-eight skills are used by
housewives in their role; some of these are marketable skills.[9]

The trick is to make them look as impressive to a potential
employer as they really are. Remember that in résumés you list what
you have *done*, not whether the work was full- or part-time. You
must, of course, explain what work was part-time or volunteer during an interview. But by then, you have one foot in the door. If a
part-time task was a consistent, important contribution to an organization or business, do not undermine it, or you, by listing it as
part-time on your résumé.

Exhibits 7.1 and 7.2 are sample résumés written in traditional
format for those who have been out of the workforce for a while.
Some of the jobs listed were part-time or voluntary, but notice that
there is no indication of this in the first résumé. How much time
you spent at a particular job can be discussed in an interview with
a potential employer.

Exhibit 7.1.   Sample Résumé.

Résumé of
Name
Address
Telephone number

Objective: To find a position in retail management at a large urban
department store in Fabric Department

Accomplishments:

Sewing instructor   1994–Present in Town Hall After-School Program.
Responsible for teaching sewing and educating children in fabric origins,
textures, and cultural history of American crafts for ages 6–10. Reported
to school director.

Retail sales and advertising   1991–94 for Babies Are Special (clothing
and furniture resale shop). In charge of consignment clothing; wrote
copy for print media ads and arranged for newspaper ad placement.
One of duties included interview for state TV program on burgeoning
resale businesses in tri-state region. Reported to owner.

Sales and management   1984–91 for City Store. Began as a sales
associate in Fabric Department, working my way up to position of head
buyer. Transferred to Junior Department in 1984, becoming head buyer
and then manager of department. Responsible for entire inventory and
sales force of four associates. Reported to store manager.

Education:

Diploma, South High School, vocational program, 1982
Certificate in textiles and merchandising, Design Tech School, 1984

Professional Organizations:
Member, National Association of Child-Care Providers
Member, Fabric Institute of America

Publications:
"Sewing for Teens," "The New Washable Silks," "Throw It Out? Perish
the Thought!" published in "Living" section, *South City Times*, summer
1992.

Exhibit 7.2.   Sample Résumé.

Résumé of
Name
Address
Telephone

GOALS: Accounting position in growing firm, with opportunity for further education culminating in earning CPA.

SKILLS

- Accounting • Implementing bookkeeping systems for nonprofits
- Cost estimates for residential rehabbing • Investment counseling
- Small business start-up assistance • Teaching

EXPERIENCE

1997–Present   Eastside Episcopal Church, Treasurer and Investment Counselor to Board; Instructor, "Money Sense," After Hours Seminar, Eastside Chamber of Commerce

1995–1997   Treasurer, State Economics Club. Reorganized bookkeeping operations of state professional organization. Discussion Leader, "Money Sense," spring conference, Eastside Chamber of Commerce, 1997

1988–1995   Full-time parenting for daughters, Janet and Lisa. Refurbished 1920s duplex with husband, Ted.

1983–1988   North Bank: Trust Department, Investment Accounts. Responsible for investing and for counseling clients. Reported to Vice President, Trust Department.

EDUCATION

1983   B.A. in Economics, State University
1995   Fundamentals of Accounting I and II, Evening School

PROFESSIONAL ORGANIZATIONS

County Professional Women's Association
Women in Economics

When writing your résumé, present everything you've done positively. If you've built an efficient greenhouse out of old storm windows or organized evening lectures on filling out income tax forms, present these as skills. "Employers will take it seriously as long as you take it seriously and communicate exactly what you've been able to accomplish."[10]

Here is an example of how one mother said she would describe her years at home full-time if she were looking for a job: "Responsible for the management of a 2,000 square foot facility. Schedule and supervise daily activities and education of two preschoolers. Constantly utilize my organizational and management skills and knowledge of child development. Able to work in chaotic environment with few breaks. Required to be patient, creative, and resourceful. Qualified for similar management position outside the home."[11]

If you need help in writing a résumé and cover letters, borrow the appropriate books and manuals from your public library (for a book with specific examples, see Appendix A). Make your résumé succinct—a page is good—but also detailed. If you are especially nervous, try to see an adult education or community center career counselor who specializes in women who are reentering the workforce. Also, do some role-play interviewing with your spouse or a good friend. Once you have a résumé written and some confidence, give the résumé to friends and acquaintances who seem appropriate, either for giving advice or for helping you make contacts. More jobs are found through personal contact than through the want ads.

One way to find employment is by applying for a job (or devising a job yourself) for a school, church, synagogue, hospital, or organization where you have volunteered. I know of one newly divorced mother of two who got a three-quarter-time job at a hospital where she had volunteered for years. Another woman who had trouble making ends meet after the birth of her second child got a job teaching Hebrew in her congregation for fifteen dollars an hour a few hours a week. So look around and ask around. Volunteer work may not seem like an obvious option because it is unpaid work, but it is valuable and can lead to other things.

Staying in Contact

Many women who quit their jobs to stay home with children do not have much to do with their profession or former colleagues after they leave. Sometimes this can be a big mistake. First, being at home with little children, though fun and stimulating, can get wearing. It's good to have adult stimulation and conversation now and then with someone other than an adult you live with. A successful entrepreneur suggests that you drop in occasionally at your old job at the end of a day or at lunch. The opportunity for a part-time or job-sharing position can sometimes turn up during such casual visits. Keeping up contacts will enable you to build, not burn, the bridges behind you.

If your former job—or a profession you're interested in getting into—has a professional organization, consider joining it. Keeping a membership in such an organization usually costs only pennies a week and is another good way to maintain old friendships and to gain knowledge about developments in your field. You may not care as much as you once did about the latest tax laws, the best whirlpool for physical therapy patients, or how to teach English as a second language, but keep up the professional membership anyway. If your professional organization publishes a newsletter or journal, maintain your subscription and read it occasionally. Consider becoming an officer, too. One woman I interviewed who was a job sharer became an officer in her professional organization after her twins were born and she was home. She found that having the professional affiliation and holding an office resulted in having her name better known after she quit than when she was working full-time. It also contributed to her finding a good position when she wanted to return to work and locating another professional to share the position.

If you have no professional affiliation but are a college graduate, consider joining AAUW (American Association of University Women), a group looking for young members. A good feminist organization to join is NOW (National Organization for Women), for contrary to what many may think, NOW has housewives in its membership. Most cities and counties have business organizations that offer networking opportunities and are not expensive to join.

If the years have gone by and you haven't kept up old contacts or made new ones, it's certainly not too late. You can join organizations now. If you've lost contact or moved away from your old job-hunting ground, that's manageable too. Contact night schools and organizations like the YWCA to see what courses and workshops are available on reentering the labor force. Find out what opportunities there are in your area for networking, and make contact with other women who've returned to part-time or full-time work after years of being at home. If you feel you lack self-confidence, do what you can to build it by learning as much as possible about the field you're interested in so you'll feel knowledgeable in interviews. For psychic bolstering, enlist the emotional support of friends and family, give yourself pep talks in the mirror, get a new haircut—whatever will give you a boost.

It's OK to Dress for Success

Until I actually read the book, I laughed at the idea of *Dress for Success*—it seemed part of the Have It All mentality of the 1970s and 1980s. But John T. Molloy, the author of *Woman's Dress for Success Book*, who also wrote the original book for men, is a down-to-earth fellow with a blue-collar background who has a lot of good tips for succeeding in the business world. I liked his book in spite of myself. My feeling after completing *Woman's Dress for Success Book* was that, whether we like it or not, appearance matters, appearance creates an impression. When I went back to work full-time, I wanted to feel I had some control over the impressions I made. With the prejudices against at-home mothers that exist in the business world today among both men and women, I felt that, even with published writing samples and a good résumé, I might be at a disadvantage. Therefore, I wanted to look as professional as possible, and I used tips from *Woman's Dress for Success Book* to help me. I interviewed in, and later wore to work, suits and coordinated outfits rather than more casual pants and sweaters. The latter were fairly acceptable at the publishing house where I found my job, but did not project the image I wanted.

The initial problem I had was being able to *afford* the kind of clothes I needed. But I found an answer to the problem at the thrift shop where my mother worked. Because when pricing items she was the first to see new arrivals such as lined wool skirts and Evan Picone jackets, she was able to snatch up the best and mail them to me. I also found bargain suits at my local church thrift shop, at a commercial resale shop, at outlet stores, and, occasionally, on clearance racks at the back of traditional retail stores. Sometimes the outlet merchandise that was drastically reduced had loose stitching or missing buttons that I would have to fix or replace. But the small amount of sewing required was well worth the lower price of the item. By the way, resale shops are another burgeoning business that parents wanting to stay close to home are getting involved in. With names like Second Hand Roze, Neat Repeats, and Man to Man, these shops appeal to people's desire to recycle as well as save money. There are now more than fifteen thousand resale shops in this country, and the number is growing.[12]

If you don't like the idea of getting involved in all the accoutrements of the business world, including the dress-for-success dictum, look for a job that is more casual: landscaping services, garden shops, carpentry, behind-the-scenes retail, child care. Admittedly, it is hard to give up sweats and jeans for a full-time job. But if you want to get the highest pay possible in order to meet a specific goal, such as buying a house or sending children to college, be savvy about the look that is expected in the business world today. The rigid navy-blue-suit-with-silk-bow-tie "professional woman's uni-form" is out today (thank heavens!), but the need to look busi-nesslike is not. So whether your collar is blue, white, or pink, look professional and appropriate for the work you seek.

Opportunities for Part-Time Work Outside the Home

Because raising children is a job in itself, even when the children reach school age, many women prefer to find part-time jobs. There-fore, the remainder of this chapter concentrates on part-time oppor-tunities outside the home. Chapter Eight focuses on part- and full-time paying work at home.

Contrary to what many people think, there are thousands of job possibilities for part-time work. During the last thirty years, there was a 69 percent increase in the number of Americans voluntarily engaged in part-time work.[13] Researchers estimate that part-time positions will continue to grow. Those occupations that lend them-selves best to part-time work are research, service, computer, legal, and "project-oriented" positions.[14] Poll taker Daniel Yankelovich has called part-timers and others involved in alternative work styles the "New Breed."

In deciding what exactly you want to do part-time, it's a good idea to assess your marketable skills, the jobs that are available, and what you like doing. There are many, many resources available to help you do this (see Appendix A for further readings).

It's particularly important to pay attention to what I call personal quirks. Are you a morning person or a night person? Do you like steady work for a fixed number of hours a day, the same days each week, or do you thrive on change and variety? Do you work well in spurts, twenty minutes here, five minutes there? Or do you like to work for long, intense periods under pressure for a few days and then have complete freedom for several days? Are you a high-, average-, or low-energy sort of person? Do you want a "bread and butter" job that will simply help feed your family well, or do you want a profes-sional career? Do you want to learn new skills, or do you prefer to do the same type of work you did before having children?

While we're on the subject, it's important to consider the quirks and personalities of your child(ren). Do you have kids who feel pretty confident and happy when you're not around? Do you have access to a really good sitter or a relative your children love to be with? If not, would your spouse or other adults you live with look after your chil-dren in the evening, or would this be too exhausting for them?

Sometimes child care by people outside the family can be avoided completely by concocting a combination of short-term jobs, some of which you do at home when your children are playing, in school, or asleep, and some of which you do outside the home with your children in tow or while they're at home with a relative or spouse. For example, a writer for the "Making Money at Home" fea-ture in the newsletter *Welcome Home* describes doing everything from political analysis for a presidential campaign to updating mail-ing lists to market research to candy tasting. Some of these things she did at home with her children nearby, and some she did alone outside the home in the evenings or during school hours. A combi-nation of individual short-term jobs requires organizational skills, a sense of humor, and an interest in constantly keeping an eye out for possible jobs. Some people thrive on this method of making money part-time, and others say that they would go crazy fast doing it.

Obviously, there are lots of things to think about. It's a mistake to feel that evaluating them all is not worthwhile because the job will be "just" part-time. There is nothing inconsequential about how you spend ten to thirty hours of your life each week. So take time to evaluate your individual situation and the possibilities for work.

"Group Permanent Part-Time"

As a result of several social and economic developments, today there is a wide range of part-time work available. A growing area of clerical part-time work is what is called "group permanent part-time," through which a group of workers all work part-time shifts, often receiving the same hourly pay as full-time workers and, if they work more than twenty hours a week, usually half the benefits. These jobs are permanent, and because you work within a group of other part-timers there is a sense of camaraderie and continuity that some part-time jobs lack. Banks, hospitals, insurance companies, data-processing firms, schools, retail stores, the food industry, and the U.S. government have such groups of part-time workers.

Temporary Office Work

One type of part-time work that has been around for years is temporary office work. Traditionally, temporary agencies were the only places where you could get these jobs, and such agencies are still a very good source. But something new in this field is the increase in "temp banks" run by large companies or firms. Their personnel departments create a group or bank of temporary workers whom they recruit and call on as needed. Because no intermediary agency is involved, you can sometimes make more money than you would at a temporary agency. These banks are made up of former employees, well-recommended friends, and people answering want ads who have the clerical or bookkeeping skills the company requires.

Both the newer and the traditional types of temporary work are good for a mother with young children because if your child has an ear infection on the day you get a call for work, you can say no and the next person on the list is called. The national temporary agencies like Kelly and Manpower are still good and have improved over the years in some important areas. They now offer a variety of positions in addition to secretarial and clerical jobs, can sometimes give you pay close to or equal to that of permanent employees, and offer their own benefits packages. Kelly and Olsten also offer training and retraining programs, which can be a big help to anyone who's been out of the labor force for a while or was never in it.

Professional and Semiprofessional Jobs

Increasingly, there are also professional and semiprofessional jobs available part-time. Approximately two million men and women are involved in such positions, including nurses, doctors, economists, lawyers, statisticians, writers, computer specialists, speech pathologists, reading specialists, and government employees. According to Helen Axel of the Conference Board, a business research group, "more jobs lend themselves [today] to offbeat schedules—project-oriented work, research, computer operations and other service activities."[15] Such jobs pay much better than clerical positions because of the advanced education and experience involved. And, if you work twenty-five hours a week or more, you can often get benefits.

Job Sharing

This is another option for professional part-timers and is becoming increasingly sought after by women with children. Job sharing means that two, and occasionally three, employees share one job, including the various responsibilities and tasks of that job. Fringe benefits and pay are prorated according to how duties are divided. Some people consider job sharing a fad. But as Caroline Bird states in the foreword to *Working Free*, "What's alternative today is mainstream tomorrow."[16]

One of the reasons job sharing may become more and more acceptable as time goes on is that once all the benefits and salary divisions have been negotiated, the employer fares as well as or *better than* the job sharers. Two employers in Wisconsin describe the improvements in work done by job sharers:

> Not only has the productivity of the department increased, but also the quality of the overall service is rising very quickly. Time is not wasted through simple inactivity or through performance of an it-makes-me-look-busy task.

One positive and quite unexpected spin-off we have noticed is that our office has been forced to re-examine and streamline certain processes and abandon or transfer others. It's possible that this might not have occurred if the job sharers hadn't observed how much time they spend on routine paper shuffling. Apparently one gets a much better view of what constitutes wasted effort from a [in this case] four-hour-per-day perspective.[17]

Employers also benefit because they are getting two employees for the price of one, each employee contributing his or her unique background, education, and expertise. They are also getting two fresh, enthusiastic employees who give 100 percent for the period of time they are on the job. As two job-sharing editors in Massachusetts said, "We're a good deal."

With such advantages, one question to ask is, Why don't more employers schedule more job-sharing positions? One answer is that there is some math and paperwork to do in figuring out how to divide time, salary, benefits, and duties. Another reason is that some jobs, like high-level managerial positions, are not easily adapted to job sharing. The third reason it isn't more popular is that job sharing is new. Employers are often slow to change.

But in spite of some employers' reluctance, job sharing is catching on and is especially popular in California and Hawaii. In thinking about the possibilities of job sharing, it's important to know a few facts. Sixty-five percent of job sharers were already working for their employer when they began sharing, and one half of individual job sharers knew each other before splitting the responsibilities of a position.[18] A man or woman who has been out of the labor force to raise children has the best chance of finding a good job to share if he or she is a former long-standing employee at a firm or has a good track record at a similar company, school, or agency. To find a shared position, you should contact former employees, analyze want ads for full-time jobs that could be split, and advertise for a job sharer through a college alumni newsletter or a professional journal.

Job sharers I spoke with said that the two most important things for initially landing the kind of job they wanted were (1) good communication with their sharer and (2) careful preparation of a job proposal and joint résumé for their present or potential employer. (Appendix A lists books and organizations that will help you do this.) Table 7.1 gives an example of a job-sharing discussion between potential partners, Exhibit 7.3 gives an example of a joint résumé, and Table 7.2 outlines a proposal to be presented to an employer.

Obviously, you have to do a lot of preliminary work to set up a job-sharing arrangement, especially if the employer is conservative

Table 7.1.   Preliminary Discussion Between Job-Sharing Partners.

Are our philosophies compatible and our skills complementary? Can we communicate well? What strengths and weaknesses would we bring to the position? Can we trust each other and follow through on decisions?

Do we operate at the same level of commitment and exert similar amounts of effort?

What do we expect from each other?

How will we schedule our time—how will we overlap our schedules? Will we be flexible and cover for each other in the event of a child's illness or other emergencies?

How do we wish to divide benefits?

What communication method(s) will we use to transfer all necessary information to each other?

How can we best approach problem solving and decision making as a team?

Noting all ongoing yearly, monthly, weekly, and daily responsibilities, how will each be handled? What about new responsibilities?

What about housekeeping, desk, files, equipment, and so forth? Who is entitled to the position if it is made full-time?

Source: Kathleen Sciarappa, unpublished material. Reprinted with permission of the author.

Exhibit 7.3.   A Sample Joint Résumé.

Job-Share Résumé of

Name	Name
Address	Address
Phone number	Phone number

Education

1990: B.A., English, Anycollege

1994: Publishing Procedures
Certificate, with honors

1993: B.A., journalism,
Upstate University, night school

1994–95: Evening classes in
editing, City Women's Center

Experience

1986–90: Editorial Assistant,
City Publishers (summers)

1990–94: Freelance copyeditor,
Fine Publishing Co.

1994–97: Senior editor,
Fine Publishing Co.

1997–present: Contributing editor,
Anytown Gazette

1993–94: Reporter, City Herald
1994–96: Ad writer, City Herald

1996–present: Copywriter,
Ads, Inc.

Summary of Skills

Writing press releases	Research	Videotape editing
Copywriting	Interviewing	Management
Scriptwriting	Substantive editing	Photography

Professional Organizations

Women's Press Club, college alumni associations, college recruitment
committee, American Association of University Women

References and publications furnished upon request

Table 7.2. Outline of Proposal to Employer for Job-Shared Position.

Definition of job sharing

The prevalence of job sharing

Profiles of experienced sharers

The advantages of job sharing

Schedule and proposed work plan:
  Weekly schedule
  Dual coverage
  Conferences
  Illness/emergencies
  Communication
  Referral and feedback
  Office housekeeping
  Philosophies
  Relationships with other employees and clients

Benefits, taxes, and social security payments

Specific responsibilities

Accountability

Source: Kathleen Sciarappa, unpublished material. Revised and reprinted with permission of the author.

and is a stranger to you. But the more work you do writing a proposal—thinking of all possible objections and planning to discuss the many advantages with an employer—the better your chances are of landing a well-paying job and enjoying it to the fullest. Notice that the job-sharing résumé does not state that in 1989 and 1991 these two people had babies or that work for the *Anytown Gazette* and the freelance writing involve only a few hours of work a week or less. These specifics can come out in an interview or not at all. Experience is what matters.

Starting Your Own Business

If you have skills and experience in a particular area and don't want to work for someone else, you might be interested in starting your own small business. The most prudent way to begin a business without a huge outlay of capital is to start at home, later expanding to an outside location. But if this sounds undesirable, consider a business with a former business associate. Be sure to get professional advice from the start. If you're hooked up to the Internet, you can find various organizations for franchisers and small business partners, or get advice free of charge from SCORE (Service Corps of Retired Executives), your local chamber of commerce, small business administration office, Internal Revenue Service, or business network.

You may also wish to spend a few hours with a lawyer and an accountant and to talk with others who are in business for themselves. For a full-scale business outside the home, at least a hundred hours of study and legwork will be needed before you even talk to a realtor about renting space. (For a discussion of smaller-scale part-time businesses that can be adapted to working at home, see Chapter Eight.)

In deciding what exactly you will do and where and when to do it, consider your children. If they are in school every day till 2:30 or if you're married and plan to work at night, then child care is no problem. At most, you might have to ask a neighbor or high school sitter to come in when you have an occasional conflict. But if this is not your situation, your children may have a lot of influence on your choice of work.

Part-Time Work and Caring for Children

Although it is unusual for a single mother to survive financially with part-time work, it has been done. It helps if you have only one or two children and some savings, dependable child support, and close friends or relatives willing to help out occasionally. One single parent who did not want her child in a daytime baby-sitting situation had a neighborhood teenage sitter who could care for her daughter in the evenings and an ex-husband who wanted to spend time with his child every weekend. This woman's skills were wallpapering and painting and singing. Her most productive time of the day was evening. So she freelanced, setting up gigs for the weekend with a fellow entertainer and doing commercial wallpapering for restaurants and office buildings weekday evenings after her child was asleep. Another single mother found that a combination of evening teaching jobs and at-home work was an improvement for her over what she at first thought would be ideal hours at her long-time, "prebaby" job arranged on a flex-time schedule. "Ironically, it has taken all my feminism and activism to find the place where I can parent and be content . . . that place is home."[19]

Flexibility is important, especially when you have the privilege of setting your own hours. A young Nebraska mother writing to the newsletter *New Beginnings* described her experience bringing her children to the small clothing store she owned. She set up an area away from the main activity of the store with a crib and a playpen. Sometimes she had her son in an infant seat on the counter or sat with him in a rocker. With the help of a part-time salesperson, she was able to talk with sales reps, help customers, and do the general business of the store. Her child obligingly napped a great deal, which meant late nights for him but also more time with his father. All this worked "wonderfully" for two years, but things changed with the birth of a second child who was "fussy and very demanding." At that point her two-year-old was "feeling cramped in the store" and needed to be outside playing. So she sold the store to stay home for a few years with her children and took courses to further her education.[20]

For many of us in such a situation this would be a healthy decision. Every child is different, and every child changes constantly. The only thing you can really count on is that they'll grow up faster than you can believe. If things that worked well at one stage in a child's development don't continue to, you have to make changes. The highest rate of job satisfaction for working mothers is among part-timers, but choosing part-time work outside the home is no guarantee that things will turn out perfectly. As one job sharer said, "It's often a tradeoff. You can't get the ideal situation all the time with everybody in the family. You simply try to set up the best possible situation for your child's care for the hours you're not home."

One option that many part-timers choose for their children is a few hours of day care while they are working. Although day-care centers and family day-care homes cater to families needing full-time care, there are facilities that will take children part-time. An even more popular option for parents with children over the age of three is preschool. Nursery schools have excellent morning programs and sometimes extended afternoon hours, too. Neighbors, relatives, and friends who don't feel that they can make a full-time commitment to baby-sitting are sometimes happy to sit on a permanent part-time basis. If you work in the afternoons, you could consider having a high school student come in to sit. Some high schools have baby-sitting courses that include instruction in first aid and simple cooking. Three of the best people who cared for my children on a part-time basis were responsible fourteen-year-olds.

Disadvantages of Part-Time Work Outside the Home

In almost any type of part-time work performed outside the home, there are some disadvantages. Women in conventional part-time office or retail jobs where they are in the public eye have to spend as much money on clothes as women working full-time. Anyone who works half-days but every day has the same commuting expenses as her full-time colleagues. Women in part-time jobs that aren't professional or semiprofessional sometimes find that the pay is "not worth leaving home for." In short, for some mothers, there can be all the expenses and disadvantages of full-time work without the advantages of full-time pay. Because of these disadvantages, many women who must make money for their families turn to work at home.

Making Money at Home
Nap Time, Nighttime, Anytime You Can

A mother making money at home is following an old tradition of American women. Women in both colonial and independent America ran boarding houses and inns, kept books for businesses, made and sold cheese and other foodstuffs, and assisted in operating farms, dairies, and various small businesses. Most women also manufactured many goods for home consumption. In fact, in the 1770s, one way of thwarting the British and evading their taxes was for women to make their own items—candles, soaps, clothing, and the like. The British government preferred that the colonists sell raw materials to the British, who would manufacture goods from them to be sold back to the colonists. "Making your own" was an effective method of boycotting such British household goods and was an expression of independence. In general, women enjoyed greater independence and fewer social restrictions in the early United States and Canada than in England and Europe.

Today there are virtually no restrictions and therefore no limits to what women can do to earn a living. At this writing, millions of men and women work from home, with thousands of new home-based businesses opening every day. Nearly 75 percent are operated by women.[1] Parents who want or need to work at home are finding a variety of ways to do so. Here is a list of only a few of the possibilities:

Gourmet caterer

Manager of bed-and-breakfast inn

Seamstress

Writer/editor

Web site designer

Designer of computer software

Typist/word-processor

Accountant

Sprout and herb farmer

Direct sales representative

Psychologist

Sweater designer

Tour boat reservationist

Commodities broker

Career counselor

Paralegal

Upholsterer

Commercial artist

Foreign language tutor/translator

All that's really required in devising an appropriate job is an imagination. (For specific examples of parents who earn income at home, see Appendix B.)

One of the best things about working at home that parents cite is that, for the primary-care parent, work can take up only a few hours while children are little but can later expand to three-quarter time or full-time. As one interior designer said, "By working part-time I manage to keep my foot in the door. I can push that door wide open later on in my life, when the time is right."[2]

Assessing Your Children's Needs

As when considering part-time work outside the home, a mother
wanting to work at home should make certain assessments, particularly in regard to children. Ask yourself: Do your children take
naps frequently and regularly? Are they active? Loud? Quiet?
Dependent? Self-sufficient? Do they like playing outside in the yard
and at friends' houses? Do they fight or get along reasonably well
with siblings? Is one (or more) able to help with household chores?
Do they happily watch TV programs you approve of, or is an older
child likely to switch the channel to the kind of videos that would
have been X-rated movies when we were in school? And finally, are
your children at an age when they can understand that you are a
separate person with your own needs and responsibilities?

After asking such questions, you will probably be able to identify some potential problems. As long as you are not looking for
an unreasonably large block of time for yourself (and therefore
unusually good behavior from your children), you can usually work
things out. But it is important to ask the initial questions. Lately
there have been many books and magazine articles on entrepreneurial mothers that paint an ideal picture of the woman working
at home. It runs something like this: Sylvia Smith, who studied
dress designing in Paris, designs and makes exquisite sequined gowns
at her home in suburban Chicago (*and* has a seven-figure income),
while twin two-year-old daughters Susie and Sarah play happily in
a corner of her workroom hour after hour. We all know quite well
that, in fact, Susie and Sarah are restless after only an hour of playing dolls and creatively cutting up fabric. They stick pins into each
other when they get on each other's nerves, and periodically their
mother, Sylvia, screams at them.

It's wise to be realistic. Some of the published entrepreneurial
stories are just the flip side of the Supermom record. Kathleen
Christensen, author of *Women and Home-Based Work,* conducted a

study that confirms this. She found that half of the women with young children who were involved in clerical or professional work at home had paid or unpaid child care at least part of the day. Women who didn't have access to day care said they often stayed up late to finish work after their children were asleep. Christensen also found that for some women, particularly those who were not working at home out of choice, there was a good deal of stress. This was largely because "[w]orking at home eliminates the boundary between work and family, so that the women often find they never can leave their work." Christensen concluded at the end of her study that "Like any job option [working at home] has unique advantages and disadvantages. The idea that it is a relatively simple solution to complex work and family problems is a cruel illusion, implying that a woman will be able to resolve these problems by simply changing the place where she works."[3]

You will have to consider a number of things if home-based work is to be pursued realistically and accepted by everyone in the family. A good deal of money-earning labor *can* be done at home, and millions of women prove this every day. But, depending on the ages and personalities of your children, the work will probably not be steady for any more than a couple of hours at a time. Even when my children were in school, I found that the income-producing work I did was woven under and over and around breakfast, laundry, math drills, errands, dinner, and bedtime. This no longer bothers me much because I've also had two full-time jobs working in an office in recent years and found that my work day was interrupted by phone calls, questions from colleagues who were coworkers on a project, conferences, and talk around the coffee machine. Few people work two solid four-hour blocks of time punctuated only by the lunch hour. The important thing is to be as focused as possible while working, to be flexible about necessary interruptions, and to refocus quickly.

Here is what I think is a realistic view of how much work you can hope to get done at home, according to the age of your youngest child:

Baby, birth to 4 months	Zero work; enjoy the baby and rest
Baby, 4–18 months	2–3 hours a day
Child, 18 months to 3 years	2–4 hours a day
Child, 3–5 years	2–4 hours a day, sometimes more
School-age child	5–8 hours a day

With this in mind, it is often a good idea to set up a schedule that you alter as your children grow and change. The key to working happily at home with small children can be summed up in one word: *manageability*. It's important to avoid taking on too much. During the fleeting years before children go off to school, I think the goal should be to help pay the rent while enjoying the kids. If you find that your goals for income-producing work are not manageable when your child is a terrible two-year-old, for example, cut back for a while and resume the same work load later. If you find that being at home is not workable because either you simply are not earning enough to make ends meet or you have cabin fever, then a reassessment is in order. You might be better off combining a smaller degree of at-home work with a part-time job outside the home.

Assessing Your Own Capabilities and Interests

As far as your capabilities for at-home work are concerned, it is good to ask yourself some of the same questions that are asked in Chapters Six and Seven. When is your "prime time"? Are you a self-starter? Well disciplined? Easily distracted? Are you reasonably well organized? Even if the answers to some of these last questions are no, it's all right. It just indicates where you need to make some changes—or it may mean that you'd be better off getting a part-time job outside the home.

According to Georganne Fiumara, the organizer of Mothers' Home Business Network, the most important personal attributes you must have to succeed in at-home work are "a willingness to work hard, build a positive self-image, believe in your abilities, build relationships with others who can help you advance your goals and know who your customers are and fulfill their needs."[4] The general dictum "to sell your product, sell yourself" applies to success in an at-home business just as it does for any other business.

One of the most thorough "tests" to determine whether working at home is right for you is the "Suitability Survey" in the book *Working from Home* by Paul and Sarah Edwards. The survey profiles various office environments and asks questions that give insight as to whether at-home work is appropriate for you. The authors also provide a great deal of information on the range of at-home opportunities, and details about taxes, zoning, and operating expenses. See Appendix A in this book for other materials, and check your own public library and local bookstore. Find out, too, whether there are workshops or classes at local colleges and vocational or technical schools, adult education classes, small business administration seminars, lectures at the local chamber of commerce, and courses given by the IRS or private firms on small businesses.

The most important consideration in all of this is, of course, what exactly you're going to do. Entrepreneur David Birch of Cambridge, Massachusetts, stresses the need to find something you like to do. "If you're in it [only] for the money, it just won't work. It should flow out of something you really enjoy." Sometimes parents know exactly what they want to do. If you don't, most experts suggest that you list in writing all the things you've ever done—athletics, jobs, hobbies, interests, travel—no matter what your level of experience in each. The list should include activities and tasks you weren't paid for. It's then best to analyze what exactly you liked about each. This should help you to determine what you're going to do.

Basically, at-home employment, or worksteading as it's also called, falls into two categories: providing a service or providing a product. Within these two areas, there are thousands and thousands of possibilities.

Providing a Service

Examples of a service include landscape design, legal counsel, accounting, or word processing. Many women provide a service using skills they learned when they were working full-time that they can easily adapt to a home working situation. But often the service that these women can offer their community has grown out of an interest that began while they were at home, such as doing kitchen renovations or children's portraits. These kinds of services frequently offer the best opportunity for professional growth while you are at home with children, and can be expanded as the kids get older. Generally, they give you the best opportunity for making money.

Day Care

A significant number of opportunities are found in what are called social services or human services. One of the most common for women at home is day care, because it's such a good way to combine caring for one's own children with making some money at home. But I strongly urge anyone who is interested in day care to regard it as an important *profession*. If you have no background in child care or teaching, take a couple of courses in such areas as child development and creative play. If you cannot afford to do this, read as many books, magazines, and journals as you can find. It is true that the most important qualification for being a good day-care provider is love and respect for small children. But it is also true that the job of caring for several preschoolers close in age is an awesome one, so you need as much guidance as you can get.

Join a family day-care association if there is one in your area, and if there is not, contact the state agency that oversees child care and make contact with other mothers on their child-care list. One way or another, find a way to network with other day-care providers so that you have people to exchange information with and to work with on joint activities and field trips. Day care is very hard work and therefore has a high turnover rate. You will be less likely to join the turnover statistics if you can minimize your sense of isolation and increase your enjoyment of the job.

Direct Sales

Another common at-home service job is that of representing a direct sales company. Though you sell a product, you don't produce it yourself. Rather, you make it easy for customers to buy a product, usually in their homes. Two of the best-known direct sales companies are Tupperware and Mary Kay Cosmetics. These companies sell directly to their customers through you and therefore avoid the expense of distributors and all kinds of middlemen. They therefore make quite a profit. The question for you then is, Will *you?* With most of these companies, you initially have to invest your own money, although admittedly it is usually not much. Generally, in order to make more than a few thousand dollars a year, you have to build a network of people selling for you in your region; you receive a share of their profits because you've brought them into the system, in addition to your own profits from the sales you make yourself.

If you like selling, direct sales might be for you. One of the biggest advantages of direct sales is that solid marketing ideas for the product are devised by professionals at the company's headquarters. So you are not alone and ignorant about the best methods of reaching customers. It's a good way to start out, to learn about marketing and how to project yourself effectively.

One objection to direct sales is that some of the market strategies that are devised at headquarters involve conducting parties in your home, complete with silly hats and sillier games. If this turns you off but the product doesn't, find out if these parties can be modified or dispensed with. Another objection is that the products themselves are often geared to the domestic scene or to the makeup mirror. The number of exceptions, however, is increasing. A young mother from Manitoba, Canada, wrote to tell me about a line of children's music that she feels very good about promoting and selling. There are also books and other educational materials that you can sell.

Occasionally, direct sales advertised in a newspaper involve a scam, and the person selling is as much a victim as the person buying and being cheated. For information on the reputation of a direct sales company that you are interested in, contact the Direct Sales Association (DSA) in Washington, D.C. Check out the reputation of any company that is not a member of the DSA with the local Better Business Bureau.

Franchises

In the first two editions of this book, I did not include a discussion of franchises because the initial outlay of cash to buy a franchise is usually so high. But there is a lot of interest in them, and they do have some distinct advantages.

First of all, if you do your homework, you can find a business that's pretty much a sure bet, with a good word-of-mouth reputation and numerous locations that are already financially successful. Also, franchises can take a lot of the worry out of a start-up business. Coming up with the cash to buy the franchise is the largest initial hurdle. If you have enough of your own money from a before-kids bank account to invest, or if you can borrow from relatives, split the cost with one or two friends you know you work well with, or go in with someone who'll put up the cash if you'll do all the work, you're in.

Franchises often come as a packaged deal, with marketing and advertising procedures; merchandising (such as special deals, discounting, "value days," and the like); attractive uniforms; accounting and inventory systems; and one or more training videotapes to train you and your workers in how to do your jobs. You get what you pay for, and sometimes that's quite a lot.

However, franchising isn't for everyone. For one thing, franchises usually aren't very creative—somebody else has figured everything out, so you just follow their lead. Franchises can also be like a mom-and-pop store. Especially if you've *just* managed to come up with the cash to buy a franchise, you may not have the money to hire any help the first year, which means putting in long, long hours. You should do a lot of reading, such as *Best Home-Based Franchises* or *Franchises You Can Run From Home* (see the Chapter Eight listings in Appendix A). Also, get a list of names of other franchise owners from the company selling you the franchise, and make some long-distance phone calls with a set list of questions to ask current owners.

Mail-Order

One of the advantages of direct selling and most franchises is that you do paperwork at home but get out of the house to do the actual work. But if you would rather spend most of your time at home, consider starting a mail-order business. Read the stories of other people who've done this successfully in *Inc.* and other entrepreneurial and business magazines. In mail-order, you are both creating a product and providing a service to customers who enjoy the convenience of ordering things from their home. Most mail-order businesses are thriving right now, but be sure that you learn all the details of the business before beginning.

Producing a Product

An appropriate product to create at home is virtually anything you can think of that someone else would want to buy. Although it helps if you are doing something fun or interesting, the most important consideration initially may be how easily it blends in with your family life and how important you feel the work is. For some parents, the at-home work they do is just something to make ends meet for a few years; for others it may become a lifelong passion. I talked with a woman who made catheter bags for hospital supply houses when her children were tiny. She felt her work was valuable and, because no one else in the region where she lived was making the bags, it was profitable as well as easy to do at home. But by no means was this something she wanted to do for the rest of her life. As when doing your budget, it's important to do a little analyzing and a good deal of brainstorming to find the right product, if nothing evolves out of your previous work experience.

Handwork

Handcrafts lend themselves well to mail-order as well as to other types of selling, particularly if they are lightweight so that the customer does not have to pay much for shipping. If you have skills in a handcraft, you might want to take advantage of the interest today in handmade, high-quality goods. Making and selling such items is one of the most creatively satisfying ways to make money at home and, if you find the right item, is quite profitable. A handmade table or handstitched quilt can sell for upwards of $400.

But there are some things to watch out for, according to two experienced people I talked with, especially if you are producing small items. There is often a lot of repetition. One said, "You may like making one pot holder with an appliqued pineapple, but will you want to make ten in one weekend?" Sometimes, there is also considerable pressure right before Christmas and summer shows. And "a woman has to decide if she wants to have her favorite hobby turn into a business with all that that entails." Another word of caution: profit margins are often slim. One woman I interviewed was enormously talented in handcrafts, but said that they weren't worth doing as a business because her supplies were so expensive. She wound up doing computerized bookkeeping instead while her children were young.

Supplies and Other Expenses

Before you begin a handcraft business, find out the most efficient and least expensive way to buy supplies, preferably wholesale. Be sure to buy the highest-quality materials possible. For most potential customers, the whole point in buying handcrafted items rather than mass-produced is the quality. If the materials you use are obviously excellent, you can sell items for more money. One craftswoman found that if she sold small, quilted squares as "folk art" wall hangings instead of making the intricate squares into pot holders, she could charge what her time and thought and detailed handwork were worth. Remember that the labor you expend making something is the same whether materials are cheap or very good. Your labor is important, and it's unwise to waste it on something that may wind up looking shoddy. If you're going to go cross-eyed at 2:00 A.M. to fill a big order, you might as well get the best possible price.

Fairs and Shows

These get you out of the house on the weekends. But usually they also get you out of town, and, for some parents, that's too far. Fairs can also be exhausting, and there are a number of expenses involved. You must buy space and pay for transportation, food, collapsible display tables, and signs. This outlay of cash means that some people make no profit their first year going to fairs (although this *is* typical of almost any new business). But many at-home artisans love fairs and shows. According to one couple who initially sold only at craft fairs: "You get to know other craftspeople and see what they're doing. You learn a lot about the business end of the business: wholesalers, shows coming up, marketing devices, attractive display techniques, and how to generate a mailing list. You also learn what the basic response of the public is to the items you are selling. You can tell when one of the things you think is clever is a real bomb to the public."

Marketing Representatives

For parents who don't like the idea of being away from home on a weekend or don't want to pay the fees involved in shows, craft fairs, or flea markets, there is an alternative: marketing representatives. Marketing reps are go-betweens for the artisan and the marketplace, especially gift shops. Initially no expenditure of money is required on your part. You sign a contract with a rep to market and sell the items you produce. He or she peddles your goods to gift shops or in other appropriate markets nationally and makes money by selling in volume. You get an order from the rep, mail out the order to the shop, and pay 10–20 percent of the order to the rep within thirty days. If the rep can't sell your stuff, you are free to get out of the contract by giving written notice to that effect within thirty days; the rep has the same right.

The only disadvantage to marketing reps is that they are sometimes hard to find. Your best bet is with someone who is new in the business and eager to get new clients. To find out where a regional trade mart is (and the offices of marketing reps), call local gift shops and stores and ask them where the local mart is located, or look in the yellow pages under "Gifts, wholesale." You can also go to a regional gift show, buy a catalogue, and look up the names and addresses of the marketing representatives listed (see Appendix A for the address of the Rep Registry, another good resource).

You can, of course, sell your goods yourself at local stores. You can also sell products from your home if this appeals to you and the zoning laws allow it. Sometimes, there is no zoning restriction as long as you do not have a sign outside your home.

Co-ops

Many parents who work at home creating a handmade product join a co-op. If there are any in your area, your state or county craft league should have a list. If there aren't any nearby, you might consider starting a co-op with friends. The basic rules for starting such a co-op are the same as those for starting a food or baby-sitting co-op. (In fact, some handcraft co-ops may resemble a baby-sitting co-op in that a corner of the co-op's shop or work area is often set up for little children to play in while their parents wait on customers or work.) Co-op participants join forces to share ideas, space, and advertising expenses. They divide up the time spent selling their wares to customers in the shop so that they have more free time to devote to making their product. Sometimes they share space with business owners such as antique, brass, or art dealers who are not involved in actually making a product but who sell a product or provide a service that complements the items being made.

Diversifying and Expanding

Some at-home parents have become financially successful selling a handmade product by diversifying and slowly expanding outside the home. Two quilters I talked with who started out selling large and small quilted items at local fairs also took orders for custom-made quilts. Their custom-order business slowly expanded, and later, when their children were all in school, they opened a quilt shop selling their own and fellow quilters' handcrafts, as well as fabrics and notions, stenciling materials, craft books, and patterns. They also taught classes in quilting and later hired additional teachers and salespeople in order to expand further.

Teaching a Handcraft

A number of craftspeople I interviewed found that their craft was something that other people wanted to learn how to do. Although it would at first seem that teaching someone your "tricks of the trade" would only result in increasing the competition or destroying the market for your product, this doesn't seem always to be the case. For one thing, the people who take a class are not necessarily those who would buy your product, if it's fairly expensive. And teaching a craft can simply be one more way for your business to offer another "product."

Windsor chair maker Mike Dunbar and his family provide a case in point. Now nationally known, with examples of his work in the Smithsonian in Washington, D.C., Dunbar started out making chairs with hand tools in his basement twenty years ago. Reproducing the exacting details of seventeenth-century American furniture, he later began writing about Windsor chairs in magazines that focused on fine woodworking techniques.

Dunbar sold the handmade chairs to those who could afford them, but at $600 per chair, this left out a lot of people who appreciated his product. Occasionally asked to teach a class in various locations around the country, he had considered teaching to be only a sideline. The birth of a late-in-life, much-loved child resulted in his wife, Sue, leaving her career as a political consultant to stay at home. The couple decided they might be able to increase Mike's income with a regular schedule of teaching, and that Sue could use her expertise to manage and market Mike's expanding business while caring for their new baby.

Mike and Sue sold their large city house and bought several acres of wooded land in a commercially zoned area in the country, where they could build both a small house and a workshop. Today, Mike teaches classes on a rotating basis on how to make several different styles of Windsor chairs, and he and Sue produce a professional-looking newsletter on their home computer. They also market a line of miniature Windsor chair jewelry, distributed nationally. They share child care, although their son, now in elementary school, is very much at home with the hand tools in the Tim Allen atmosphere of his father's workshop.

If you decide to teach your craft, remember that the same standards of instruction apply as in a good school classroom. You need to find effective, clear teaching methods, and each "lesson" needs to have an instructional objective. Photocopied handouts, overhead projected images, step-by-step procedures, and hands-on practice are all valuable teaching aids. People learn best by doing and like to have a feeling of accomplishment when completing a class—two criteria that are par for the course when teaching handcrafts.

Cottage Industries

A cottage industry is an at-home business run by one individual that becomes so successful that outside people have to be hired to help.

The most common types of cottage industries have traditionally been in the garment and furniture business. An example is The Silent Woman, a small sewing business headed by a Ripon, Wisconsin, housewife, Jean Bice. Mrs. Bice provides the women who work for her with notions, fabric, and a picture of the garment they are to make, and then pays them for their labor.[5] Cottage industries have been around for hundreds of years. The industrial revolution in Europe and the United States in the 1800s ushered in the era of work away from home and the later practice of commuting long distances to work, but cottage industries have made a comeback in handmade production in this country. They have recently had a rather dramatic transformation into what are sometimes referred to as "electronic cottage industries." The term was coined by futurist Alvin Toffler to designate those people who work at home at a company-supplied computer terminal, with a national telephone hook-up, or with their own personal computer. (For more information on running a computer-based, at-home business, see Chapter Nine.)

The Value of Networking

Many parents operating a small venture from home find that it's possible to avoid the negative aspects of competition by networking. This approach works particularly well for businesses that provide such services as accounting, word processing, public relations, editing, legal advice, or psychotherapy. There are a number of national networks for people working at home (see list and addresses in Appendix A), but there are also state and local networks in many areas, as well as guilds, clubs, and other organizations that can provide a network of referrals and information. Use your phone book, local library, community center, or chamber of commerce to find an appropriate network.

Apart from making life more pleasant and profitable, networking can also help you make friends who can help in a pinch. If you are ever overwhelmed with business but hate to turn away a cus-tomer completely, you can call on someone in your field to do the extra work. Although there is always the risk of losing a customer this way, women who network say that they give customers better service as a result. Also, networkers usually get as many referrals as they give. According to a word processing entrepreneur, it's best to "try cooperation instead of competition."[6]

Financing Your Home Business

If you need to get financing in order either to buy something like a computer or to expand a business when your children get older, you should take a how-to-get-financing seminar at your local chamber of commerce or small business organization. It's also a good idea to read magazines like *Inc.* and *Money* to get tips. If you cannot find financing after going to several banks, consider contacting a ven-ture capitalist. This is someone with "disposable income" who likes investing in small, promising companies instead of more conven-tional businesses. He or she is usually most interested in successful ventures that are expanding because their market is increasing. To find a willing capitalist for a business partner, contact the National Venture Capital Association or professional advisers, such as the Entrepreneurship Institute (see Appendix A).

If, on the other hand, you run a nonprofit business, such as a health care service or a children's museum, you might look into applying for a grant from an appropriate organization. Also, look into federal and state loan programs.[7]

I recommend that women planning to work at home avoid bor-rowing money either privately or from a bank. Women constitute the fastest-growing group of entrepreneurs in the United States, but more businesses fail than succeed. So start out thinking small. If you have to borrow, be sure to have a solid business proposal to show your potential lender. The proposal should be based on a business plan, which is something everyone should have whether starting out big or small. In a business plan, you identify potential customers; determine how you will reach them; decide on a monthly budget and on collection procedures; determine where you will buy raw materials; decide how to package and deliver your product (if that's relevant); and consider whether you'll need to hire seasonal or occasional help. It may seem ridiculous to write down things like this if you're planning something small in scope, but it's a good idea to force yourself to do it. As one writer-entrepreneur put it, "Refusal to commit your plans to paper may reflect an unwillingness to face potential problems involved with any new business venture or may be a way of fooling yourself into believing that problems do not exist."[8]

No matter how modest an enterprise you start, you will face some basic expenses in getting the word out about your service or product. In some businesses—such as child care—demand is such that all you need to do is put an ad in the paper for a few dollars and your phone will be ringing off the hook. But in a good many part-time, at-home businesses, marketing and advertising are important, and there are some important steps to take. First, think about your potential customers. Be calculating enough to consider what income group you will appeal to. If you appeal to a general middle-income group you will sell more but will probably have to charge less for your product or service. With a higher-income market, the reverse is usually true.

Office Hours and Scope of Business

If you want to put up a sign for your business, find out what zoning regulations are in force where you live and what is involved in getting a variance. Think also about whether or not you want to have clients or customers coming to your house and "seeing your two-year-old's Dr. Denton's draped over a chair or peanut butter smeared on the kitchen counter," as one mother put it. For many of us, part of the point of working at home is for the privilege of cleaning the house later and working half the morning in a bathrobe if we feel like it. But if you need or want to have people coming to your house, think about maintaining specific office hours.

Another general area to think about is scope: How big is your business going to be? Will you stick to one community or reach out to others through advertising and mail-order? Do you want from the beginning to plan on gradual expansion, or do you prefer simply to start small and see what happens? Do you want to stay home to do all your work or have a combination: some at home, some at the customer's place of business, and some "on the road"?

Your Potential Customer

Ask yourself how the product or service you want to provide will benefit your customer. What would he or she be most interested in, and what are you best qualified to provide: Low price? Special service? Attention to detail? Accessibility? What do you know about your customer's lifestyle and spending inclinations? It is important to focus all your efforts directly on this potential customer. Then be sure to compare your product or service with that of the competition. List your competitors' products and their prices and special services. How will you be different from your competition?

It may seem that these are awfully serious questions to be asking yourself. I think at first the natural tendency is to say, "But I'm just going to be selling my homemade banana bread at sports events on Saturday afternoons." If Mrs. Fields had had that attitude about her cookies, she wouldn't be a millionaire today. The fact is, you will put a lot of time, effort, and thought into making and selling your product. There is nothing sadder than high hopes and wasted effort. I spoke to a young mother with two preschoolers who spent two weeks making quilted handcrafts, paid fifty dollars for a booth at a craft fair, spent several dollars on gas to get there and back, sat for ten hours at her booth at the fair, and *sold nothing*. The reason she did so poorly was that the craft fair was crammed with quilted handcrafts.

If you can see that your product or service could meet the same fate in the market you are considering, don't become discouraged. You may simply be looking in the wrong place, where the competition is too stiff. One couple I spoke to in Maine had difficulty selling their New England–theme products to New Englanders in the three-state area they first targeted, but did fantastic business in the West and Southwest through national market representatives. So be flexible enough to work around the problems of competition.

Getting the Word Out

Whatever the scope or sphere of activity of your business, you should have a business card. If you want a really super-looking card with a logo (a symbol representing your business), you can have a card designed professionally. But it's also quite satisfactory to select lettering from a catalogue at a printer and have cards made up for you on heavy stock paper. This is an inexpensive way to get cards and is adequate for those of us who have a no-frills kind of business. In deciding what exactly to have printed on your cards, be sure to be very specific about what you are offering. If you are too vague, you may wind up with a lot of phone calls from people you can't help, and telling them so means a lot of work time lost. The most important thing about business cards is to *get rid of them:* give them to people every chance you get, put them up on appropriate bulletin boards, and, if you can find someone willing, leave a stack of them in a dispenser at a related business.

The same rule applies to brochures, folders, and printed descriptions. If you go to the trouble of writing them and printing them out on your computer or having them commercially printed, *get them out, give them away.* One successful entrepreneur suggests that every time you get an order, send a description of something else for the customer to buy and an order form. Descriptions of new products can be printed out on heavy stock paper and inserted into your brochure or folder, or placed on top of the order you're mailing out.

If you're good at calligraphy or hand printing, you can create a notice each time you develop a new product and then photocopy it. You can produce folders inexpensively, by the way, by printing out a description of your business lengthwise on a legal-sized piece of paper, photocopying it on colored paper, and folding and mailing it yourself. Mailing lists can be bought, but you can also make them up yourself by consulting the phone book or trade lists, and by getting referrals through networks and friends and relatives. Enlist the aid of everyone.

If you think that you want to advertise your service or product to the public in the local media, look into methods that are free. For example, many local newspapers have a "new businesses in town" section. A reporter may interview you in person or on the phone and then write a sizeable description of you and your venture. Often the paper will take a photograph, too. There are other local publications, such as shoppers' flyers, regional magazines, and business digests, that also list or do articles on new businesses. You yourself can also write about your business by doing press releases for local newspapers when you first start working at home. Whenever you have the slightest change in your business—an improved product, a new service, a person you've hired to assist you, a visit from a school group—write another press release.

Establishing Your Professionalism

Most people working at home part- or full-time suggest that you devise a name for your business. It's a good idea to register that name with your state's secretary of state in order to protect yourself from having your business's name duplicated. If someone else is already using the name, the state office will let you know, which can save you confusion and legal hassles. It may also be a good idea to fill out an IRS form for an Employer Identification number, which the IRS will send you free after receiving the form. The advantage to an EI number is that it enables you to look more professional to the IRS and minimizes the chances of your having any problems with it.

In the past, men and women working at home have been criticized on the assumption that they do not declare income and therefore get out of paying income taxes. Some of this criticism is valid. However, one trend among parents with at-home businesses is to make every effort to be professional: declare all profits, pay federal and state taxes, *and* take all the allowable deductions when tax time rolls around. All the books, articles, entrepreneurial newsletters, and small business consultants point out that there are many professional and financial benefits to "doing it the right way." Making out all the necessary state and federal forms and paying required sales taxes legitimizes the at-home worker's endeavors and can have some nice results in lowering personal taxes.

Setting Up a Work Space at Home

If you want to take your work space as a deduction, you can as long as the area is used *exclusively* for your business. The IRS has become extremely strict about this in recent years, and many tax experts now advise caution in using this deduction. There was so much abuse in the past that a home office deduction has become a red flag to IRS auditors. Just be sure your space qualifies. "If [it] . . . is used for both business and personal purposes (for example, a bedroom that is used for business during the day . . . which reverts to a family room at night), the exclusive-use test is not met. To support deductibility, one should be able to document the extent of the work done in the office and be able to document and describe the office furnishings, all with a view toward demonstrating their appropriateness to the business."[9]

Apart from any concern with the IRS, it is important to have a space that is used only for your work. Some people can simply use the kitchen table and clear it up at the end of the day with no problems. But most of us are not this well organized or clean. If finding "your own space" is difficult, make a list of possible work areas: an attic, cellar, enclosed porch, entryway, storage closet, or hallway corner. If none of these places yields space, consider using one end of a reasonably large room like the living room or master bedroom. You can define this area by placing a desk or a wide bookcase across the width of the room. You can hang planters or decorative objects above the desk or bookcase to create the illusion of a wall. The space between the end of the desk or bookcase and the other wall is the "door" to your workroom.

Once you have a specific work area you will need to furnish it, perhaps with secondhand furniture or furniture you already have that you adapt to your business needs. You can buy metal or cardboard filing cabinets if you need them or simply get cardboard liquor boxes the size of file folders. However you set up your space, make it efficient and pleasant and be sure everyone understands that it is *yours*.

In organizing your work space, consider whether you will be working during hours other than nap time, evenings, or school hours, that is, times when your children are not occupied. If you will be working at least part of that time, you should position your desk or work table so that the children can see you from the room where they play, use a playpen in the area where you are working, or set up a "children's corner" near you with small toys and books and maybe a beanbag chair to rest in. Once children get to be four or five, it is usually enough to be close physically for reassurance and talk now and then.

If you use the same telephone number for business and personal use, consider giving a different family name or your maiden name as your last name to business people. Use your married name with friends and neighbors. That way, when you get a phone call and are asked for by your business name, you and your children will know immediately that the call is for business. If the name used on the other end of the telephone line is your married name, you will know that it's a nonbusiness call. This simple practice can give you a lot of mental space.

In any business, it's important to get all telephone calls. With a home business that may have crunch times, it is also important to be able to screen calls when you are at home but cannot answer each call because of a tough deadline. If your family does not already have an answering machine or service, you will probably need to get one.

There are a number of options. Perhaps the most professional sounding is the service you can buy from the local telephone company. It is also more economical than an answering service with real human beings. You simply call in every time you get back to your desk or work table, and get your messages on a recording with various prompts. One disadvantage with this option is that everything goes silently through the electronic service. In other words, if you have a deadline and can only take essential calls, and one *particular* call is very important, you cannot listen to the callers' messages and then jump up breathlessly to answer the phone when that one special call finally comes through. You also cannot screen nuisance callers trying to sell you vinyl siding. I therefore think it best to buy an answering machine that allows you to listen to calls as they come in.

Children and Your At-Home Business

If you have preschoolers, it's a good idea to write out a work schedule for yourself and read it to them. You can then display it in a prominent place for older members of the family to see. Most women I talked to and corresponded with felt that children handle the idea of an at-home working parent pretty well as long as they know when they can count on the parent's full attention. Most parents find that it's best to spend an hour or more in the morning doing something exclusively with the children and then getting them busy with something they can do unassisted. Initially, be very firm about the time you need for work. Explain the reasons you are working at home and how your child can contribute by doing his or her own "work" while you do yours. This is not stifling children, and it does not mean that they are in the same position as a child whose mother works full-time outside the home. You are teaching your child responsibility and consideration and *reality*.

But if there is a big problem or you find that your business takes more time than you had expected, consider joining a baby-sitting co-op or play group. If you schedule your turn to baby-sit to coincide with the time when you would ordinarily be playing with your own child, your basic work schedule will not be disrupted.

If you can afford it, there is also the option of taking your children to a private preschool or a day-care center. One mother who made medical supplies for hospitals on fairly large equipment in her home found that her children, whom she had adopted in fairly rapid succession, were happier—and she was too—when they were in a day-care center across the street from their house. When they were sick or when there was an emergency, she still had the freedom to have the children home with her. As with anything, you have to be flexible and work out whatever is most comfortable for everyone in the family.

By the age of three or so, most children can become actively involved in some aspects of an at-home business—for example, stuffing envelopes or sorting fabrics. As they get older, they can be responsible for answering the phone and taking messages while you are "out of the office." One of the many benefits people working at home cite is that children learn what is involved in putting food on the table: "It's important that they see how work is done. For most kids, work is a place parents go away to, not something they understand."[10]

Children can help a parent working at home simply by doing chores. For very young children it helps to break down chores into mini-tasks. Don't underestimate how much your child can do, but if he or she shows obvious stress, alter the way you instruct the child to do the work, or have him or her do only a manageable portion of the job. There is nothing exploitative about having children be responsible for a number of chores, especially if they are of school age. As an at-home newspaper publisher in South Dakota put it, "A few chores each day gives them something to do, makes them feel part of the whole plan, and lessens the workload for parents."[11] Two of the most common problems cited by teenagers with drug problems and by those who try to commit suicide are low self-worth and a feeling of malaise. Kids with work to do at home that a parent really *needs* them to do don't have much opportunity to have these problems.

To reward them for their part in helping Mom or Dad get an order out or do important chores, some parents give their children a small portion of the money they earn in their own "pay envelope." Computer consultant Cynthia Harriman sometimes gives her children five dollars out of a freelance paycheck. "But it doesn't necessarily have to be five dollars. A giant cookie at the bakery en route to the bank to deposit my check can work just as well. The point is that this is their share of Mom's pay for the work they did to help her."

Harriman addresses still another issue that is important to those of us who feel strongly about women's having a specific occupation and being capable of self-support. "I feel I'm a good role model for my daughter. She sees me working at home every day. She also sees me when I occasionally have to visit clients dressed in my dress-for-success uniform. With a mother who works at home, both sons and daughters get a good sense of the value of both work and family."[12]

Taking Care of Your Future

Some people express concern that mothers working at home cannot have Social Security exemptions set aside for them by a company. However, women working at home can make their own financial plans. In order to set aside money for retirement, a Keogh plan, an IRA, or a combination of both is a much better investment. The Keogh is especially attractive because you don't have to be self-employed full-time to qualify, and you can put up to $30,000 or

25 percent of your income from at-home work (whichever is less) into the plan each year. You can arrange for both IRA and Keogh plans at banks or with brokers.[13]

The idea of putting as much as $30,000 a year into a retirement plan may seem rather remote from the modest goal most of us have set for ourselves in our work at home. But one entrepreneurial mother warned against what she calls the "Church Bazaar Syndrome": charging too little for work well done. She was referring specifically to beautifully crafted items sold for only a few dollars, but the syndrome can affect anyone producing an item or providing a service. So be certain to find out the going rate for whatever you are doing, deliver a professional job, and get paid what you should.

Working at home is not for everyone. You have to be disciplined and well motivated. You have to balance responsibilities to children and work, with children as the main priority, and yet remain professional so that you can bring in a decent amount of money each year. But for those parents who are enthusiastic "home workers," it's the best possible life.

Do Try This at Home
Computer-Based Businesses

The first time I learned about computers was in a science class in college—my genetics textbook pictured a mammoth computer that took up an entire room. I could appreciate that such a machine could solve the riddle of the genetic code, but that was it. The different languages some classmates were learning to program computers (COBOL, FORTRAN, BASIC) were intimidating to me, and, although I felt a bit guilty about my lack of adventure, I had no desire to learn anything more about computers. They would never be something I had to concern myself with.

Wrong. I could never have imagined then that the machines I associated with math and science would be something I could use to write a book or article. They have saved my skin on more than a few occasions when I had tough publication deadlines, and have made at-home work with kids infinitely easier for all of us.

Fifteen years ago, about the only people sitting in front of a computer at home were working directly in the computer industry devising software, writing and editing computer instructional manuals, or telecommuting for large banking and insurance companies. Five to ten years ago, that group was joined by stock and commodities brokers, designers, engineers, cartoon artists, designers, medical and financial newsletter editors—the list goes on and on. The applications for computers are so many and the advantages of padding around the house unshaved or half-dressed so great, it was only natural that people would think of more and more things that could be computerized and accomplished at home.

Initially, national union officials leveled some criticism of the trend toward computerized work at home. They charged that some of the women doing clerical work at computer terminals installed in their homes or taking orders over the telephone for national retail networks were paid less per hour than office workers and had no benefits because they were part-time workers: "rather than looking at the cottage industry of the future, we may be looking at an electronic sweatshop, which takes us backwards, rather than forwards."[1] However, parents at home doing this kind of work insist that they make the same or more than their office counterparts because they save money on clothes, day care, and commuter costs. Most of them are married and have health insurance through their spouse's employer. Although they caution that this type of work at home has all the advantages and disadvantages of other home-based work, they are enthusiastic.

Telecommuting

For those who are already computer literate and whose jobs outside the home are computer dominated, the changeover to home work can be easy. You just use a computer at home instead of at the office, with the employer's blessing, of course. If you have a long track record with a large company that could install a computer in your home, you might be able to get a job working either part-time or full-time. Generally, companies will not install expensive telecommunications equipment unless the employee is well known or highly recommended.

Telecommuting means commuting to work by telephone rather than by car, train, bus, or subway, because the information you work on is transmitted by telephone lines. You could say that any at-home setup with a modem or fax machine is engaged in telecommunication because these are hooked up to other modems and facsimile machines via telephone lines. But the term *telecommuter* has come to mean anyone who works in this way for a company full- or part-time rather than in their own entrepreneurial business. As Lisa Shaw states in her book, *Telecommute! Go to Work Without Leaving Home*, "telecommuting appeals to people who want to work at home but who don't necessarily want to start a business. They want to start living their own lives, but they don't want to give up all of their security."[2]

Usually, when you telecommute you still go into the office for meetings and other responsibilities once or twice a week, although there are a few telecommuters who make it in only once a month and rely on conference calls and faxes to keep up. It really depends on the individual company.

In determining whether or not telecommuting would be ideal for you, it's important to consider first of all whether it is feasible at the company you work for. Then it's necessary to consider whether you want to work full- or part-time. Some parents shift to part-time work when they begin telecommuting, if they have that option. Finally, the usual issues apply for anyone working at home: Are you a well-disciplined self-starter? Are your children at an age where you can realistically work at home when they are home after school or at night? Will a refrigerator one room away be too great a temptation? Will neighbors and friends drop by or call on the phone once they find out you're home? Can you really *get the work done* for the company?

Lisa Shaw suggests that employer and employee sign a contract that spells out the responsibilities of both in a telecommuting arrangement. Sometimes, for the new mother commuting to work the usual way and crying in the parking lot, the contract is really a proposal to an employer who may or may not be amenable to telecommuting. As in the case of two workers who want to job-share, telecommuter wannabes have to make the proposal very attractive, pointing out such advantages as higher productivity.

Be well prepared when making your proposal. Shaw cautions that older bosses are often the most resistant simply because telecommuting is a new concept to them. Anticipate their objections and show them "what's in it for them." You can also suggest just working one day a week at home or starting out on a trial basis only. Sometimes, you can find an ally in a middle-level manager who's middle-aged and can see both points of view—and help you present yours successfully. The most effective strategy is to point out the benefits to the bottom line: less time wasted going to and from work or talking by the water cooler, less stress, higher energy, greater productivity. As extra "ammunition" for your boss, you can also present photocopies of articles describing and praising telecommuting in the press. If there are other employees who would like telecommuting, you can work together to present the benefits, as did the employees who wrote up the agreement in Exhibit 9.1.

Working Independently

In addition to those who work for a company telecommuting, there are even more people who work independently for a number of clients, and they buy and install their own computer equipment. The computer hardware and software and Internet time are business expenses that are taken off their income tax as a business deduction.

If you have not used computers before, you may find that an interest or skill you have can be computerized, thereby saving time and money and allowing you to be at home. I found that a surprising number of women who had once worked as typists simply converted to word processing and did a lively business at home typing various documents, sometimes expanding into editing or proofreading. The same is true for bookkeepers and accountants who keep business accounts and orders straight for retail and other small business owners. The number of occupations—both blue and white collar—that are being adapted to home work is growing impressively. Magazines like Inc., Entrepreneur, and Black Enterprise are full

Exhibit 9.1.   Telecommuting Program Agreement.

Introduction
(Name your particular company, describe your particular responsibility(ies), and propose that telecommuting be considered as outlined below.)

Explanation of Telecommuting
Telecommuting is working from home, from an office near home, or from a telecenter instead of commuting to official headquarters. Telecommuting occurs on a regular schedule or on an as-needed basis with prior approval of the employer. _____
[the company] could benefit greatly from instituting new policies encouraging telecommuting.

Policy
It is the policy of _____
[the company] to provide a work environment that will allow for the maximum productivity, efficiency, safety, and well-being of staff.
    In concert with this policy, _____
[the company] could adopt telecommuting as a work option for employees, and as a means of meeting the objectives of _____
_____ [the company] in these general areas:

   A. Facilitating increased employee productivity

   B. Improving the effectiveness of _____

_____ [the company] as an employer

   C. Making optimum use of _____
[the company] facilities

   D. Reducing absenteeism

   E. Improving employee recruitment and retention

   F. Continuing the productivity of employees who need to remain home for medical reasons or maternity/paternity leave, thereby avoiding expenditure of resources to hire and train temporary help

   G. Demonstrating the commitment of _____

_____ [the company] to reducing traffic congestion and pollution in

_____ [city]

Locations
Official headquarters continue to be _____

_____.

    Telecommuter(s) work at a home office.

Exhibit 9.1. *continued*

Supervisors

A. Must oversee the day-to-day performance of telecommuting employees, just as with other employees under their supervision.

B. Are responsible for ensuring an employee's work is performed in accordance with the policies of _____
[the company], in particular:

1. Home systems run antivirus software, which is updated regularly.

2. Backup copies of all important computer files are maintained.

3. Sensitive and/or confidential files are handled in a manner consistent with the policies and procedures of _____
_____ [the company].

Employee/Employer Responsibilities

Telecommuting is carried out with the understanding that it is the responsibility of the employee to ensure that a proper work environment is maintained at the home office site. (For example, arrangements are made to ensure that dependent care does not interfere with work and that personal disruptions, such as nonbusiness telephone calls and visitors, are kept to a minimum.) Employees who telecommute will be expected to work at the official headquarters on non-telecommuting work days unless otherwise noted on the schedule. _____

_____ [the company] may deny an employee the opportunity to telecommute or may rescind a telecommuting agreement based on an unacceptable home office environment.

A. All forms of telecommuting imply an employer-employee relationship with the employee receiving the same benefits and incurring the same responsibilities as a non-telecommuting colleague.

B. The telecommuter work option must not alter personnel management practices such as rest periods, leave, holidays, etc.

C. Telecommuting is based on company requirements as determined by management.

D. Each *Telecommuting Program Agreement* must be discussed and renewed annually.

Source: Adapted from parts I and II of New Hampshire DCA Telecommuting Program Policy and Procedures, courtesy of Charles LeBlanc.

of articles about individuals working as independent contractors who have adapted their occupation or avocation to at-home work.

The wonders of using a computer *are* many, with features that result in easy mailing-list management, accounting, graphic design, word processing (read: smart typewriter), scheduling, contract management, research, project management, and computer-aided design (also called CAD). You can find a software program to help you do just about anything. A computer is really no more complicated to use than a food processor or lawn mower. If you can run these—and if you are reading this book—you can run a computer. To practice, go to a computer store that has demos, try out a willing friend's, or look up information on the local public library's computers. Begin familiarizing yourself with the basic equipment.

It always takes several frustrating hours (or, for some of us, days) to become computer literate enough to use a machine efficiently, but the amount of time you eventually save is pretty astounding. It is also very good to have a computer at home for children in the family to use on the weekends and other off hours, because most kids will be using computers in the future in *their* jobs—whether your daughters plan to be auto mechanics or dress designers.

Computer Basics

Conscious that there are some readers who are as in the dark about computer technology as I was, I'll begin with a few basics, which those more knowledgeable can skip.

Often new industries and movements (computers are a little of both) develop a language of their own. The computer industrial–social transformation of the late twentieth century is no different. Its nomenclature is like one big pot of acronyms, abbreviations, and mixed metaphors: CAM, CAD, AIM, ASCII, EPROM, e-mail, Java, bits, bytes, chips, bugs, web, net, surf, dump, drive, crash, boot, Apple, mouse, motherboard, gopher. This mix makes it easy to feel lost, intimidated, illiterate, and left behind in the dust of a dying century and not at all ready for the next. A few simplified definitions of basics are therefore in order. Some of the definitions in Table 9.1 (at the end of the chapter) are not absolutely necessary to the daily, mundane use of a computer, but when you go shopping for computer equipment or talk with business colleagues, it's a good idea to be familiar with these terms. I have left out dozens of other words in this table, and, by the time this book is published, there will no doubt be new terms reflecting new developments in the computer marketplace. Ken Ryan, author of *Computer Anxiety*, suggests that novices increase their vocabulary and basic understanding of hardware and software by going to a newsstand or bookstore and buying a minimum of three computer magazines to read (including the advertisements). The public library also has computer magazines to take out.

Computer catalogs are an inexpensive resource on what is available (see Appendix A). If you call the 800 number of one catalog company, you can get free catalogues from them and soon also be on the mailing list for many other catalog companies. You can buy fairly inexpensive paperback books on computers, but be sure to skim first to make certain that the book is not already obsolete. If it talks about WordStar, you're in trouble. One of the best paperbacks that is updated annually is the *Consumer Reports Guide to Personal Computers*, which is very thorough and includes a number of appendixes and a glossary of terms.

Buying a Computer

A great many places now sell computers, even department store chains. Take time to buy the right machine. It is always tempting to go to a computer store with someone who knows more and simply let them take care of things. This is especially tempting for anyone who has a spouse or younger sister or brother who knows more. The problem here is that you may wind up with a computer that would fit *their* needs, not yours. Ask everyone you know who has a computer for recommendations and advice, read computer and entrepreneurial magazines, attend meetings of "user groups" in your area, and visit stores, outlets, and shows to see what is available and to play on the displayed machines.

Computers come in a variety of sizes and capabilities. Although computer salespeople may tell you that you'll have to replace any computer you buy in a few years because they become obsolete quickly, this is not really true for those of us who need only the basics and are doing work that is not particularly exotic. Besides, who wants to fork over more money five years later for something as expensive as a computer? Most of us simply don't have the profits to do this.

The first thing you will want to decide is whether to buy a Macintosh (Apple's business computer, affectionately known as "the Mac") or an IBM (or, more likely, a good IBM clone). You will then need to decide whether or not to buy a new or used computer.

As you probably know, the two most famous computers on the market are Apple and IBM. Most people first become familiar with Apple because it is in our schools and is, or was, easier to use than IBM. Windows software changed all that, so that IBM applications are as easy to use as the happy-face icons of Apple. The Macintosh is still preferred by many designers, graphic artists, writers, and editors. Many of us are now loyal users too stubborn to switch and, for those involved in graphic arts, the Mac is definitely preferred.

In most other fields, there is much to be said for IBM run on Windows software, which imitates some of the most user-friendly aspects of software for the Mac. *Windows* refers to the operating system software made by Microsoft Corporation. (Basically, the operating system is a program that tells your computer how to work.) Little "windows" graphically represent and organize various tasks the computer can perform; each task is symbolized by a small picture, or icon. You can initiate tasks by clicking on icons with the mouse. Thus, clicking on an icon picturing the ABC's means: *check my spelling,* a clock means *tell me what time it is,* and so on. You can also run a number of different programs at the same time, switching, for example, from word processing to a database and back again quite easily.

If you are going to be serving the general business world, a personal computer or PC (an IBM or an IBM clone) is the way to go rather than a Mac. Most businesses, both national and international, use PCs. You will need the basic computer—the fastest one you can afford—with the biggest hard drive you can afford. Make sure you can add to the basic system as new things come out. The operative word here is *upgrade*.

Buying New

You can get some very good deals from computer stores, and obviously there are some advantages to buying from them, as you can easily track them down if anything goes amiss. They can become the one place where you buy software and get advice. Sometimes, too, if you acquaint yourself with computers at a neighborhood store, you will get to know the people who work there and can get a good deal simply because you're a "regular," and they know you'll be back to buy software from them to run the computer. Also, because small computer stores don't have the space to keep nearly obsolete machines, they sometimes sell off discontinued stock that was the top of the line six months ago.

If you live in a large city, and there's no chance of finding a neighborhood computer store, find a place where you feel comfortable. If anyone talks down to you—or up to you—find another salesperson and, if the same thing happens again, walk out. There's another computer store down the street.

Don't rule out discount stores, which will give great deals on name brands and dependable clones, because it's their policy to keep their stock moving. They often will also leave you alone when you're planted in front of a computer for an hour. They don't have enough staff on the floor to send someone out to hover.

A good resource to check before buying new hardware is *Consumer Reports Guide to Personal Computers*, mentioned earlier, which will give you an idea of makes, models, and components. It reviews and compares the latest hardware and software available. You can check out the ads in magazines like *Computer Shopper* and *MacWorld*, too, though sometimes small-time manufacturers will put money into ads instead of into reliable internal components, and the bargain computers they offer will break down. Be wary of "no-names"—computer companies you've never heard of. Their hardware can be bought without risk only by those who are extremely knowledgeable.

The dependable IBM is too expensive for most of us to consider, but IBM clones are another story. The most important considerations are to buy a brand name and get a warranty. Dell, Compaq, and Gateway are good, dependable clones and are readily available at national discount stores. An extended warranty will cost less than $200, and if you're buying a clone be sure to get one. If the salesperson says a warranty is not available, do *not* buy the computer.

Buying Used

It's also extremely important to get a warranty if you buy a used computer. As long as you have a warranty, a two- or three-year-old computer is usually OK to buy, and the same goes for basic software. Strictly speaking, such computers are obsolete, but unless you're doing a lot of sophisticated spreadsheets or graphics, this is not a problem. You won't really need the latest to be competitive.

The back of *MacWorld* and other computer magazines have ads for factory-refurbished machines and, although these are not state-of-the-art, they are acceptable as long as they have a good warranty. Sometimes it's also good to buy a used Macintosh from a business that has to buy new constantly to stay competitive. They're not getting rid of the machine because it's unreliable but because they have to have state-of-the-art equipment.

Still other home-based workers believe that it's better to buy used hardware from an individual, rather than a business, because the machine will have been used less. To do this, look in the newspaper and in the back of the computer magazines. College campuses and private schools in the late spring are good places to look for a four-year-old computer with relatively little mileage. As with a used car, it is wise to have someone knowledgeable check out the innards of the machine you propose to buy. Apple stores and some others will issue you a warranty after checking out a computer and ascertaining that all is well.

Notebooks

Notebook computers are some of the most impressive computers on the market because they are so small and so portable. But their advantage is also their disadvantage. Because they can be lugged around from one place to another, they are more prone to breaking down than a stationary desktop computer. However, if you go to a lot of meetings where you need to take notes quickly and completely, these are invaluable. They also are good for those who live in small apartments and simply don't have the space for a desktop computer.

It's not a good idea to buy used notebooks because their portability means they get banged around a lot. A used one may therefore be unreliable, breaking down within a few months of purchase. You can usually pick up new, brand-name discontinued models for a reasonable price at computer stores, outlets, or through a reputable catalog. As usual, comparison shop.

Modem

A modem connects computers so that they can communicate with each other via telephone lines, sending and receiving data. If you can afford to, it is best to buy a computer with a modem built into it. If it's financially impossible at the time you're starting a business, you can always add a modem later to a computer that takes an external modem. Get the fastest modem you can afford.

Having a modem is not necessary for home workers who don't need to fax customers, communicate by electronic mail with colleagues, do any research, or use the Internet. But sooner or later, a modem may be a necessity. A modem's greatest asset is that it gives you and your family, as well as your business, access to all the information on the Internet.

Necessary Software

This is whatever you need to do the job at hand—a myriad of possibilities depending on whether you are designing brochures, keeping inventories and accounts, projecting sales figures, or editing manuscripts. To find out exactly what you need, talk to others who are already doing the kind of work you want to do at home, and read magazines. Start out with a minimum of software and then expand.

To try out software, go to Kinko's or a computer store that has software running. Work with it to see how it operates and if it fills your needs. At this writing, Microsoft has become the standard, largely because of its ease of use, but time will tell. No matter what you are planning to do, the basics you will probably need are word processing software and database software. To make any more specific recommendation than this is difficult because computer software changes constantly and everyone's needs are different. Computer magazines, entrepreneurial magazines, and *Consumer Reports Guide to Personal Computers* are a big help in making decisions.

The Internet

Depending on your business, you will probably want to plug into the Internet, simply because it provides an astounding amount of information from every source under the sun. The computer networks that you connect to worldwide provide electronic access to documents, data, applications, and electronic mail (e-mail—much faster than U.S. "snail mail"). The World Wide Web (electronically "www.," and usually referred to as the Web) allows you to "browse the Net" for information. It has spiffy graphics, and sometimes audio and video.

Also, there are special forums you can "plug into" that connect you to people in your same field or to potential customers. You can "talk" to other computer users, share tips and information, advertise skills, and leave messages on computer bulletin boards. For example, the authors of *Working from Home,* Paul and Sarah Edwards, communicate with other computer users through their "Working from Home Forum." Mothers at Home (who publish *Welcome Home*), Parents Place, Adoptive Families, and dozens of other organizations and advocacy groups have their own Web pages.

You can access the Net by way of general online services such as America Online or CompuServe; national access providers like AT&T WorldNet; or local access providers, which you can find out about through your local computer store, public library, or user group. AT&T and locals are the best bargains. If you're going to be using the Internet a lot, it pays to get a flat rate per month, not per hour of use.

Some cable companies can give you Web access that is significantly faster than other access providers, and you don't need a modem. Because it's cable, you also don't tie up the phone lines. Cable is expensive, however, and only worthwhile if you do a great deal of business on the Internet or need high-speed access to the Web for research several hours a day.

Other Equipment

Beside basics like computer hardware and a telephone, there are only a few other things you might need in your office.

Printers

The first printer I had was a dot matrix Imagewriter that came as a package deal with the Macintosh computer I still use, though it turned out not to be such a deal. The Imagewriter was slow and unreliable, and the little smudgy dots made anything I printed out look less than professional. I now have an inkjet printer that is very reliable, produces professional looking material, and is cheaper than a laser printer. You can buy inkjet printers new at sales offered at neighborhood computer stores, or at discount stores. Occasionally, a computer store will offer a computer with a new inkjet printer for free as a special deal. As always, be sure that you buy a brand name (Hewlett Packard and Canon are both good) and comparison shop. Printers are reviewed and rated in various computer magazines.

If your business requires high-volume printing or if you are going to be doing a lot of graphics, it is wise to invest in a laser printer. These are definitely more expensive than inkjet printers, but they are faster, the quality is excellent, and they can shoot out a lot of stuff in a day.

Fax Machines

Some businesses will assume you have a fax machine because you have a bona fide business, and it can be embarrassing if you have no access to one. A modem allows you to hook up to a fax machine to send and receive messages and important documents in minutes, by way of the telephone lines. If you have a friend or colleague who has a fax machine and you can share, picking up messages at an agreed-upon time that is convenient for the person, this can work pretty well. In some cities you can also go to a printing service that has facsimile services. I did this for a couple of years when I did not fax many things and didn't want to spend the money on my own machine.

But the price of fax machines has gone down, and many more business people use them—to the extent that sometimes they want a fax when there is no rush or real reason for sending one instead of using the U.S. mail. It depends on the nature of your business and your potential customers whether you can wait on the purchase of a fax machine. You probably should buy one new rather than used, as they're not too costly (although we bought one from a trusted friend and it has been fine). When buying a fax machine at a store, be sure to ask how to hook it up. Each machine is different, and it can be frustrating if the printed instructions are inadequate. Most computers are capable of direct faxing. The only problem is that you can't fax something like a newspaper article. So you might need to buy a fax machine even if your computer has an internal fax.

Photocopiers

A photocopier can be a godsend, but you might not *have* to have one, and photocopy stores *are* on every street corner. If you do anything requiring multiple copies, photocopiers *are* necessary. They are also helpful if you fax back and forth a lot and want to keep the faxed messages. It's nice to be able to get a clean copy of a fax message by photocopying it immediately after arrival. The print on fax paper tends to deteriorate into a pale tan color after a while, and the usual thermal fax paper itself is gray and almost slimy to the touch.

If you do need a photocopier, it is definitely best to lease rather than buy one. A good one is extremely expensive, and there's no point in buying a no-name that might be unreliable and prone to jamming. Leases usually include repair services, and a good leasing company will get someone to you within twenty-four hours of a breakdown.

Computer Furniture and Supplies

Although some computer stores have furniture especially designed for desktop computers, you will know what you need to be comfortable once you've spent some time in front of a computer at the local public library or at the computer store itself. Most of us get by with an ordinary desk and a small adjacent table to hold the printer or a fax machine, as these items can clutter a desk. Some people like to have the computer keyboard lower than the computer or to have some kind of support under their arms. This is another very individual consideration. It is important to have your desk or work table deep enough so that the computer can be set back a bit. No, the rays will not cause cancer, but having some distance is a precaution. For most of us, having a little distance is also easier on the eyes.

Speaking of eyes, when buying your computer, pay attention to what the monitor screen is like. There are some differences. A salesperson may talk about active matrix, dual scan, and passive matrix in describing how dull or bright the screen is. All that matters is whether the screen hurts your eyes. It's easy to tell if you spend enough time in front of one at the store—another good reason for hanging out there a while. To minimize eyestrain while you work, whenever possible print out material in order to force yourself to sit at a desk with a "hard" copy. Also be sure that the graphic background on your screen is pleasing rather than glaring, and take frequent breaks from computer work.

Carpal Tunnel Syndrome

At one time, carpal tunnel syndrome was confined to butchers and perhaps to those who spent a lot of time at a typewriter or drawing board, such as typists, draftspeople, and architects. As more and more people have begun to use computers for long work periods, this malady has become much more common. Sometimes it seems that 10 percent of the population is walking around with padded supports strapped to their wrists. Carpal tunnel syndrome is a repetitive-motion injury that can make your wrists and hands feel numb, tingling, or extremely achy. At its worst, carpal tunnel syndrome requires surgery.

To minimize the possibility of problems with your wrists, it is wise to take frequent breaks from the keyboard. This is easier on the eyes, too. Finally, try to key in as many commands as possible rather than use only the mouse to point at a Windows graphic command or to pull down the menu commands. Gripping the mouse can produce wrist stress. Using one index finger to press the Command key and the other index finger to press P for print or C for copy moves the wrist up a little in a gentler movement than what the mouse affords. It's a small thing, but it seems to help.

Bits and Bytes and Babies

Many people worry about having a baby or small children around expensive computer equipment. If you have a baby with flailing little hands, or rambunctious kids going through the Terrible Twos, you might want to keep your electronic equipment under lock and key. But kids who grow up with computers from, say, age four or five, and are taught a healthy respect for them are rarely a problem. In fact, it is possible for a business computer by day to be a place for play by night, as long as special times are made clear and kids are taught what is and is not OK. Not acceptable would be banging on the keys or having beverages within spillable distance of the computer—just as it would not be acceptable with a fine piano (something I grew up with).

In addition to having special times for using the computer, it's also important to have special spaces. Individual floppy disks that are for business should be write-protected and stored in a specific place. All material should be saved onto a back-up disk at the end of each work session. Crucial documents can be saved onto additional disks and put in a safe deposit box. Kids should be given their own computer disk with their name on it and a special box or desk drawer for storage. They should also be told what files on the hard drive are for business and not to be used by them or their visiting friends. If, in spite of these precautions, you continue to have misgivings about having children around a computer, don't give in to any demands until *you* feel comfortable. Children can become acquainted with computers at the public library or at school initially and, when you feel OK about it, move to the computer sitting on your desk later.

When you and your kids are ready, you can start out by playing computer games, holding a young child on your lap. A number of excellent educational and recreational games are on the market, and you need buy only one or two for hundreds of hours of fun. School-age kids who have friends with home computers often trade game disks back and forth. If you have relatives or out-of-state friends who have a computer and modem, you and your kids can e-mail them. Children who like drawing cartoons and other figures can draw on the computer. You can also browse together on the Internet for information about favorite sports figures or upcoming movies, as well as information for school projects.

Recently, there has been a good deal of concern about kids and pornographic material on the Internet. The concern is largely unwarranted with small children because it's not as easy for kids to happen upon this stuff as alarmists would have us believe. For one thing, America Online and other service providers block porn for their customers and, for another, a user has to know exactly where to look for smut and give the computer a number of specific commands. With teenagers it's different. They can find out those commands from friends or get a porn floppy disk to insert in the computer. But it's also true that they can find somebody to buy them a porn magazine or videotape. If they really want this stuff, they can get it. As parents, we can hope that all those hours of at-home parenting will suffice to steer them away from violence against women or exploitative sex in any form. Recreation and information of a more wholesome nature are easy to find with kids, and there is no question that having a computer at home gives them a competitive edge in school.

Another reason it is good to use the computer together is that this helps us, the adults. Kids remind us to have a sense of play while using these machines. Initially, computers are *very* frustrating to use. In learning how to use them adeptly, it's important to have a sense of playfulness and a willingness to fail. Kids have this. They are not as intimidated as adults; they accept computers the way we accepted TV and cross-country airline travel.

Even if you decide that a computer-based business is not the way you want to make some or all of your income, it is wise to become acquainted with the language of computers. If for no other reason, you should become knowledgeable for the sake of your kids, because computers will be in their world someday—or are already.

Table 9.1.   Definitions for Novices.

Backup disk   An extra copy of material you are working on that protects you in the event that your original is damaged. Most people back up their files at the end of a work session or at the end of the day as a regular routine and as a precaution against viruses.

Bit   An abbreviation for *bi*nary digi*t*; the smallest unit of information in a computer. (To refresh your memory: a binary system simplifies letters and numbers into combinations of two symbols. A good example is Morse code, made up of dots and dashes. In a computer, the binary code is made up of combinations of ones and zeros; a pulse of electricity is a "one," and no pulse is a "zero.")

Byte   A unit of eight bits. (Just so you don't get intimidated by any computer sales reps: a kilobyte is 1,024 bytes, a megabyte is 1,024 kilobytes or 1,048,576 bytes, a gigabyte is 1,024 megabytes or 1,073,741,824 bytes. What this means for us is that a computer can process and store a *huge* amount of information.)

CD–ROM   An abbreviation for Compact Disc–Read Only Memory. A way of storing and using enormous amounts of information on disks that look like music CDs.

Cursor   A blinking or stationary symbol (usually an I-beam shape or underline) on a computer monitor connected electronically to the keyboard and to the **mouse** that is used to "navigate" through the document.

Database   A collection of information. This can be as simple as a mailing list or as complex as a compendium of NASA instruments and their capabilities. Different categories of a database are called **fields.**

Disk   A medium for storing information.

Diskette   A three-and-a-half-inch square wafer of plastic, partially covered with a thin metal plate on one side and a metal disk on the back. It stores information and fits into a slot on the computer or adjacent **drive** where it is "read" electronically. The word was originally used for separate, individual disks and referred to their small size, differentiating them from **floppy disks.**

Download   To move information from one computer to another, especially from the Internet to a personal computer. (People will sometimes refer to "downloading software"; this simply means that software is electronically transferred to their machine.)

Drive   A device that "drives" or "reads" information that you or someone else puts in (or "inputs") to your computer. A **hard drive** is usually inside the computer, but you can also have additional drives that are external, located in what is essentially a little plastic box that is hooked up to and sits next to your computer.

Floppy disk   Originally, this term referred to a disk that actually was floppy instead of rigid and had a big hole in the middle of it. These are now obsolete. For some reason, all external portable diskettes are now called floppies to differentiate them from internal or **hard disks** in computers, and the term *diskette* isn't used much anymore except by some Macintosh computer users.

Hard disk   A permanent storage disk, usually installed inside the computer; it has a much greater capacity than a floppy.

Hardware   The plastic-encased machine that is what most of us think of as a computer, even though it cannot compute or process anything until it is hooked up to electricity and fed with **software** (another mixed metaphor).

Icon   A user-friendly symbol or picture on the computer screen that represents a specific command. Users click on various icons to tell the computer what to do instead of having to remember different commands to key in.

Mainframe   A large, extremely powerful computer usually owned by a large company or government agency rather than an individual. A term often used when referring to telecommuters who are hooked up to a mainframe at their company.

Modem   A device used to transmit or receive information over ordinary telephone lines, allowing a person access to e-mail, fax machines, the Internet, and other useful things.

Monitor   The television-like screen that allows your computer to display information.

Mouse   A device about the size of a large mouse with a "tail" connected to the computer. It allows you to control a cursor on the monitor that moves from one area to another and, when you click a button on the mouse, positions the cursor in one spot.

Program   A specific, carefully sequenced set of instructions that a computer follows in order to perform a task. (You do not have to know any computer programming languages simply to use a computer for standard data computations or word processing.)

RAM   An abbreviation for *random access memory*, which is the "working memory" of the computer. Each program uses a specific amount of RAM. People talk about RAM when they discuss the capabilities of a computer. Having more RAM allows you to run several programs simultaneously, so the more RAM, the better.

ROM   An abbreviation for *read-only memory*, which is the memory stored on microchips within the computer. Not something an average user has to worry about.

Save   A command that "tells" the computer to keep the information it's been given. It's a good idea to give this command every ten minutes (or even more frequently) in the event of a power failure or in case the computer "crashes"—inexplicably severs communication—and information is destroyed.

Software   A program or set of instructions recorded on floppy disks or CD–ROMs that tells your computer what to do. The largest and most powerful manufacturer of software is Microsoft Corporation, Bill Gates's company.

Spreadsheet   An application that presents statistical information projecting a number of possible financial scenarios or "what if's." Spreadsheet software can make complex mathematical computations and help managers predict costs, sales, profits, demographic influences.

Virus   A destructive code that can damage files and your system, easily detected by inexpensive virus protection software.

Word processing   Software that enables your computer to act like a smart typewriter: to cut and paste, delete, copy, add words, move single words or whole pages of type to a different location within a document or to a completely different document, duplicate, check spelling, you name it—the greatest thing since sliced bread.

10

Moving Beyond the Traditional
Nurturing Ourselves and Others

Computers have made possible a new way of staying home instead for millions of mothers. In finding the balance between caring for their families at home and providing income for their needs, modern women might find it helpful to look beyond the conventional definition of *traditional* to what truly is traditional: a blending of home and work. To most people, the word *traditional* brings to mind a family with father as sole breadwinner and mother as nurturer, spending her days exclusively caring for children and making the home a place of repose. People using the term this way often seem to think they are talking about a familial configuration that has existed for centuries, that it is "natural" or immutable. Yet this conception of the traditional woman and her family is actually relatively new. In the United States it was common for only a century or so and only among certain classes.

During most of the history of the United States, a mother's primary, traditional function has been *care for her children while contributing to the family's economic survival*. She did this in the home in a variety of ways: producing goods for family members so that they would not have to buy outside the home at higher prices; producing additional goods to sell to others; running a business or farm with a spouse; managing a cottage industry; or (especially in the first half of the twentieth century) economizing carefully in order to save rather than make money. In some periods, the economic dimension of the mother's role was a brutal one, as in the lives of nineteenth-century New York sweatshop seamstresses who were grossly exploited workers. At other times, the role of women was a congenial blending of tasks that saved or brought in money; the challenge of raising children was an integral part of this role.[1]

A father's traditional role was that of chief provider, but he too was often at home or close at hand. He was working in the fields, cutting lumber or hunting in the forest, tending sheep or cattle in a pasture, or building fences or outbuildings. Fathers had an important part in child rearing in the sense of giving children, especially sons, guidance and companionship and discipline. Traditionally, the father was a presence.

Today, in staying home to rear their children themselves, women, and in some cases men, are getting in touch with time-honored family traditions but also moving beyond historical tradition to find fulfillment and value. The entrepreneurial businesses and the creative economizing they engage in are not prescribed for them in the way that farming tasks or assistance with a husband's trade were, many decades ago. Parents today do have many choices open to them and have the opportunity to be truly liberated, as hackneyed as that word may now sound.

Women's Historical Roles

At this point it will be useful to review the history of women and work and of women in the home to understand some of the conventions, assumptions, and prejudices that influence American life to this day. It was not until the mid- to late nineteenth century that society encouraged women to consider the rearing and educating of children as their primary concern at home—what many people now think of as the traditional mothering role. The change occurred for a variety of complicated political, social, and economic reasons. But one impetus for the change was a growing concern about the problem of "hooliganism" in both cities and rural areas. Young boys without supervision—hooligans—were guilty of vandalism and generally reprobate behavior. Their sisters were sometimes in the streets for reasons other than vandalism.

Social reformers believed that if low- and moderate-income women were able to spend more time attending to these children and teenagers, some social problems could be alleviated. This idea began in England among the middle and upper-middle classes, who were gaining in numbers and in political and social influence. The idea spread to the United States and was embraced by the social reformers of the late nineteenth century. So a "tradition" was born, of the mother as educator and authority in the home. At its best, it eroded the notion that women were not much higher than beasts of burden; it gave them status and their own realm: the home. At its worst, it became a genteel prison for intelligent, spirited women. But it became a goal among all classes. The industrial revolution and the growth of labor unions, with their emphasis on a "family wage" to be earned by male breadwinners, made it possible for an increasing percentage of the population to achieve this goal by the twentieth century.[2]

There are some misconceptions about what family life was like in the nineteenth and early twentieth centuries. One of the most prevalent is the myth of the "extended family" in the United States. Until the medical advances of the twentieth century increased the life span of the elderly, many young children's grandparents had died by the time the grandchildren were born, or did so shortly afterward. Even in families in which the grandparents were still alive, younger members were mobile, moving fifty miles away from the family homestead—or five hundred. The "extended family" was simply not as common in the United States as it was in Europe. And, at that, plenty of families left Mama behind in the old country when they emigrated to the New World.

It is also important to remember that in spite of all that has been said about the "bored housewife," the average woman in the late nineteenth century and in the first half of the twentieth century had a great deal to do: tending gardens; canning and preserving fruits, vegetables, and meats; sometimes taking care of chickens and other small animals; making clothing; caring for children; sometimes educating children; and, particularly in the country, working to produce or grow something to sell. If a married woman worked for pay outside the home or took in work (laundry, for example), it was usually menial, low-paying drudgery that she did because she was poor. Having a wife who worked became almost a stain on a man's character, and the widowed working woman was often an object of pity.

There was little encouragement for women to become professionals, though for a time it looked as though this might change in the 1920s, especially at some of the women's colleges. In the early twenties, Smith College founded the Institute to Coordinate Women's Interests to help educated women have both a family and career; however, it lasted only six years. College-educated women who wanted a professional career often were celibate or married late and remained childless.[3]

Though for decades it was common for young working-class women to hold a job prior to marriage and for well-educated middle-class and upper-middle-class women, both married and single, to work hard at volunteer jobs, it was not until World War II that married women worked outside the home in significant numbers. By V-J Day, married women outnumbered unmarried women in the workforce for the first time in U.S. history. After the war, those women either left the workforce voluntarily, were forced out, or, tragically for some war widows, were pushed out of high-paying industry jobs into low-paying "women's work." The reasons for this were various: some economic, some "patriotic," some plain sexist. The pay inequities that had been common for decades persisted. The Equal Rights Amendment, which had first been proposed in 1923, looked as if it might pass as a "thank you" to women for their war effort, but it did not.

However, one result of married women's working outside the home during the war was that afterward, there was a steady increase in the entrance of married, middle-aged, middle-class women into the workforce. It was acceptable and respectable for a woman whose job of raising children was essentially over to get a job outside the home. Without any strong feminist movement urging them on, the numbers of middle-aged women entering the workforce, mostly in teaching and clerical work, steadily grew in the postwar years.[4]

In the 1960s and 1970s, the combination of high inflation and increased Social Security and personal taxes caused many younger families to feel that they needed two paychecks to maintain a middle-class standard of living. The growing divorce rate made it necessary for still more women, including those with babies, to join the full-time workforce. It is my belief that these economic and social realities *coincided* with the burgeoning women's movement, but were not necessarily caused by it. The movement offered ideological support for women who were young mothers who also wanted to go back to work. But it is my belief that had the women's movement of the 1960s and 1970s never taken place, there would still have been a large increase in the number of women with children in the workforce today. Inflation, no-fault divorce, the low tax exemption for dependents, and the fact that so many of us grew up accustomed to a middle-class lifestyle have been the significant influences on the decision of many women to leave young children to go out to work. The women's movement gave us the theoretical reasons to work, but the economic realities and social pressures would have been the same.

We responded the way women have for centuries—by finding a way to bring income into the family. The trouble was and is that in the last 150 years, the means of earning an income have moved from the home to spheres outside the home in business and industry. As I pointed out in Chapters Eight and Nine, in the coming decades this situation may well change. Let's hope it does, because what the average working mother has experienced in the last thirty

years has not always been liberating. There are murmurings, growing louder by the day, that some women may have lost as much as
they've gained. "Many women have concluded that all feminism
ever got them was more work."[5]

Misunderstandings Between Generations

One of the things that may have been lost is something that, ironically, the rhetoric of the women's movement referred to a great
deal: sisterhood. I see growing polarities between young women
and older women; mothers who "work" and mothers at home who
"don't work"; child-care providers and the mothers of the children
they care for. I first became aware of the polarity between young
and old when I was working and found myself being misunderstood
by older people. When I told anyone over fifty that I worked, they
sometimes gave unsolicited opinions, acting as if I were deliber-
ately doing something awful to my children. If I explained that I
didn't want to leave my kids but had to, this provoked a pitying
response, which I found irritating. Pointing out that my job was a
likable one caused them to revert to treating me like a selfish
destroyer of the home. It was very frustrating. Somehow, to them
it was OK to leave your children if you hated your job, but if you
liked it, you were suspect.

There are always misunderstandings between the generations,
but they seem to have become greater. There is sometimes jealousy
on the part of older women because of the material things that some
working women have. And some young women seem to think that
older and middle-aged women have nothing to teach a new generation of mothers.

It is no wonder that some older women feel resentful, considering that some young working women with children (and without)
act as if older women were once exploited, uncreative, and smoth-
ering as housewives and mothers, as if they had been "nonpersons."
This attitude can be pretty insulting, particularly to the women of

the 1950s who were well educated and considered themselves resourceful and creative in the home.

I think that, to a certain extent, mine was a generation of know-it-alls; we weren't keen on the tradition of the younger generation receiving information from the older. If our mothers or grandmothers told us about pain in childbirth we viewed them with tolerant amusement. After all, *we* had Lamaze. We would therefore have *contractions*, not *labor pains*. We would "stay on top of the contractions," we would breathe fast and never lose control. Some of us had rude awakenings in our less-than-perfect Lamaze birthings.

When mothers and grandmothers tried to tell us that having a child would change our whole lives and our marriages, or that we would feel an attachment for our babies like none we'd ever felt before, some of us figured that they "hadn't had much else in their lives." When they warned us that during the first few weeks after having a baby we'd be more busy and tired than we'd ever been, we thought *they* were ignorant, not us. After all, times had changed; women had changed. "What a shock it was to all of us . . . to discover that children really do not lie quietly in their cradles waiting for quality time."[6] Or to find that "you can have it all if you don't sleep much."[7] It never occurred to us that babies hadn't changed or that we might search forever and never find the perfect person to take care of the baby: "Babies have not changed their nature in the course of human history. They have not been liberated by the changing family styles of the past decades. . . . It has taken millions of research dollars to find out what anybody's grandmother knew 50 years ago. Babies know their parents and prefer them to other people as early as the first few weeks of life."[8]

For those women who divorced after several years of marriage and after having a child or two, the concern of our parents about our not insisting on alimony or the family house was met with protests that we would not be "leeches"; we would do fine on our own. In dividing possessions equally in a no-fault divorce, women did not recognize that they would not have an equal chance with their former husbands in the marketplace for pay or positions commensurate with their education or abilities.

We had much to learn from older, experienced women. They could have taught us a lot of what we've learned the hard way if we had only believed that they were *worth* listening to, if we had only been less arrogant.

As part of the early research for this book I interviewed older "career women" to try to understand what it was like to combine paying work and child rearing two generations ago. But I discovered that none of the impressive women I interviewed had gone out to work before their children were in kindergarten. One of the women had strong opinions about the young women in the office she was about to retire from who left their children to work: "They have a baby and come back a few weeks later. They feel confined; they miss people at work and a regular paycheck. And they don't want to go through the adjustment to motherhood that everybody goes through when they're at home with a baby."

These same young mothers may, of course, cry in the parking lot every day the first week they come back. But to older women it looks as if children's lives are being sacrificed for money, and maybe some of them are. One flinty, resourceful widow who had lost her husband in World War II and supported their three small children on a widow's benefits and a variety of at-home jobs was highly critical of mothers leaving their children. "They have to buy clothes instead of making them. I used to make summer dresses out of flour sacks. . . . They have to have disposable diapers instead of washing out cloth diapers. They're used to things being so easy. And you have to have a paycheck to buy what's easy."

A New Jersey woman in her seventies who had worked outside the home for almost forty years, but only after her last child entered public school, made similar comments: "I think young people in this country have lost the art of waiting. They want so much, so soon, and they truly believe this is the way it's got to be: a nice apartment, new furniture, a full china closet, then a beautiful house—all before they're twenty-eight. I was forty before we owned our own home."

It is no wonder that as a nation we cannot get together to solve the problems of those children whose mothers work. There is valid criticism of the younger generation by the older generation, but there is also jealousy and lack of understanding. Older women need to recognize that the reason a working mother may be wearing a fashionable suit is that she has to dress like that for work. Or that she may have some extra cash because although for financial reasons she needed only a part-time job, she was unable to get anything but a full-time position.

At the same time, women suffering separation pangs from their babies shouldn't have to pretend that they are not. Those suffering stress or uncertainty should admit it to older relatives and neighbors. If nothing else, they would at least no longer come across as cold, heartless princesses of narcissism. They might also get some concrete help in the form of backup baby-sitting.

Those of us who got out of the rat race to stay at home with children need to pay more attention to how women over fifty managed things like raising three children on a postal worker's salary. I don't think that the higher tax exemption for dependents is the only way to help at-home mothers. Admittedly, the days are over when a young woman learned from older women all the tasks and traditions that she needed to conduct her life. But we could still gain from each other. The polarity that now exists does nothing for anyone.

Women Who "Work" and Women Who "Don't"

Another division is between women of the same generation: mothers who work full-time outside the home and those who don't. Asking a woman I've just met at a cocktail party how she spends her day is something I may never try again. Women who "don't work"—that is, who work at home as mothers—sometimes visibly bridle. Mothers who work full-time outside the home often feel compelled to mention how worthwhile their work is or how wonderful their day-care center is. The feelings about both lifestyles have heated up tremendously in the last several years: "Some man, woman, or child is always holding forth on whether or not mothers should work. As a result, some listener is feeling very guilty, or thinking he or she would like to scalp the speaker with a dull knife. Despite clear evidence that we're causing real injury to people's feelings and reinforcing narrow-mindedness, we continue to pipe up with hard-and-fast declarations."[9]

Both working moms and at-home moms have ideas about how the world may view them negatively: "Working women are stung and enraged by the guilt-provoking suggestion that their careers are more important to them than their children; that if they loved their babies more they'd be willing to put their work aside. And full-time mothers are angered and shaken by the low esteem with which many career women regard them."[10]

Women in each camp (it's hard to get away from the embattled images) find that what they do is unacceptable to *someone*. It used to be that only mothers who worked felt guilty. Today, everyone can feel guilty.

The Fast-Track Versus the Rut

Within the ranks of full-time working mothers, an additional division exists between women who have "ordinary" clerical or human service jobs and professional women who have "high-powered" jobs. The latter are almost always in business, banking, or industry. So those in fields traditionally dominated by women are not regarded as "high powered." What this means is that an elite has formed among working women. Generally, the more time a woman spends with men in a male-dominated occupation, the higher the status. Women who work with other women or with children are considered lower in status. Consequently, school teaching, one of the most stimulating and demanding jobs around—and one that allows you to do some of the work at home and have the summer free for your own children—is sometimes looked down on by bright young women.

Day-care director Marian Blum points out an interesting irony resulting from this situation that can be seen in day-care centers: "Many contemporary parents, some of whom consider themselves feminists, emphasize the importance of nonstereotyped role models. And then, they enroll their children in institutions where, all too frequently, depressed women do what is perceived as menial work. The role model of the successful woman in the gray flannel suit with the leather briefcase does not work at the day-care center."[11]

A day-care worker or a baby-sitter can feel uncomfortable with the accomplishments of a professional woman. On the other hand, a mother, especially a new mother, can feel inexperienced compared with a woman who has over the years cared for dozens of children. In the words of a former day-care worker, there can be "a clash in social class" and therefore sometimes "a clash in values." She thinks that there needs to be "a good fit," but with so much of day care underground and underpaid, this goal can be tough to accomplish. Consequently, hostility sometimes exists between the two people concerned with the well-being of the child. The mother needs understanding, and the child-care provider needs respect.

Dimensions of the Day-Care Problem

I do not believe that a nation can truly prosper when economic and social pressures combine to push mothers into the workforce, even though, at the same time, no system exists for providing consistently good care for their children or much respect for those who provide it. Mothers and fathers who work outside the home need worry-free day care for their children, and those parents who wish to provide that care themselves need adequate tax breaks to do so.

Thousands of low-income, single women who wish to work in order to raise their standard of living have difficulty doing so, because there is no space for their children in federal- and state-subsidized child-care facilities. According to a report by the San Antonio Coalition for Children, Youth, and Families, some of the children on waiting lists in San Antonio, Texas, are left during the time their parents are working "in a variety of situations—with relatives, neighbors, older siblings, and in startling and ever-increasing numbers, are left at home alone, with no supervision whatsoever!"[12] Many child-care experts are warning of the danger of the United States's becoming a nation that supports a two-tier system of child care, in which the working poor have the worst for their children and upper-middle-income working couples have the best.[13] Poor care—or no care—has been associated with cognitive and language deficits, low self-esteem, suppressed immunity in infants, and poor social relationships.[14]

Perhaps we also need to consider that encouraging low-income women to join the workforce full time is not necessarily the best thing to do for the health of their individual families or of the nation. Poor women might benefit more than any other group from at-home paying work. Therefore, it seems wise to expend more energy helping these women become self-supporting at home or helping them find work outside the home during hours when their children are in school.

At other times in our history, our government has supported parental care for children by giving families generous personal and dependent tax exemptions. The personal exemption on federal income tax, which was introduced in 1913, allows each taxpayer to deduct a certain percentage of his or her income for the expenses of being alive. The dependent exemption, enacted in 1917, allows the taxpayer to deduct an amount for each household member. Historically, this was the wife and dependent children of a male breadwinner. The dependent exemptions allowed were largely responsible for maintaining the American custom of having mothers care for babies and young children at home. Until recent years, the exemption kept pace with inflation. Now it most certainly does not.

Adjusting exemptions for inflation and taxing more fairly could make a significant difference for millions of two-parent families who would prefer to have one parent at home as principal caregiver and for some single parents who might be able to afford to work part time instead of full time. Those who continued to work full time would have many more take-home dollars with which to buy better-quality child care. Perhaps making it easier for both those who stay home and those who work outside the home could also ease some of the tensions that have grown up between them.

Stereotyping of Women at Home

Sometimes the polarities and social divisions are more funny than sad. Since deciding to stay home, I have found that all kinds of assumptions are sometimes made about the woman at home: that she is conservative in her politics, religion, and social views; that she's probably rich; or that maybe her husband doesn't "let" her work outside the home.

For example, I once appeared on a television program about the crisis in child care in the United States and was presented by the program's host as a mother who solved her day-care problems by working at home. At no time did I express any political or social opinions that were either Left or Right during the early part of the discussion. Yet halfway through the program I was referred to as "representing the Right" and then asked a question. I tried to keep from choking and finally, unable to think of any rejoinder, simply shrugged and looked blank. But I have since found that if you stay home with your children, some people will automatically place you in a right-wing slot.

In fact, there are women at home who are feminists, neoliberals, neoconservatives, moderates, trade unionists, anarchists. They are left-wing, right-wing, "pro-life," "pro-choice." Lesbian Moms At

Home now has a web page on the Internet. As *Welcome Home* newsletter founder Cheri Loveless has said, "The choice to stay at home crosses all political and socioeconomic boundaries. You cannot pigeonhole us as a group."[15]

The "Backlash" Against Feminists or Feminists' Fear of Individualism?

Yet women themselves are pigeonholing other women, and some of the hostility is getting more and more intense. As increasing numbers of men and women have begun questioning the rigors of life in a two-paycheck family, some feminists have become increasingly vitriolic. There are now all sorts of labels and accusations that are flung about: "revisionists" are accused of "turning the clock back" and being in cahoots with the "male chauvinist backlash."

The literature that is now coming out of the women's movement has become more and more bizarre and their perceptions and causes more questionable. The titles of their books reveal a great deal: *Backlash: The Undeclared War Against American Women; A Fearful Freedom: Women's Flight from Equality; Feminism Without Illusions: A Critique of Individualism*. The gist of most of these books is that our decadent culture is dominated by men out to put down women, who are having a hard time thriving in the "malestream."[16] Further, too many women have retreated from the battle; they've gone all mushy—missing their kids, worrying about strains in their two-paycheck marriages, and questioning whether it really is better to be a doctor than a nurse. Such women, which includes most of us, are politically incorrect "individualists" and "revisionists" who threaten "the movement." We're not given any slack for using common sense or trying to find our own way to solve problems.

What this means to me, after clearing away all the iconoclastic debris of their writing, is that the most outspoken feminists do not really want diversity or individualism. It's really not OK to find your own answers to your working-parent woes. Any questioning of the working-mom status quo represents betrayal of the cause and is supposed to be part of the "backlash" conspiracy against women. Staying home is verboten. One critic reviewing some of these feminist books said, "Those of us who cherish true diversity, who believe that women have rights as individuals and not as a gender, can only say: Please ladies, start the get-together without me."[17]

The Power to Be Yourself

We need to stop listening to those feminists who tell us how it's "supposed to be" for all working women. Listening to them and following their lead has been a little like taking flying lessons from people who don't have pilot's licenses. Many of the most famous feminists who advise us, patronize us, or castigate us are childless and unmarried. Many have never run a household or had a long-term relationship. Although they may give strongly held opinions on everything from the corporate world to women in the military, they often have had no experience in either business or the military. They are more ignorant than arrogant. They simply do not have the *experience* to instruct us. It is no wonder that today many working mothers feel as if they are flying off course.

Those who feel caught in the working-mom rat race need to know that combining full-time work with motherhood *is* hard, *for everybody*. We need to admit this to other women, to husbands and lovers, to bosses, to parents, to our mothers-in-law—to everyone who has anything to do with our lives. Acknowledging this truth does not mean whining or beating our breasts, but stating clearly that having it all, all at once, is exhausting for the average woman. If we do this, some changes may become possible.

Admitting to others as well as to ourselves that Supermom doesn't live in *this* house requires one important thing: power. We all hear so much rhetoric about power that the word has "become heavy with the weight of emotional and political overtones."[18] But in the best sense of the word, if a woman is powerful, she is confident about her life choices and strong enough to get what she needs. It takes power to admit that a problem exists and to work out a solution. An unhappy working wife and mother who says, "I'd like to quit but I just can't" is often behaving in a passive, powerless way. She *can* make an effort to look at options and find alternatives. If she fails in the effort, then she has to work at accepting the situation and move on, but at least in making the effort she is behaving like a strong, free woman.

Gains from the Women's Movement

In sometimes criticizing the women's movement, particularly the radical element, I do not mean to deny what we have gained in the last thirty years. As individuals, women can now get credit ratings and bank loans on their own. We have a better chance of being admitted to law school or medical school. There are legal mechanisms now in place to discourage sexual harassment on the job. We enjoy marriages to men who are often more involved in the birth and rearing of children than their fathers were.

In the last thirty years, we have gained as a society because the country is now less likely to lose out on using the talent and intelligence of half our population in areas outside the home. A young woman with high intelligence and great dexterity is more likely to become a surgeon today, for example. But I don't think we've gone far enough in enabling her to conduct a half-day practice, to go home once she's performed brilliantly in the operating room at 8:00 A.M. Most people would not think of her time at home with a child as a significant contribution. This can be just as true for the woman who works in a factory or department store.

We need to guard against a tendency in our country to regard a job as a means to great joy and fulfillment for women. We have to make it clear that for the ordinary working mother the reality is just to try to make a buck at work and to keep everybody's socks matched at home. There is really not much glamour in most jobs, and when there is, a good deal of stress is usually involved too. This doesn't mean that life is grim; it just means that life isn't simple, and a job, like everything else, is usually both good and bad. If we are willing to look, there are often a series of answers that emerge from the conflicts, responsibilities, and joys of the different seasons of a woman's life. We need to avoid rigid responses and a fear of diversity. According to writer and psychologist Elaine Heffner:

> Women were for a time told that the only way to be a real woman was through motherhood. In order to be whole they would have to sacrifice those parts of themselves that longed for expression in other ways. Now women are being told that in order to be whole they must sacrifice the impulse to mother. . . . Neither view addresses the full range of women's feelings. . . . We appear to believe that perfection is an attainable state. When we encounter a problem that grows out of the conflicts of living, we imagine the problem is the result of the existing solution, rather than part of life itself. We are quick to conclude that an opposite solution would achieve the life free of pain that we are seeking.[19]

The solution to "'liberate' women from the mother role rather than by helping them become successful within it"[20] often does not work.

Social Responsibility

As a society, we may mimic the words of the politicians, who say, "Our children are our greatest natural resource." But when it comes to supporting funding for children, many of us don't seem to care. Our society does not seem to have the same sense of common "ownership" of children that it once had. For one thing, not as many people have kids as they once did. It's no longer assumed that when a couple marries, a family will follow within a few years. Most neighborhoods are not as unified as they once were. Compared to past generations, we have become disconnected.

> We have shifted from a family culture to a job culture. The primary source of adult definition and achievement now comes from the workplace, not the home. . . . The notion that we contribute most to the overall well being of society as workers, not parents, is a very big shift in public philosophy that has been harmful to parents specifically and to the nation as a whole.[21]

Career Women and Pressure

Women who make it to the top in professions are under tremendous pressure to keep their noses to the grindstone. Ironically, some of the top professions lend themselves best to half-days and "mother's hours" because of a heavy reliance on scheduling by appointment. Nevertheless, the pressure is often greatest in these professions for parents to keep strictly conventional office hours. Our society would benefit greatly if we could reexamine the various conventions and assumptions that govern working customs.

Some feminists have called for business and the professions to become "more sensitive" to women's needs and more responsive to the American family. Although I am certainly in favor of this, some of the specific proposals to make this possible are unworkable, especially for small enterprises—the majority of businesses in the United States. For example, the push for parental leaves of absence to care for a newborn is worthwhile. But the demands attendant in bills proposed in Washington have often been impractical and unrealistic.

A business is a business is a business. Its purpose is to make money in the most efficient way possible. Parental leaves will become more common when some room is given for negotiation and flexibility. Large, wealthy corporations will establish on-site day-care facilities when they see that this improves productivity. Both big and small business employers will establish flex-time and job sharing when they see that it is to their benefit to do so, and when we tell them how badly this is needed. We have the chance now to change slowly what has been unfair to us, but we will not succeed by demanding what is unrealistic or naïve or unfair to the business community.

In some situations, women of talent and ambition will have to strike out on their own. It is therefore important that we safeguard and promote our right to earn money in our own homes, to revive and make strong the American tradition of independence and entrepreneurship.

The Importance of Education

I think one of our major goals should be to continue to encourage teenage and young women to attain the highest education possible. Education is important as a means to being independent and self-supporting, but it is also a great resource for problem solving, at home and in outside work. But I think we need to do more to educate people about the very real difficulties of combining work outside the home and rearing children.

We also need to continue educating our partners in the importance of sharing responsibilities at home. Eighty-five percent of working couples cannot afford full-time household help.[22] Men's participation in household work has increased slightly, but not enough. Apart from the issue of fairness, men's doing housework goes a long way toward solidifying a marriage. In general, women consider divorce more frequently than men do today. In one study on divorce, researchers found that "for each daily household task that the husband performed at least half the time, the wife was about 3 percent less likely to have thoughts of divorce."[23] This may sound almost laughable, but when you've got two square feet of dirty dishes and baby bottles on the kitchen counter at the end of a long day, it's not a bit funny. Shared responsibility has to be regarded as important by both partners and carefully negotiated.

The Changes to Come

American society faces many changes in the coming years, but not necessarily the kind some demographers and feminists are predicting. As long as men and women feel economically insecure, increasing numbers of families will have both parents in the labor force. But a number of factors could militate against increasing numbers of young mothers working full time outside the home. For one thing, millions of women are getting fed up with full-time work outside the home. In their "Trendicators" column, even *Working Woman* magazine acknowledges that "more people are dropping out of the rat race," citing the desire to reduce hours or quit working outside the home completely.[24] Generally, the younger the woman, the more likely she is to question the lifestyle of the fast-track working mother.[25]

A second important factor is the technological change that may make more telecommunication jobs at home possible, even likely. A number of social changes are encouraging the growth in at-home businesses: the transportation crisis in North American cities and the attendant air pollution and parking problems; the escalating costs of real estate and office maintenance; the interest in small city and rural life; the average worker's distaste for commuting; and, in the midst of a high divorce rate, the desire to "glue the family unit together again," with both children and parents helping each other at home.[26] As work at home using a computer becomes more common, it is likely that women who cannot do this specific type of work will search for other ways to combine paying work with child rearing at home.

One additional factor may bring more working mothers home to stay with their children, and that is the tide of social opinion that seems to be turning away from radical feminism. We are beginning to suffer from " 'Eve Fatigue' . . . an affliction that comes over a society that has had all the feminism it can stand."[27] We are finally questioning the excesses of a movement that is no longer doing much for us. I think this is the essence of the supposed "backlash."

About four months after I quit work, I was standing one autumn morning at the kitchen window washing dishes and keeping an eye on my then-four-year-old son playing outside, just beneath the window. He was sitting under the big maples in our backyard playing with an old chipped dump truck we had given our daughter years before. The wind came up and blew the maple leaves down around him. An equally brilliant shift of yellow-gold sunlight shown down through a space between the maple boughs, lighting up his bowl-cut, wheat-colored hair. It was one of those incredibly perfect moments that a parent never forgets and, as I stood there, in the midst of an ordinary task and an extraordinary sight, I thought to myself, "This is where I *want* to be."

Many women of my generation have finally realized that they cannot bear a child or go through the anxious years of the adoption process and then leave these children with ease—either physical or emotional—to work full time outside the home. It isn't just that children are a responsibility. They are—more than anything—heart pullers. We've found, as our grandmothers could have told us, that it's hard racing ahead on the fast track when a baby is pulling our hearts the other way.

Appendix A

Resources

Chapters One and Two

Publications

The Time Bind: When Work Becomes Home and Home Becomes Work, Arlie
Hochschild. New York: Henry Holt/Metropolitan Books, 1997.
The Second Shift: Inside the Two-Job Marriage, Arlie Hochschild. New York:
Avon, 1990.
When Work Doesn't Work Anymore: Women, Work and Identity, Elizabeth Perle
McKenna. New York: Delacorte Press, 1997.

Chapter Three

Publications

Mother Care/Other Care, Sandra Scarr. New York: Basic Books, 1984.
Nanny News newsletter, ed. M. Jane McIntosh. Knowledge Source Publications,
P.O. Box 277, Hopewell, NJ 08525; 609-737-8050. For both child-care
providers and their employers.

Organizations

Child Care Action Campaign, 330 Seventh Ave., 17th floor, New York, NY
10001; 212-239-0138. Send a letter with a self-addressed, stamped
envelope for help in finding good child care where you live.
Child Care Aware, coordinated by the National Association of Child Care
Resource and Referral Agencies, 1319 F St., N.W., Suite 606, Washington,

---

Note: Some of the older books may be available only at a public library or used
book store.

D.C. 20004; 800-424-2246, 202-393-5501. National referral service.
Free information packet on choosing good child care.

Fatherhood Project, Families and Work Institute, 330 Seventh Ave., 14th floor, New York, NY 10001; 212-268-4846. Referral service for custodial fathers seeking good child care, support groups, and companies with family-oriented policies.

Parents Without Partners, 401 N. Michigan Ave., Chicago, IL 60611; 800-637-7974, 312-644-6610 in Chicago. Call the 800 number for information about joining or starting a local support group, or check your local phone book.

Chapter Four

Publications

The Family Handyman: Helpful Hints, Reader's Digest. Pleasantville, NY: The Reader's Digest Association, Inc., 1996. In spite of the macho title, a useful book for anyone who wants to save on maintenance and repair costs.

Terry Savage Talks Money: The Common Sense Guide to Money Matters, Terry Savage. New York: HarperCollins, 1993. Easy-to-understand guide for the novice in money matters.

Chapter Five

Publications

The $5 Chef: How to Save Cash and Cook Fast, Marcie Rothman. Santa Rosa, CA: Five-Spot Press. Available at bookstores or through Five-Spot Press, P.O. Box 4559, Santa Rosa, CA 95402-4559.

Cooperative Housing Compendium: Resources for Collaborative Living. Berkeley, CA: University of California, 1993.

Freebies magazine, 1135 Eugenia Place, Carpinteria, CA 93013; 805-566-1225. Great for getting free things for kids.

Globe Pequot Press, P.O. Box 833, Old Saybrook, CT 06475; 800-243-0495, 203-526-4930. They have a free catalog listing budget-minded books on a variety of subjects.

Mary Ellen's Best of Helpful Hints Book II, Mary Ellen Pinkham. New York: Warner Books, 1981. An old standby.

New York Times Season by Season Guide to Home Maintenance, John Warde. New York: Random House, 1992.

See also Sunset paperback books on making and maintaining things.

Organizations

Shelter Institute, 38 Center St., Bath, ME 04530; 207-442-7938. The institute
   has catalogs and books of house, boat, and cabinetry plans and a list of
   books they sell by mail-order. The Shelter Institute also offers a variety
   of classes in planning and construction, with single and couple rates and
   weekend winter rates.

Chapter Six

Publications

Great Vacations with Your Kids, Dorothy Jordan and Marjorie Cohen. New York:
   NAL/Dutton, 1990.
How to Get Organized When You Don't Have the Time, Stephanie Culp.
   Cincinnati, OH: Writer's Digest Books, 1986. Humorous, step-by-step
   approach that helps you get control of your time and your life.
Meditations for Women Who Do Too Much, Anne Wilson Schaef. New York:
   HarperCollins, 1990.
The Nurturing Father, Kyle Pruett. New York: Warner Books, 1987.
   Available at used book stores and public libraries only.
Parent's Resource Connection, ed. Deanna Sletten, 5102 Deerwood Lane, N.E.,
   Bemidji, MN 56601; 218-751-3136. A directory of more than two
   hundred parenting publications and support groups. Includes home
   business profiles.
Speed Cleaning, Jeff Campbell and The Clean Team. New York: Dell, 1991.
   The glory to this book is that it involves a team approach, not a lone
   drudge approach.
Take Your Kids to Europe, Cynthia Harriman. Mason-Grant Publications,
   P.O. Box 6547, Portsmouth, NH 03802; $12.95. Clever ways to arrange
   a jaunt to Europe for the middle-class family by renting out your home in
   the United States and renting a house in Europe. Includes information
   on transportation savings and other details.
The Tightwad Gazette: Promoting Thrift as a Viable Alternative Lifestyle, Amy
   Dacyczyn. New York: Villard Books, 1993.

Organizations

FEMALE (Formerly Employed Mothers At the Leading Edge), P.O. Box 31,
   Elmhurst, IL 60126; 630-941-3553; e-mail: femaleofc@aol.com.
   A support and advocacy group for mothers at home, with local chapters

throughout the United States. Publishes the newsletter *FEMALE Forum*.
For help in starting a new group, write to FEMALE at the Illinois address
or contact the organization via e-mail.

Mothers at Home, 8310A Old Courthouse Rd., Vienna, VA 22182;
800-783-4666; e-mail: mah@netrail.net. Publishes the newsletter
Welcome Home.

Mothers Matter, Kay Willis, 171 Wood St., Rutherford, NJ 07070;
201-933-8191; e-mail: momsmatter@aol.com. Mrs. Willis gives lectures
and workshops on parenting and self-esteem, primarily in the Northeast.

National Parent Information Network, 800-583-4135. This parenting network
based in the Midwest has the largest database in the nation and answers
questions about kids and parenting free of charge.

Chapter Seven

Publications

Buying Your First Franchise. Crisp Publications, 1200 Hamilton Court,
Menlo Park, CA 94025-9600; 800-442-7477, 650-323-6100.

Careers for Women Without College Degrees, Beatryce Nivens. New York:
McGraw Hill, 1988. Available only at used book stores and public
libraries.

The Complete Guide to Job Sharing, Patricia Lee. New York: Walker, 1983.

How to Turn an Interview into a Job, Jeffrey Allen. New York: Simon & Schuster,
1986. Also see his other books on interviewing published by Simon &
Schuster.

Power Resumes, Ron Tepper. New York: Wiley, 1992.

Organizations and Contacts

American Association of University Women (AAUW), 1111 Sixteenth St.,
N.W., Washington, D.C. 20036; 202-785-7700. Has grants and
fellowships available for women who wish to go back to school for an
advanced degree.

Association of Part-time Professionals, 7700 Leesburg Pike, Suite 216,
Crescent Plaza, Falls Church, VA 22043; 703-734-7975.

National Network for Work Time Options, c/o New Ways to Work,
985 Market St., Suite 950, San Francisco, CA 94103; 415-995-9860.

Women Employed, 22 W. Monroe, Suite 1400, Chicago, IL 60603;
312-782-3902. Provides information on companies in the Chicago area

with enlightened flex-time schedules, part-time employment opportunities, and good parental leave and child-care policies. They also have support groups for women working in the greater Chicago region.

Women Work! The National Network for Women's Employment, 1625 K St.,
N.W., Suite 300, Washington, D.C. 20006; 202-467-6346.

Women's Network for Entrepreneurial Training (WNET), Office of Women's
Business Ownership, Small Business Administration, Washington, D.C.;
800-8-ASK-SBA, 202-205-6673. A mentorship program that matches
successful entrepreneurial women with new business owners who have
been in business for a year or more.

YWCA. See your local phone book for address and phone number. Workshops
on reentering the workforce and alternative employment opportunities.

For minority and low-income women: free or low-cost advice on entering the
labor force is available at some universities and city or state nonprofit
organizations. Call your local small business administration or city hall.

Chapter Eight

Publications

Best Home-Based Franchises, Philip Lief Group. New York: Doubleday, 1992.

Directory of Wholesale Reps for Craft Professionals, Sharon Olson. Eden Prairie,
MN: Northwoods Trading Co., 1992. Contact the publisher at 13451
Essex Court, Eden Prairie, MN 55347.

Books by Paul and Sarah Edwards: *Best Home Businesses for the 90's, Finding Your
Perfect Work, Home Businesses You Can Buy, Making Money with Your
Computer at Home* (2nd ed.), *Getting Business to Come to You, Secrets of
Self-Employment, Teaming Up: The Small Business Guide to Collaborating
with Others*, and *Working from Home* (4th ed.). Tarcher/Putnam, 200
Madison Ave., 16th floor, New York, NY 10016; 212-951-8577. The
Edwards's e-mail address is 76703.242@compuserve.com. They also have
a home page on the Internet: www.workingfromhome.com.

Encyclopedia of Business Information Sources. Gale Research Inc., 835 Penobscot
Bldg., Detroit, MI 48226-4094; 313-961-2242.

Franchises You Can Run from Home, Lynie Arden. Somerset, NJ: Wiley, 1990;
800-225-5945.

Free Help from Uncle Sam to Start Your Own Business, William Alarid and Gustav
Berle. Puma Publishing, 1670 Coral Dr., Santa Maria, CA 93454.

Growing a Business, Paul Hawken. New York: Fireside/Simon & Schuster, 1992.

National Directory of Mailing Lists. Oxbridge Communications, Inc., 150 Fifth
    Ave., New York, NY 10011; 212-741-0231.
Small Business Sourcebook: The Entrepreneur's Resource (10th ed.), ed. Amy Lynn
    Park. Detroit: Gale, 1997.
Start Up Guide (2nd ed.), David H. Bangs. Dover, NH: Upstart Publishing, 1984.
    Available from Upstart Publishing, 12 Portland St., Dover, NH 03820.
Tradeshow Week Data Book. R. R. Bowker, 121 Chanlon Rd., New Providence,
    NJ 07974; 800-521-8110.
Trade Shows Worldwide. Available from Gale Research Inc., 835 Penobscot Bldg.,
    Detroit, MI 48226-4094; 313-961-2242.
U.S. Small Business Administration pamphlets and videotapes on management,
    planning, and marketing are available through SBA Publications,
    P.O. Box 30, Denver, CO 80201-0030; 202-653-6654 (10 A.M. to 3 P.M.).
World Guide to Trade Associations. R. R. Bowker, 121 Chanlon Rd., New
    Providence, NJ 07974; 800-521-8110. Available at most public
    libraries.

Organizations and Contacts

American Home Business Association (AHBA), 4505 S. Wasatch Blvd., Salt
    Lake City, UT 84124; 801-273-5450.
American Small Business Association (ASBA), 1800 N. Kent St., Suite 910,
    Arlington, VA 22209; 800-235-3298.
American Women's Economic Development Corporation (AWED),
    71 Vanderbilt Ave., 3rd floor, New York, NY 10169; 800-222-AWED,
    212-692-9100.
Association of Small Business Development Centers, 1300 Chain Bridge Rd.,
    Suite 201, McLean, VA 22101; 703-448-6124.
Direct Selling Association, 1666 K St., N.W., Suite 1010, Washington, D.C.
    20006; 202-293-5760. Write for their listing of member companies
    and the products they direct sell, and for the association's brochure
    Direct Selling: The Career for the '90s.
Entrepreneurship Institute, 3592 Corporate Dr., Suite 101, Columbus, OH
    43231; 614-895-1153.
Mothers' Home Business Network (MHBN), P.O. Box 423, East Meadow, NY
    11554-0423; 516-997-7394. Send a self-addressed, stamped envelope for
    information and a list of publications.

National Association for Family Day Care, 1331-A Pennsylvania Ave., N.W.,
    Suite 348, Washington, D.C. 20004; 602-838-3446. Send a self-addressed,
    stamped envelope for information on how to start a family day-care business.
National Association for the Self-Employed (NASE), P.O. Box 612067, Dallas,
    TX 75261; 800-232-NASE.
National Association of Women Business Owners (NAWBO), 1100 Wayne
    Ave., Suite 830, Silver Spring, MD 20910. Advice on networking and
    conferences.
National Business Association (NBA), 5151 Belt Line Rd., No. 1150, Dallas,
    TX 75240; 214-458-0900.
National Federation of Independent Business (NFIB), 53 Century Blvd., Suite
    300, Nashville, TN 37214; 615-872-5800.
National Venture Capital Association, 1655 N. Fort Myer Dr., Suite 700,
    Arlington, VA 22209; 703-351-5269.
Rep Registry, P.O. Box 2306, Capistrano Beach, CA 92624. Contact: Jill Ford.
    They have a handbook called *Working with Wholesale Giftware Reps . . .
    A Beginner's Handbook*.
Service Corps of Retired Executives (SCORE), 409 Third St., S.W., 4th floor,
    Washington, D.C. 20024; 202-205-6762. Provides free counseling and
    marketing advice. Call the Washington number to find out the nearest
    branch, or look in the local telephone book.
Small Business Institutes. Free advice from M.B.A. students at universities and
    colleges. Ask about these at your local SBA office.
Small Business Network (SBN), P.O. Box 30149, Baltimore, MD 21270;
    410-581-1373.

Chapter Nine

Publications

Home Business: The Work-from-Home Magazine, 9582 Hamilton Ave., Suite 368,
    Huntington Beach, CA 92646.
Home Office Computing magazine, P.O. Box 53561, Boulder, CO 80322;
    800-631-1586.
Consumer Reports Guide to Personal Computers, Olen R. Pearson and the editors
    of *Consumer Reports*. Yonkers, NY: Consumer Reports, 1997.
Telecommute! Go to Work Without Leaving Home, Lisa Shaw. New York: Wiley,
    1996.

Chapter Ten

Publications

Being There: The Benefits of a Stay at Home Parent, Isabelle Fox and Norman
  Lobsenz. New York: Barron, 1996.

Sequencing, Arlene R. Cardozo. New York: Macmillan, 1989.

What's a Smart Woman Like You Doing at Home? (2nd ed.), Linda Burton, Janet
  Dittmer, and Cheri Loveless. Washington, D.C.: Acropolis Books, 1993.
  Also available through Mothers at Home, Inc., 8310A Old Courthouse
  Rd., Vienna, VA 22182.

When the Bough Breaks: The Cost of Neglecting Our Children, Sylvia Ann
  Hewlett. New York: HarperCollins, 1992.

Appendix B

Alternatives to 9-to-5 Jobs

The businesses described below demonstrate how to use skills, resources, and personal interests to earn money. The people who are profiled have fictitious names but real businesses.

A Home Baking Business

Susan Anders had a two-year-old daughter she loved taking care of, a high school diploma, an extra stove on the back porch of her apartment, and a gift for making great cheesecake. When she started Andre's Gourmet Cheesecakes, she lived in a resort community that had to import cheesecake from bakeries in New York or Boston. She took advantage of the fact that a relative worked in the dairy department of her local supermarket and could get eggs, sour cream, butter, and cream cheese at a discount. Susan bought several springform pans, and after making the rounds of the resort's most expensive restaurants with generous samples of her cheesecake, she was in business.

Five mornings a week, after playing with her daughter for an hour, Susan is ready to mix up and bake her cheesecakes. In the afternoon, when they're cool, she places them on cardboard rounds, wraps them, and seals them with her gold "Andre's Cheesecakes" sticker. Her carpenter husband brings home their truck in the middle of the afternoon and looks after their daughter for an hour while Susan delivers her cakes.

Susan does not have a six-figure income. But she does take advantage of the fact that the local restaurants' clientele will pay top dollar for freshly made cheesecake, and she charges accordingly. She makes enough to supplement her husband's income and occasionally take her husband and daughter out for their own dessert treat.

A Tourism Business in New England

Jack and Diana Marquette are a New England couple who operate a successful brochure distribution service. The two met in the Virgin Islands and, after their marriage, moved to San Francisco, where Jack ran a tugboat in San Francisco Bay and Diana used her economics degree as a research coordinator in the banking industry. Although Jack was reasonably happy, Diana was disappointed in her job. "I thought I'd love it, but I didn't feel in control. . . . Some other entity was always telling me what to do and where to be." Jack and Diana decided to return to their New England roots to raise a family and start a business. By the time their first child was born, they had done just that and parlayed their knowledge of tourism into a successful business.

In the Virgin Islands, Jack had had a contract with a distributor to display the brochure he used to attract tourists to his business. In the area where he and Diana relocated in New England—a few miles from the ocean and only a couple of hours from ski areas—there were quaint restaurants, inns, and historic buildings and museums, but no distributors for the brochures generated by these attractions. Diana and Jack started out with only ten contracts to set up brochure racks, but seven years later, they have nine hundred contracts, cover three states, and, in the summer, have twenty part-time employees. Although their workload is heaviest in the summer months, they have plenty of business in the fall and winter for the two of them to share. In the spring, they are busy preparing for the summer season.

Working out of the large farmhouse they recently moved into, the Marquettes have an office set up in what was originally a four-seasons porch. They have one part-time employee who comes in a couple of times a week to help Diana with accounting and customer contacts. "We don't have a fax machine and we could be more computerized, but we mainly use the phone and send out letters to make contacts. We use our computer primarily for word processing." Diana and Jack keep overhead low by storing brochure racks in the root cellar beneath their garage. Maintenance and repairs are also done here. In the summer, they rent ministorage units to store brochures in the regions they cover, another way to keep overhead low. Their part-time distributors use their own cars or trucks to restock the racks each week, so Jack does not have to keep a fleet of expensive vans.

Jack says the people he hires part-time "are great—dependable, well educated. We get a lot of retired people, a lot of overqualified people, really. They like the independence of the job and the fact that we're actually offering them flex-time; they can distribute the brochures whenever it's best for them as long as they get the brochures out there."

Diana and Jack now have another child and find that working together from their home suits them and their family's lifestyle. "We try to keep a balance," says Diana. "We maintain a clear division of responsibilities and have a good complement of skills and talents. What I like to do, Jack doesn't, and vice versa." Jack covers operations, field work, and sales. Diana takes care of accounting and other office work with the help of their part-timer. In dividing business tasks and child care, the couple has a system of working "four and four," meaning each works four hours, either in the morning or in the afternoon. In the evening, after the kids are in bed, they put in more hours, "sometimes till one in the morning in the summer, but then we may spend the afternoon at the beach with the kids the next day."

The down side of working at home for the Marquettes is that they sometimes feel isolated. "There's no longer the opportunity to make friends at work, to enjoy the camaraderie of the workplace. We really have to nurture outside friendships." The business is logistically complicated at times. For example, at an inn or motel using their service, they can leave dozens of restaurant brochures, but not at the restaurant just down the road where such brochures would only be competition. "So, it's a lot more complicated than you'd expect." At the moment, the Marquettes have no plans for expansion. They also have no desire to move out of their home office at any time in the future. They like the fact that, for them, "a tough commute is when there are toys on the stairs."

Computer Consulting and Writing at Home

Marjory Zell works as a computer consultant and writer. She has an eight-year-old and a five-year-old and works from an office that was once a formal dining room. She has a bachelor's degree and had a variety of part-time jobs in and out of the home before she got interested in computers. She took a couple of good computer courses, "played" with a computer that a storekeeper friend had, and got to know some people in her area who made their living working with computers, before she bought a small desk computer. She gave free "helping sessions" at the public library on Saturday mornings for adults and children who had just bought new computers, and then managed to sell a local newspaper on the idea of a weekly column on computers in exchange for free advertising. She soon became known as an expert.

She now writes instructional manuals on computer software for a large publishing company, teaches courses on how to use computers, and serves as a consultant to area businesses and schools. Marjory uses networking a great deal to get business and to pass on business. She also networks to get free use of the best computer software, telling manufacturers that if she can have free use of their software in her classes, she will, in effect, be encouraging students to buy the manufacturer's products. They get free advertising and promotion, she gets the software.

Marjory works each morning until her son arrives home from kindergarten, takes a long break, and then works another hour or two while he reads or watches *Sesame Street*. She does errands and some household chores during a break in the afternoon when her daughter arrives home. She later works another two or three hours in the evening while her husband cares for the children. Marjory makes a very good living, though she points out that she usually works six hours a day and, before publishing deadlines, eight or more hours a day—something not everyone is willing to do. "But I can do my work in jeans or my bathrobe if I feel like it. I have the freedom to work a lot or a little."

Paralegal Work Partly at Home

Claire Donovan wanted to get out of the house and out of her jeans when she started her own business as a paralegal. She had worked for several years as a legal secretary before giving birth to a son and a daughter. She enjoyed the years at home when her children were babies but felt restless and a little confined as they grew older. She worked part-time as a legal secretary but found that she felt guilty when there was an emergency and she needed time off for her kids. "Feeling guilty and having divided loyalties between my kids and my boss was my main motivation for starting my own business."

Today the main focus of that business is on residential and commercial title searches for attorneys practicing law in the area where Claire and her family live. The work is very precise, and Claire found she could not do it at home because of all the interruptions. She therefore works occasionally at her clients' offices and, more often, at a desk at the county office. Since the office is a public building, there is no charge for this space, and documents and records she must consult are within easy reach.

At home, Claire has an answering machine to receive calls when she is away and a desk where she can do billing and other record keeping in the afternoon. Although the work is demanding and Claire had to take some difficult courses to qualify as a certified paralegal in her state, she loves the work itself and the stimulation of the people she works with. Currently, the only drawback is that the demand for Claire's services has become so great that she could "easily spend sixty hours a week on the business." Now that her children are both in school, she works about forty hours a week, tailoring her schedule to her children's school hours and extracurricular activities. When too much business comes her way, she refers potential clients to other certified paralegals, and after seven and a half years in the business, she has hired an assistant and given herself the entire month of August for time at home for rest and family.

Buying and Refurbishing Old Houses

Like Claire Donovan, Ann Minotti works outside the home, but her eight-year-old son is often at her side. Five years ago, when she was just divorced, she had a degree in biology, half the money from the sale of her home, and a great reluctance to leave her then two-and-a-half-year-old to go out to work. She and a friend, who was also going through a divorce, decided to form a partnership to do something they had talked and dreamed of for years: buying and refurbishing old Victorian houses and renting out the finished rooms to university students and the elderly. Ann had some carpentry skills and had previously taken a couple of courses on the history and restoration of old houses, but most of all, she had a strong commitment to doing interesting work that could include her son.

In order to organize a work crew, Ann and her friend advertised in the local newspaper for women with or without repair and decorating skills and said they could bring their children. The phone "rang off the hook," and Ann was in business. She now buys and refurbishes three-story Victorian houses—about two a year—and does some restoration projects for individual clients as well as some consulting.

People outside the business are still amazed at her success. "The most common question I get about our mom-and-kids crews is 'How can you possibly work with little kids around?' Yet in all the years I've been doing this, we've never had one problem. Kids understand that they can help Mom out by being good, and there's surprisingly little fighting among the children. We keep all dangerous tools away from the kids, instruct them in safety, and let them do some of the work themselves, like spackling nail holes. If one of us has to leave to pick up an older child at school and take him to gymnastics or something, that person just leaves for half an hour and resumes work later."

Ann now has an office with two full-time employees in the town where she has many of her rental properties. When her son was a preschooler, Ann worked with him nearby. Now that he is in school, most afternoons he gets off the school bus at her office instead of at home. She has a snack of homemade cookies and milk for him, which he eats at an office table. He then does his homework while Ann works, or if he has an after-school activity, she drives him to the extracurricular activity and then returns to the office or goes to one of the houses she is refurbishing. Some of the original crew members still work on projects with her, and others have struck out on their own to do the same kind of work. But there are still lots of children at the job sites.

Commodities Broker Working from Home

Mike Dorss is a commodities and real estate broker who had built an enviable reputation in the business by the time his daughter, Dina, was born seven years ago. His wife, Sherry, works as a public relations director at a resort a few minutes from their home. When their daughter was born, Sherry took time off for several weeks and then went back to work three days a week, splitting child care with Mike. When the time came for Sherry to go back full-time, Mike moved everything in his office to the house and set up office space there. "All I really needed to earn a living was a telephone. I felt Sherry was very good at what she did and I always wanted her to accomplish what she had set out to do in her career." For her part, Sherry felt that Mike, as an experienced father who'd been married before, "had such patience. He had so much experience parenting and has taught her more than I ever could have."

Although Mike and Sherry live in the South, Mike was hooked up by telephone to a commodities clearinghouse in Chicago. He would handle clients and trades by telephone and send invoices and other paperwork to Chicago through the mail. The real estate business he did was local and also involved a good deal of phone work. A typical day would have Mike on the telephone, with Dina playing by herself or with a friend in the morning. In the afternoon, Dina and her dad would "take field trips," usually to the beach for a swim and an ecology lesson on marine life.

Now that Dina is school age and Mike and Sherry have made the decision to educate her at home, Mike has cut back considerably on his brokering business. He and his daughter spend three hours every morning on homeschool lessons and spend three afternoons or more on community and beach field trips. When Sherry's job takes her away from home for several days to a city like Orlando or Atlanta, Mike and Dina go along. Mike has recently become extensively involved in volunteer work that uses his financial background. His real estate and commodities business has taken a back seat to Dina's education and his volunteer efforts.

"I could be out selling. Sherry could be out selling. But I prefer to be at home, and she prefers to stay at her old job and be close to home. We decided to take care of our daughter ourselves, to give her parental protection and a good education one-on-one. . . . I'm having the time of my life. This is a very pleasant, very harmonious arrangement for us."

Part-Time Work as a Physical Therapist

As the head of the physical therapy department at a city hospital, Janet Roberts did not have the kind of profession that would allow her to bring her newborn child to work with her. When she took a maternity leave, she fully intended to simply stay home for a few weeks and then return to work full-time. She was upset to find that she hated leaving her baby all day and was physically exhausted both at work and at home.

She had a "hellish" three months before she set up a job-sharing arrangement with another professional in her department who was qualified to divide the management and supervisory responsibilities of the job. "But even this didn't work," she recalls, "because even though I was paid for twenty-five hours a week, I was constantly on the phone on my off-days discussing decisions that had to be made with my job sharer. I was overly conscientious and could not seem to get over the fact that I had once been sole head of this department and had worked sixty hours a week at the job."

After several months, Janet finally decided to make a complete break and go to another hospital as a part-time employee working twenty hours a week with no supervisory responsibilities. "For me this is perfect. I give my all for three days a week and then I'm home, really home. Yet I'm not climbing the walls the way I know I would if I weren't working at all. A lot of people might say I've taken a step down, but I don't give a damn what people say I 'should' be doing. I'm still involved in a profession I love, I'm still contributing to the household economically, and, best of all, I'm spending most of my days with my son, which for me is a step up."

Notes

Preface

1. John Chancellor, *Peril and Promise: A Commentary on America* (New York: HarperCollins, 1990), pp. 76–77.

2. Excerpts from Arlene Rossen Cardozo, *Woman at Home* (Garden City, NY: Doubleday, 1976), pp. 3–4.

Chapter One
Introduction: Is This Liberation?

1. Lee Morical, *Where's My Happy Ending?* (Reading, MA: Addison-Wesley, 1984), p. 49.

2. Edith Tarbescu, "Conflicting Choices: Three Decades in a Woman's Life," *Christian Science Monitor*, May 11, 1988, pp. 30–31.

3. Betty Friedan, lecture at the University of New Hampshire, March 1982.

4. Anne Merewood, "Sperm Under Siege," *Health*, April 1991, p. 55.

5. Lynda Hurst in an article for *Breakthrough* newsletter, cited in Betty Friedan, *The Second Stage* (New York: Summit Books, 1981), p. 33.

6. Morical, 1984, p. 29.

7. Richard Louv, "What Do Mothers Really Want? Working Life Survey," *Parents*, May 1996, p. 40.

8. Lee Bergman, telephone interview, March 9, 1982.

9. Suzanne Gordon, "Excerpts from *Prisoners of Men's Dreams*. Fear of Caring: The Feminist Paradox," in *American Journal of Nursing*, February 1991, p. 46.

10. Ellen Goodman, "Just Woman's Work?" in *At Large* (New York: Summit Books, 1981), p. 185.

11. Lesley Alderman, "Why It Pays to Keep Working," *Working Mother*, February 1997, p. 18.

12. Judsen Culbreth, interview on *Today* show, NBC, January 22, 1997.

13. Christopher Hayes, interview on *Today* show, NBC, January 22, 1997.

14. Alderman, 1997, p. 19.

15. Rep. Frank Wolf, cited in Carol Felsenthal, "Congress Getting Involved in Day Care Issues," *Chicago Sun Times*, May 6, 1984, p. 18.

16. Dan Rather, *CBS Evening News*, April 4, 1984.

17. Howard V. Hayghe and Suzanne M. Bianchi, "Married Mothers' Work Patterns: The Job-Family Compromise," *Monthly Labor Review*, June 1994, pp. 24–25.

18. Ibid., p. 25.

19. Shannon Dortch, "Moms on the Line," *American Demographics*, July 1996, p. 27.

20. Deborah Churchman, "A Close Look at Labor Statistics Bursts the 'Supermom' Myth," *Christian Science Monitor*, July 9, 1987, p. 18D.

21. Deborah Fallows, *A Mother's Work* (Boston: Houghton Mifflin, 1985), p. 134.

22. Brad Edmondson, "Work Slowdown," *American Demographics*, March 1996, p. 4.

23. Cheri Loveless, telephone interview, January 21, 1985.

24. Deborah Churchman, "Women in Business: The New Entrepreneurs," *Christian Science Monitor*, August 25, 1982, p. 15; and Phyllis Gillis, *Entrepreneurial Mothers* (New York: Rawson Associates, 1983), p. 5.

Chapter Two
The Working-Mom Rat Race

1. Program notes on Pay Equity, 1987, pp. 1–2, from The Great American Family Tour.

2. U.S. Department of Housing and Urban Development, "Fiscal Year 1997 Income Limits," http://www.huduser.org.data/asthse/fmrdata97/sect8.html.

3. Dr. Estelle Ramey, lecture at Phillips Exeter Academy, Exeter, NH, June 23, 1983.

4. Lee Morical, *Where's My Happy Ending?* (Reading, MA: Addison-Wesley, 1984), p. 128.

5. Dr. Avodah K. Offit, cited in Natalie Gittelson, "Success and Love: Do I Have to Choose?" *McCall's*, November 1982, p. 182.

6. Richard Moore and Elizabeth Marsis, "Sisterhood under Siege," *The Progressive*, January 1985, pp. 30–31.

7. Patricia L. Dombrink, "The Gender of Success," *Christian Science Monitor*, August 9, 1982, p. 23.

8. Marian Blum, *The Day-Care Dilemma* (San Francisco, CA: New Lexington Press, 1983), p. 115. Reprinted by permission of the publisher.

9. Marjorie Hansen Shaevitz, *The Superwoman Syndrome* (New York: Warner Books, 1984), p. 55.

10. Lynne S. Dumas, "The Split-Shift Solution," *Working Mother*, April 1995, p. 32.

11. Katherine Yost, cited in Gay Norton, "When Spouses Pass in the Night," *Family Weekly*, August 7, 1983.

12. Anita Shreve, "The Lure of Motherhood," *New York Times Magazine*, November 21, 1982, p. 43.

Chapter Three
Anxiety Attacks at the Baby-Sitter's Door

1. William O'Neil, cited in Carol Hymowitz and Michaele Weissman, *A History of Women in America* (New York: Bantam, 1978), p. 321.

2. Linda Baker, "Day-Care Disgrace," *The Progressive*, June 1994, p. 27.

3. Sylvia Ann Hewlett, *When the Bough Breaks: The Cost of Neglecting Our Children* (New York: Basic Books, 1991), p. 148.

4. The 1990 National Commission on the Role of the School and the Community in Improving Adolescent Health, National Association of State Boards of Education and the American Medical Association, as cited in Sylvia Hewlett's *When the Bough Breaks*, p. 11.

5. Hewlett, 1991, p. 12.

6. Sen. Lloyd Bentsen, "Families Need a Tax Cut," in "Opposing View," *USA Today*, October 23, 1991, p. 12A.

7. Lawrence Mishel, Jared Bernstein, and John Schmitt, *The State of Working America 1996–97* (Armonk, NY: Sharpe, 1997), pp. 4–6.

8. Sen. Lloyd Bentsen, 1991, p. 12A.

9. See Wayne Eastep, "Nomads of the Desert," *Smithsonian*, December 1984, pp. 46–56; and Bruno Bettelheim, *The Children of the Dream* (New York: Macmillan, 1969).

10. Mary B. Jones, "New Alternatives," sidebar in "From Career to Maternity," *Rutgers Magazine*, Summer 1991, p. 31.

11. Marian Blum, *The Day-Care Dilemma* (San Francisco, CA: New Lexington Press, 1983), p. 1. Reprinted by permission of the publisher.

12. Ibid.

13. Christina Robb, "Who's Minding the Kids?" *Boston Globe Magazine*, March 3, 1985, pp. 27, 36.

14. S. J. Diamond, "Women on the Job: Surge Widely Felt," *Los Angeles Times*, September 9, 1984, p. 9.

15. Child Care Action Campaign, "A Child Care Primer for Parents," http://www.voiceofwomen.com/childcare.html (June 6, 1997).

16. Maria L. LaGanga, "Experts Disagree—Child Care: Do Careers Pose Perils?" *Los Angeles Times*, September 16, 1984, sec. 1, p. 24.

17. Mary B. Jones, "The Child Care Option," sidebar in "From Career to Maternity," *Rutgers Magazine*, Summer 1991, p. 30.

18. Blum, 1983, p. 86; italics mine. Reprinted by permission of the publisher.

19. Maria Crockett, "For Day Care, There's No Place like Home," *Christian Science Monitor*, April 16, 1984, p. 31.

20. Blum, 1983, p. 87. Reprinted by permission of the publisher.

21. Marjorie Gelb, "Child Abuse: Benefits of Child Care Outweigh Parents' Fears," *Maine Sunday Telegram*, May 5, 1985, sec. A, p. 41.

22. Ibid.

23. Marilyn Gardner, "Are Day-Care Subsidies Too Much to Pay for Children's Safety?" *Christian Science Monitor*, January 9, 1987, p. 25.

24. Ibid., p. 26.

25. Ibid.

26. Carolee Howes cited in Shannon Brownlee and Matthew Miller, "Lies Parents Tell Themselves About Why They Work," *U.S. News & World Report*, May 12, 1997, p. 61.

27. Linda Burton, "What's a Smart Woman Like You Doing at Home?" in "Speaking Out" column, *Christian Science Monitor*, December 7, 1982.

28. "What Price Day Care?" *Newsweek*, September 19, 1984, p. 21.

29. Ibid.

30. "After 10–Year Day-Care Study, Psychologist Changes His Stance," *Focus on the Family*, August 1987, p. 10.

31. Mary B. Jones, "The Child Care Option," sidebar in "From Career to Maternity," *Rutgers Magazine*, Summer 1991, p. 30; and LaGanga, 1984, sec. 1, p. 24.

32. Marcy Whitebook et al., "Who's Minding the Child Care Workers?" *Newsweek*, July 23, 1983, p. 45, cited in Marian Blum, *The Day-Care Dilemma* (San Francisco, CA: New Lexington Press), p. 23. Reprinted by permission of the publisher.

33. Gardner, 1987, p. 26.

34. Letter in "Problems and Solutions," *Welcome Home*, January 1985, p. 23.

35. Dr. William Rodrigues, Children's Hospital, Washington, D.C., cited in Blum, 1983, p. 74. Reprinted by permission of the publisher.

36. Jack Levine, cited in Gardner, 1987, p. 25.

Chapter Four
Can You Really *Afford* to Quit?

1. George Barbee, cited in Peter N. Spotts, "Adding a Child and Dropping an Income: A Time for Planning," *Christian Science Monitor,* May 18, 1984, p. B5.

2. Deborah Fallows, *A Mother's Work* (Boston: Houghton Mifflin, 1985), p. 223.

3. C. F. Watts, "Home Is Where the Business Is," *Black Enterprise,* November 1994, pp. 128–130.

4. "From a Single Mother at Home," *Welcome Home,* April 1984, p. 15.

Chapter Five
Saving Money Instead of Making It

1. Mary Ann Cahill, *The Heart Has Its Own Reasons* (Franklin Park, IL: La Leche League International, 1983), p. 186.

2. Ibid., pp. 107–108; italics mine.

3. Deborah Churchman, "Manufacturers Are Cranking Out Coupons by the Billions," on the "Home and Family" page, *Christian Science Monitor,* January 10, 1984.

4. Ibid.

5. Ibid.

6. Barbara Salsbury, with Cheri Loveless, *Cut Your Grocery Bills in Half!* (Washington, DC: Acropolis Books, 1983), p. 258.

Chapter Six
How to Avoid Being Chief Bottle Washer

1. Lee Morical, *Where's My Happy Ending?* (Reading, MA: Addison-Wesley, 1984), p. 49.

2. Deborah Fallows, *A Mother's Work* (Boston: Houghton Mifflin, 1985), p. 228.

3. Richard Louv, "What Do Mothers Really Want?" *Parents*, 1996, p. 40.

4. Yankelovich and Blankenhorn findings, cited in Miriam Durkin, "June Cleaver, Is That You?" *The Charlotte Observer*, August 4, 1991, p. 2E.

5. Louv, 1996, p. 40.

6. Merck Family Fund, "Merck Family Fund Poll," *Working Woman*, August 1995, p. 14.

7. Kyle Pruett, quoted in Keith Henderson, "The 'Nurturing Father' Appears to Be Doing a Very Good Job," *Christian Science Monitor*, March 26, 1987.

8. Linda Burton, "What Do You Do All Day?" *Welcome Home*, April 1984, p. 21.

9. Linda Burton, "A Place to Come Home To," *Welcome Home*, March 1984, p. 5.

10. Beth Bennett, "Homemakers' Survival Guide," *Woman's World*, May 7, 1985, p. 47.

11. Excerpts from Arlene Rossen Cardozo, *Woman at Home* (Garden City, NY: Doubleday, 1970), p. 10.

12. Ibid., p. 2; italics mine.

13. Janet Dittmer, "The Home Manager," *Welcome Home*, March 1984, p. 18.

14. Pat Cundick, "The Home Manager," *Welcome Home*, April 1985, p. 9.

15. Excerpt from Marilyn Gardner, "Cleaning Up the Original Family Business: How to Get Everybody into the Act," *Christian Science Monitor*, January 23, 1984, p. 21.

16. Albert Scardino, "The New Baby Boom Spurs Local Magazines for Parents," *New York Times*, June 26, 1989, pp. D1, D7.

17. Bonnie Watkins, "Entertaining Children on a Limited Budget," *Welcome Home*, April 1984, p. 8.

18. Blaine Taylor, *The Success Ethic and the Shattered American Dream* (Washington, DC: Acropolis Books, 1976), pp. 28–29.

Chapter Seven
Building Bridges

1. Lee Morical, *Where's My Happy Ending?* (Reading, MA: Addison-Wesley, 1984), pp. 49–50.

2. Richard Nelson Bolles, *What Color Is Your Parachute?* (Berkeley, CA: Ten Speed Press, 1976), p. I.

3. Study by Joyce Jacobsen and Laurence Levin, announced in San Jose, California, reported by *NBC Evening News* and Associated Press, January 11, 1992.

4. Marilyn Gardner, "Mother's Hours—Custom-tailoring the Workweek," *Christian Science Monitor*, September 12, 1985, p. 29; see also John Applegath, *Working Free: Practical Alternatives to the 9 to 5 Job* (New York: American Management Association, 1982).

5. Betty Holcomb, "Time Off: The Benefit of the Hour," *Working Mother*, July 1991, pp. 31–35.

6. Julia Lawlor, "Study: Moms' Chores Still Outweigh Dads'," *USA Today*, January 20, 1992, p. 58.

7. Adapted from "How to Sell a Flexible Schedule," sidebar in "Time Off: The Benefit of the Hour," Betty Holcomb, *Working Mother*, July 1991, p. 34.

8. Shirley Sloan Fader, "A Guide to Part Time Work," *Ladies' Home Journal*, October 1984, p. 72.

9. Deborah Churchman, "Getting Back into the Work Force—Without Going Back to School," *Christian Science Monitor*, December 15, 1983, p. 36.

10. Ibid.

11. Gretchen Olson Shively, "Occupation Housewife," *Mount Holyoke Alumnae Quarterly*, Summer 1982, p. 39.

12. Denise Kalette, "Thrift-Store Shoppers Find Chic for Cheap," *USA Today*, September 26, 1991, p. 7B.

13. Bureau of Labor Statistics, U.S. Department of Labor 1991 figures, as reported by Peter T. Kilborn, "Part Time Hirings Bring Deep Changes in U.S. Workplaces," *New York Times*, June 17, 1991, p. A1.

14. Naomi Barko, "The Part-Time Path," *Working Mother*, April 1985, pp. 38–43.

15. Ibid., pp. 38–39.

16. Caroline Bird, cited in John Applegath, 1982, p. i.

17. Quoted in Patricia Lee, *The Complete Guide to Job Sharing* (New York: Walker & Co., 1983), p. 92.

18. See Applegath, 1982, p. 13, and Vivienne Sernaque with Nachman Urieli, *Parttime Jobs* (New York: Ballantine Books, 1982), p. 20.

19. "From a Single Mother at Home," *Welcome Home*, April 1984, p. 15.

20. Tami Moore, "A New Direction," *New Beginnings*, March–April 1985, p. 44.

Chapter Eight
Making Money at Home: Nap Time, Nighttime, Anytime You Can

1. Brian Doherty, "No Business Like Home Business," in "Citings," *Reason*, July 1997, p. 14; see also Watts, 1994, pp. 128–130.

2. Jaimie Day, cited in Barbara Evans Openshaw, "An Interior Design Business at Home," in "Making and Saving Money at Home" column, *Welcome Home*, August 1984, p. 25.

3. Kathleen Christensen, *Women and Home-Based Work: The Unspoken Contract* (New York: Holt, 1988), pp. 5–6.

4. Georganne Fiumara, Mothers' Home Business Network promotional letter quoting from "A Dream Come True for Mothers Working at Home," *Woman*, February 1985.

5. Rushworth M. Kidder, "The Flap Over the Cottage-Industry Ban," *Christian Science Monitor*, December 12, 1983, p. 27.

6. Lynette Smith, cited in Barbara Evans Openshaw, "Lynette Smith: Home-Based Success," in "Making and Saving Money at Home" column, *Welcome Home*, June 1985, p. 19.

7. Debra Ann Hatten, "Where to Look for Nest Eggs to Hatch Your Enterprise Soundly," *Christian Science Monitor*, June 11, 1985, p. 27.

8. Phyllis Billis, *Entrepreneurial Mothers* (New York: Rawson Associates, 1983), pp. 89–90.

9. Ed Morris, "Don't Overtax Yourself: What Authors Should Know About Home Office Expenses," *Authors Guild Bulletin*, Winter 1992, pp. 2–3.

10. Lynn Langway et al., "'Worksteaders' Clean Up," *Newsweek*, January 9, 1984, p. 87.

11. Pat Eggen, cited in Georganne Fiumara (ed.), *Homeworking Mothers: The Mothers' Home Business Network Newsletter*, Spring 1985, p. 8.

12. Cynthia Harriman, personal interviews, November 1984 and April 1985.

13. Thomas Watterson, "The Keogh Plan, a Close Cousin of the IRA, Covers Any Kind of Self-Employment Income," *Christian Science Monitor*, March 13, 1985, p. 21.

Chapter Nine
Do Try This at Home: Computer-Based Businesses

1. Harley Shaiken, in a report on CBS *Evening News*, December 3, 1984.

2. Lisa Shaw, *Telecommute! Go to Work Without Leaving Home* (New York: Wiley, 1996), p. 3.

Chapter Ten
Moving Beyond the Traditional: Nurturing Ourselves and Others

1. Christine Compston, "From Stone Throwers to Hearth Tenders," lecture at the University of New Hampshire, Durham, NH, July 14, 1982.

2. Ibid.; see also William H. Chafe, *American Woman: Her Changing Social, Economic, and Political Roles, 1920–1974* (New York: Oxford University Press, 1974); and Carol Hymowitz and Michaele Weissman, *A History of Women in America* (New York: Bantam, 1978).

3. Chafe, 1974, pp. 160–171.

4. Ibid.

5. Ed Rubenstein, "Right Data," *National Review*, March 10, 1997, p. 14.

6. "Lynn," cited in Susan Crain Bakos, *This Wasn't Supposed to Happen* (New York: Continuum, 1985), p. 152.

7. Susan Gilette, cited in Bakos, 1985, p. 153.

8. Selma Fraiberg, *Every Child's Birthright: In Defense of Mothering*, cited in "Additional Views," Select Committee on Children, Youth, and Families hearing, December 1983, Washington, D.C. (Washington, DC: U.S. Government Printing Office), p. 83.

9. Rose R. Kennedy, "Why Are We So Black-and-White?" *Special Report: On Family*, August–October 1990, p. 22.

10. Karen Levine, "Mother vs. Mother," *Parents*, June 1985, p. 64.

11. Testimony at hearing before the Select Committee on Children, Youth, and Families, May 21, 1984, Irving, TX, p. 172 of printed testimony (Washington, DC: U.S. Government Printing Office, 1984).

12. Ibid.

13. Ibid.

14. Mary B. Jones, "The Child-Care Option," sidebar in "From Career to Maternity," *Rutgers Magazine*, Summer 1991, p. 30; Cynthia Orr, "Kids Rate Working Parents," *Portsmouth Magazine*, April 17, 1986, p. 22; and Dr. Christopher Coe, Stanford University, cited in Bernie S. Siegel, *Love, Medicine and Miracles* (New York: Harper-Collins, 1990), p. 183.

15. Cheri Loveless, telephone interview, June 27, 1984.

16. Kenneth Minogue, "The Goddess That Failed," *National Review*, November 18, 1991, p. 47.

17. Cathy Young, "Phony War," *Reason*, November 1991, p. 58.

18. Lee Morical, *Where's My Happy Ending?* (Reading, MA: Addison-Wesley, 1984), p. 104.

19. Elaine Heffner, *Mothering: The Emotional Experience of Motherhood after Freud and Feminism* (New York: Doubleday, 1978), pp. 10–18.

20. Ibid., p. vi.

21. Barbara Whitehead, cited in Marilyn Gardner, "'Pioneer Parents' Put Family First," *The Christian Science Monitor*, May 3, 1991, p. 10.

22. Cynthia Gorney, "Fry It Up in a Pan Yourself, Buster," interview with Arlie Hochschild in *Special Report: On Family*, August–October 1990, p. 39.

23. Ibid.

24. "Trendicators," *Working Woman*, August 1995, p. 14.

25. Richard Louv, "What Do Mothers Really Want?" *Parents*, May 1996, p. 40.

26. Alvin Toffler, *The Third Wave* (New York: Morrow, 1980), pp. 216–219.

27. Florence King, "Eve Fatigue," *National Review*, November 18, 1991, p. 42.

Index

A

AAUW (American Association of University Women), 129, 218
Association of Part-Time Professionals, 218
AWED (American Women's Economic Development Corporation), 220

B

Baby-sitting exchanges, 112
Brown, Helen Gurley, 11
Business: advertising, 162–163; cards, 162; children and, 166–168, 188–190; financing, 159–160; history of women and, 143, 193–198; name, registering a, 163; networking, 158–159; plan, 159–160; start-up, 138–139

C

Career success. *See* Success.
Child care. *See* Day care.
Children: assessing needs of, 132, 139–141, 145–147; and computers, 177, 188–190; forcing independence on, 60–61; and home businesses, 166–168; and illness, 61–63; learning of responsibility by, 108–110, 116, 166–168
Clothing, savings on, 73, 90, 130
Computers: and accessing the Internet, 183–184; at-home work and, 144, 158, 171–190; buying, 178–182; carpal tunnel syndrome and, 187–188; catalogs, 178, 221; children and, 177, 188–190; terms, definition of, 190–192; Macintosh versus PC, 179–180; and modems, 182–183, 185; notebooks, 182; printers and, 184–185; software for, 183; and telecommuting, 172–174, 175–176; and World Wide Web, 184
Cottage industries, 157–158
Coupons, 99–100
Credit cards, 94

D

Day care, as at-home business, 149–150; centers for, 57–60; childhood illness and, 61–63; children's response to, 48–49; effects of, 48–51, 60–61, 64–65, 204; guilt about, 47, 62; national policy on, 41–44, 64–65, 204–205; part-time, 139–141; standards for, 51–53; tax policy and, 43, 204–205; two-tier system of, 204; types of, 54–57
Debt, problems with, 93–94
Direct sales, 150–151
Dressing for success, 129–131

E

Early Childhood Education and
Development Act, 42
Economizing, 67–77, 85, 113–116
"Electronic cottage industries," 158
Entrepreneurs, women as, 138–139,
145
Entrepreneurship Institute, 159, 220
Equal Rights Amendment, 196
"Extended family," myth of, 195

F

Family day-care associations, 149
Fathers, as nurturers, 104, 229–230
Fax machines, 185–186
FEMALE, 110, 217
Feminism, 13–14, 34–35, 206–210,
213
Finances, assessment of, 68–76. See
also Economizing.
Financing a home business, 159–160
Flexible time, 121–124
Food costs, 73, 96–100
Franchises, 151–152, 219
Friedan, Betty, 9–10, 30

G

Gift buying, 113–114, 117
Guilt, 47, 62, 202, 206

H

Handcrafts: as business, 153–156; sup-
plies for, 153; teaching, 156–157
Health Maintenance Organizations
(HMOs), 72, 93
History of women and work, 143,
193–198
Home-based businesses, 143–169
Home heating, 95–96
Housework, managing, 30–33, 38–39,
108–110
Housing, 70–71, 90–92

I

Institute to Coordinate Women's
Interests, 196

Internal Revenue Service, 74, 139,
148, 163–164
IRAs, 168–169
Isolation, 79

J

Job sharing, 134–138, 218
Jobs. See Work.

K

Keogh plans, 168–169

L

"Like" list, 68, 70, 75–76

M

Mail-order business, 152
Marketing reps, 154–155, 162
Marriage, stress in, 30–33, 38
Materialism, 116–117
Media, image of working women in,
16–17, 33–37
Medical costs, 71–72, 92–94
MHBN (Mothers' Home Business
Network), 147, 220
Motherhood: as an occupation,
102–103; traditional, 193–197
Mothers' hours, 121, 210

N

"Need" list, 68–74
Needs, emotional versus material,
4–5, 40, 69–79. See also Priorities.
Networking, 111, 158–159
NOW (National Organization for
Women), 129

P

Parent's Day Out services, 110–111
Part-time work: at home, 75, 131–
138; for single parents, 139–140;
"group permanent," 132–133;
mothers' hours, 121, 210; outside
the home, 131–132; versus full-time
work, 121–122, 141; V-time, 121
Preschool, 55, 141, 167
Priorities, 4–5, 104–105, 113–114

Professional organizations, 128–129
Public library, 86, 110, 177–178, 184, 186, 188

R
Recreation, 75–76, 80, 112–113
Registering a business name, 163
Résumés, 124–127, 136–138
Retirement, 168–169

S
Sales, direct, 150
SCORE (Service Corps of Retired Executives), 139, 221
Skills, marketable, 119–120, 124, 127
Social pressure, 78–79
Social Security exemptions, 168–169
Statistics, misleading, 22–23
Staying home, attitudes toward, 78–79, 102–103
Stress: of leaving child, 46–47, 54, 78, 213; in marriage, 30–33, 38
Success, image of, 16–17, 33–37, 205, 207
"Suitability Survey," 148

T
Tax: deductions, 74; exemptions, 73
Telecommuting, 172–174, 175–176

Temporary office work, 133
Time management, 104, 106–108
Transportation costs, 72–73, 94–95

U
Utility costs, 71

V
V-time, 121
Venture capital network, 159, 221
Volunteer work, 124, 127

W
Welcome Home newsletter, 112, 132, 206, 218
Women's liberation movement, 8–10, 197, 206–209
Work: expectations from, 104–105, 128–129; quitting, 67–68, 128; returning to, 119–138; versus staying at home, 201–202. *See also* Flexible time; Job sharing; Part-time work.
Work space, in-home, 164–166

Y
YWCA, 80, 129, 219

About the Author

CHRISTINE DAVIDSON was educated at Ripon College and Boston University and at the University of Exeter, Devon, England. She taught English in Boston public schools and was an instructor in nonfiction writing at Antioch-New England and the University of New Hampshire. Davidson writes on family issues, education, and travel. She lives in seacoast New Hampshire with her husband and two children.